Festive Paper Holidays

Remember the chains made from interlocking rings of paper that decorated your childhood Christmas tree? How about Valentines consisting of a construction paper heart, a paper doily, and a handwritten sentiment? Personally, I also made my share of paper plate pumpkins for Halloween — using black and orange paint plus a curled green pipe cleaner for the stem.

Holiday paper crafting has come a long way in the past decade, due in large part to the wide variety of themed products available and the development of clever new techniques and paper crafting tools. Paper Crafts magazine has been showcasing the creativity of reader-submitted designs for over seven years, and we are delighted to offer this collection of the best holiday paper projects from recent issues.

In these pages you'll find hundreds of ideas for not only Christmas, Valentine's Day, and Halloween, but also Easter, Thanksgiving, and New Year celebrations. We also cover seasonal themes (spring, summer, fall, and winter) plus a special section with ideas to show your patriotic pride.

I hope you'll find an abundance of inspiration for your next holiday paper project, and continue to find ways to adapt these ideas for many more down the road.

Jennif

Note: Because these projects are from past issues, some products may not be available. Luckily, the Internet provides a wonderful way to search for similar items so you can still create a beautiful project using these inspiring techniques. So, if you can't find a product, use your creativity to adapt the project and find a replacement.

THE
BIG BOOK
of Holiday Paper Crafts

13

249

97

116

32

125

Contents

Designer Tip

This is a great way to use up those patterned paper scraps. It would also make a great New Year's party invitation!

Celebrate 2011 Card

Designer: Kim Kesti

① Make card from cardstock. ② Trim strips of patterned paper; adhere. ③ Cut panel from cardstock; affix sticker. Die-cut year from cardstock and adhere to panel. ④ Adhere panel; stitch border.

Finished size: 5¾" x 5"

Numbers New Year Card

Designer: Kim Hughes

① Make card from cardstock. ② Trim cardstock to fit card front and adhere. ③ Trim patterned paper slightly smaller than front and adhere. ④ Trim cardstock and adhere. Adhere buttons. ⑤ Adhere stickers to cardstock, trim pieces, and adhere. ⑥ Spell sentiment on cardstock with rub-ons, trim, and adhere.

Finished size: 4¼" x 5¾"

SUPPLIES: *Cardstock:* (Beetle Black, Lily White, Mexican Poppy, KI Teal, Parakeet, Grenadine) Bazzill Basics Paper *Patterned paper:* (Compilation from Anthology collection) Studio Calico *Sticker:* (celebrate) Little Yellow Bicycle *Dies:* (numbers) QuicKutz

SUPPLIES: *Cardstock:* (Raven, white) Bazzill Basics Paper; (white glitter) Doodlebug Design *Patterned paper:* (grid) *Accents:* (red buttons) Papertrey Ink *Rub-ons:* (Alex alphabet) American Crafts *Stickers:* (Cappella numbers) BasicGrey

New Year's Party Wine Wrap

Designer: Kristin K. Tierney

1 Make sleeve from cardstock.

2 Punch circles from cardstock and patterned paper; adhere, using foam tape as desired.

3 Tie on ribbon.

4 Accordion-fold patterned paper and adhere to form circle; adhere with foam tape. Punch cardstock and patterned paper circles; adhere.

5 Stamp celebrate on cardstock. Emboss, punch into circle, and adhere.

6 Thread buttons with cord. Adhere buttons, pearls, and rhinestones.

7 Slide sleeve onto wine bottle.

Finished size: 2¾" diameter x 5" height

SUPPLIES: *Cardstock:* (gold, silver) Paper and More; (white) *Patterned paper:* (silver damask) The Paper Studio; (Dahlias from I Do collection) American Crafts *Clear stamp:* (celebrate from Damask Designs set) Papertrey Ink *Pigment ink:* (silver) Tsukineko *Embossing powder:* (Silver Pearl) Ranger Industries *Accents:* (white pearls) Stampin' Up!; (clear rhinestones) Kaisercraft; (white, yellow buttons) *Fibers:* (silver ribbon) Offray; (silver cord) Stampin' Up! *Tools:* (¾", 1", 1¼", 1⅜" circle punches) Stampin' Up!; (2" circle punch) Marvy Uchida *Other:* (wine bottle)

Celebrate Card

Designer: Lisa Dorsey

❶ Make card from cardstock.

❷ Adhere patterned paper strips around edges.

❸ Adhere patterned paper piece.

❹ Make glass, following pattern on p. 282. Mat with cardstock; adhere with foam squares. Draw inside of glass with marker.

❺ Cut circles from patterned paper and adhere with foam squares.

❻ Punch circles from cardstock. Apply rub-ons to spell "Celebrate"; adhere.

Finished size: 3¾" x 8"

Blustery Snowflake

Designer: Natasha Trupp

CHARM

❶ Stamp large snowflake on shrink plastic; trim.

❷ Punch holes in snowflake. Shrink, following manufacturer's instructions.

CARD

❶ Make card from cardstock.

❷ Cut cardstock slightly smaller than card front. Stamp snowflakes with watermark ink.

❸ Ink piece with brayer.

❹ Adhere ribbon and cord. Adhere piece to card.

❺ Tie charm with cord.

Finished size: 4¼" square

SUPPLIES: *Cardstock:* (black, white, orange) Bazzill Basics Paper *Patterned paper:* (Line Up, Bounce from Delightful Blend collection) Arctic Frog *Color medium:* (white marker) Sanford *Rub-ons:* (Ned Jr alphabet) American Crafts *Adhesive:* (foam squares) EK Success *Tool:* (½"circle punch) EK Success

SUPPLIES: *Cardstock:* (Brilliant Blue, Glossy White) Stampin' Up! *Clear stamps:* (snowflakes from Big Retro Flake set) Gel-a-Tins *Dye ink:* (Blue Frost Spectrum) Stampin' Up! *Solvent ink:* (Ultramarine) Tsukineko *Watermark ink:* Tsukineko *Fibers:* (white organdy ribbon, silver cord) Stampin' Up! *Tools:* (⅛" circle punch) Fiskars; (brayer) *Other:* (white shrink plastic)

⁵⁵ₜₑₚₛ Holiday Cheer Card

Designer: Kim Kesti

❶ Make card from cardstock.

❷ Cut patterned paper slightly smaller than card front; adhere.

❸ Cut square of cardstock, punch corners, ink edges, and adhere. Ink pine branch stamp using Rock and Roll technique (see "Rock and Roll Technique"). Stamp pine branch and adhere pompoms.

❹ Stamp sentiment on cardstock. Trim, ink edges, and adhere.

❺ Attach brads.

Finished size: 4" x 5"

ROCK AND ROLL TECHNIQUE

Add more color variety to your stamping with the Rock and Roll technique. To do this technique, simply apply a lighter ink to your stamp, roll the stamp edges in a darker ink, and press the inked stamp on paper.

Birdie Season's Greetings Card

Designer: Eleanor McGarry

❶ Make card from cardstock. Stamp Canvas Background.

❷ Adhere ribbon.

❸ Trim cardstock strip with decorative-edge scissors; adhere. Adhere cardstock strip.

❹ Stamp two birds on watercolor paper; color with crayons. Trim and adhere.

❺ Stamp bird on watercolor paper; color with crayons. Trim, mat with cardstock, and adhere using foam tape.

❻ Stamp season's greetings.

Finished size: 4¼" x 5½"

DESIGNER TIP

When watercoloring, start with the lightest color first and add darker colors to create depth and detail.

SUPPLIES: *Cardstock:* (Awesome Aqua Deep, Totally Tan) WorldWin *Patterned paper:* (Forrest Bonfire from Love, Elsie collection) KI Memories *Clear stamps:* (pine branch from Classic Holiday set, sentiment from Holiday Whimsy set) Tinkering Ink *Dye ink:* (Chocolate) Close To My Heart *Chalk ink:* (Dark Moss, Warm Green) Clearsnap *Accents:* (metal brads) Karen Foster Design *Fibers:* (green pompom trim) Fancy Pants Designs *Tool:* (corner rounder punch)

SUPPLIES: *Cardstock:* (So Saffron, Real Red, Chocolate Chip) Stampin' Up! *Specialty paper:* (watercolor paper) Fabriano *Rubber stamps:* (birds from Holiday Birds set) Hero Arts; (Canvas Background) Stampin' Up! *Clear stamp:* (season's greetings from Faux Ribbon set) Papertrey Ink *Dye ink:* (So Saffron) Stampin' Up! *Pigment ink:* (Onyx Black) Tsukineko *Color medium:* (yellow, red, green, pink watercolor crayons) Lyra *Fibers:* (light green, red gingham ribbon) Stampin' Up! *Adhesive:* (foam tape) *Tool:* (decorative-edge scissors) Fiskars

⑤ XOXO Love Tree

Designer: Teri Anderson

❶ Make card from cardstock. ❷ Trim patterned paper; adhere. Run tracing wheel through paint and roll to create lines. ❸ Adhere clouds; trim tree from patterned paper and adhere. ❹ Trim edge of cardstock strip with decorative-edge scissors; adhere. ❺ Affix stickers to spell "XOXO". Attach brad.

Finished size: 4¼" square

DESIGNER TIP

Create a faux stitched look with paint. Dispense a small amount of paint on scrap paper. Roll a sewing pattern tracing wheel repeatedly through the paint and then roll on your card. It's so easy!

SUPPLIES: *Cardstock:* (kraft) Neenah Paper; (white) Georgia-Pacific *Patterned paper:* (Smoochie Pooh, Pookie from I Heart You collection) American Crafts *Paint:* (white) Plaid *Accents:* (pink brad) Colorbok; (pink felt clouds) American Crafts *Stickers:* (Whistle Stop alphabet) American Crafts *Tools:* (tracing wheel) Prym-Dritz; (decorative-edge scissors)

Stitched Sweetheart

Designer: Betsy Veldman

❶ Make card from cardstock. ❷ Trim strip of patterned paper with decorative-edge scissors and adhere. Zigzag-stitch along edge. ❸ Stamp hearts, outline hearts, leaves, and heart line. Stamp sentiment on cardstock. Trim, ink edges, and adhere. Adhere rhinestones. ❹ Stamp heart border on cardstock; trim and adhere. ❺ Punch edge of patterned paper strip and adhere. Zigzag-stitch along seam. ❻ Ink card edges. Tie on ribbon.

Finished size: 4¼" square

SUPPLIES: All supplies from Papertrey Ink unless otherwise noted. *Cardstock:* (Rustic Cream, kraft) *Patterned paper:* (green polka dot from 2008 Bitty Dot Basics collection; red polka dot from Simple Valentine collection) *Clear stamps:* (heart, outline heart, heart border, heart line, sweetheart from Simple Valentine set; leaves from Turning a New Leaf set) *Pigment ink:* (Hibiscus Burst, Spring Moss, Fresh Snow) *Chalk ink:* (Creamy Brown) Clearsnap *Specialty ink:* (Dark Chocolate, Pure Poppy hybrid) *Accents:* (red rhinestones) Kaisercraft *Fibers:* (red ribbon) *Tools:* (decorative-edge scissors) Provo Craft; (border punch) Fiskars

5 STEPS Adore

Designer: Latisha Yoast

❶ Make card from cardstock; round bottom corners. ❷ Trim cardstock piece and round bottom corners. Trim patterned paper strips and adhere. ❸ Stamp angel and xoxo. Apply rub-on. ❹ Adhere rhinestones. Tie on ribbon and adhere piece to card with foam tape.

Finished size: 4¼" x 5½"

5 STEPS Color My World

Designer: Jessica Witty

❶ Make card from cardstock. ❷ Trim cardstock pieces and adhere. ❸ Stamp sentiment. ❹ Punch hearts from glassine bag and adhere. ❺ Thread buttons with floss and adhere.

Finished size: 5¼" x 3½"

DESIGNER TIP

Slippery materials such as glassine can be difficult to punch. Backing the glassine paper with cardstock before punching will help produce clean images.

SUPPLIES: *Cardstock:* (white) *Patterned paper:* (Jaw Breakers, Lollipop from Sugar Rush collection) BasicGrey *Clear stamps:* (angel, xoxo from Angelic Love set) Flourishes *Dye ink:* (Tuxedo Black) Tsukineko *Specialty ink:* (Claret hybrid) Stewart Superior Corp. *Accents:* (orange rhinestones) BasicGrey *Rub-on:* (adore definition) BoBunny Press *Fibers:* (orange ribbon) Papertrey Ink *Tool:* (corner rounder punch) Creative Memories

SUPPLIES: All supplies from Papertrey Ink unless otherwise noted. *Cardstock:* (Lemon Tart, Summer Sunrise, Melon Berry, Raspberry Fizz, Pure Poppy, white) *Clear stamp:* (sentiment from Tiny Treats: Valentine set) *Specialty ink:* (True Black, Pure Poppy hybrid) *Accents:* (pink, red, melon, yellow buttons) *Fibers:* (white floss) no source *Tool:* (heart punch) EK Success *Other:* (glassine bag) no source

Crazy for You, Baby

Designer: Beth Opel

① Make card from cardstock; round bottom corner. ② Trim cardstock strip and adhere. Punch patterned paper squares and adhere. ③ Affix stickers to spell "Crazy". Apply rub-on. ④ Adhere trim. ⑤ Affix flower and lips stickers. ⑥ Affix stickers to spell "For you, baby". Affix heart sticker.

Finished size: 7" x 5"

⑤ Eight of Hearts
STEPS

Designer: Wendy Sue Anderson

① Make card from cardstock. ② Trim patterned paper panel slightly smaller than card front; round right corners. ③ Stitch edge of patterned paper; adhere to panel. Adhere chipboard playing card. Adhere sentiment die cut using foam tape. ④ Tie ribbon around panel and adhere. ⑤ Thread chipboard tag with twine and adhere using foam tape. Adhere rhinestones.

Finished size: 5¼" x 6½"

DESIGNER TIP

This quilted technique is a great way to use small scraps of papers from your stash. You can choose different colors of scraps for different occasions—for example, green scraps for a St. Patrick's Day card.

SUPPLIES: *Cardstock:* (white, pink) American Crafts; (Ladybug glitter, Bubblegum glitter, Cupcake Serenade) Doodlebug Design *Patterned paper:* (red, pink, white assortment) *Rub-on:* (scalloped black trim) Jenni Bowlin Studio *Stickers:* (black alphabet) American Crafts; (epoxy lips) Anna Griffin; (black rhinestone flower) Glitz Design; (epoxy heart) Heidi Grace Designs; (black glitter chipboard alphabet) Me & My Big Ideas *Fibers:* (red pompom trim) We R Memory Keepers *Tools:* (square punch, corner rounder punch) EK Success

SUPPLIES: *Cardstock:* (red) Core'dinations *Patterned paper:* (Newsprint Word from Love Struck collection) Making Memories; (pink bird from Sweet Love pad) Little Yellow Bicycle *Accents:* (chipboard playing card, sentiment die cut) Making Memories; (chipboard tag, heart rhinestones) Little Yellow Bicycle *Fibers:* (red ribbon) Offray; (hemp twine) *Tool:* (corner rounder punch)

Love You Berry Much

Designer: Kim Hughes

❶ Make card from cardstock. ❷ Trim strawberry from patterned paper. Cut stem and leaves from cardstock using pattern on p. 284. Stitch edges of strawberry and adhere stem. ❸ Stamp retro stripes on leaves, stitch, and adhere. ❹ Cut thin strip from cardstock, curl, and adhere. ❺ Stamp sentiment on cardstock, trim, and adhere. ❻ Thread buttons with floss and adhere. Adhere strawberry to card.

Finished size: 4" x 5"

DESIGNER TIP

Wrap the cardstock strip on a round pencil or paper piercer to create a smooth curl for the stem.

SUPPLIES: *Cardstock:* (Rustic Cream, Spring Moss) Papertrey Ink; (pink) *Patterned paper:* (Eye Candy from Bloom & Grow collection) My Mind's Eye *Foam stamp:* (retro stripes) Plaid *Clear stamp:* (sentiment from My Punny Valentine set) Papertrey Ink *Pigment ink:* (Spring Moss) Papertrey Ink *Accents:* (yellow buttons) Papertrey Ink *Fibers:* (yellow floss) DMC

Love You Much

Designer: Jen Arkfeld

❶ Make card from cardstock. ❷ Trim patterned paper layers and adhere. ❸ Stamp sentiment on cardstock, punch bottom, and attach brad. Adhere. ❹ Tie on ribbon.

Finished size: 4¼" x 5½"

DESIGNER TIP

Because the patterned paper is glittered, be sure to use plenty of adhesive because the adhesive will lose some tackiness from the glitter.

SUPPLIES: All supplies are from Stampin' Up! *Cardstock:* (Very Vanilla, kraft) *Patterned paper:* (large flower, small flower, petite flower from Sending Love collection) *Rubber stamp:* (sentiment from Well Scripted set) *Dye ink:* (Real Red) *Accent:* (heart epoxy brad) *Fibers:* (brown ribbon) *Tool:* (border punch)

Be Mine

Designer: Maren Benedict

1 Make card from cardstock. Draw border. 2 Stamp trees on patterned paper; color trunks. 3 Stamp trees on patterned paper panel, color hearts, and trim tree tops. Color edges and adhere over first image using foam tape. 4 Trim sentiment from patterned paper and adhere using foam tape. 5 Tie on ribbon and adhere panel using foam tape.

Finished size: 4¼" x 5½"

DESIGNER TIP
Use a white gel pen to add details and accents to cards in a unique way.

SUPPLIES: *Cardstock:* (Aqua Mist) Papertrey Ink *Patterned paper:* (Bow & Arrow, Hearts Bloom, Postcards from Cupid collection) Pink Paislee *Rubber stamp:* (trees from Sweet Affections set) Unity Stamp Co. *Dye ink:* (Tuxedo Black) Tsukineko *Color media:* (red, brown markers) Copic; (white gel pen) *Fibers:* (pink ribbon) Offray

Sending All My Love

Designer: Latisha Yoast

1 Make card from cardstock. 2 Cut patterned paper piece, adhere patterned paper strip, and punch edge; adhere. 3 Color pearls with marker; adhere. 4 Tie on ribbon. 5 Trim sentiment block from patterned paper; adhere.

Finished size: 4¼" x 5½"

DESIGNER TIP
Most embellishments like pearls, ribbon, brads, and flowers can be customized by using a marker to change the color or texture. This technique helps to coordinate your accents perfectly with the other elements in your project.

SUPPLIES: *Cardstock:* (ivory) Flourishes *Patterned paper:* (Whoo Loves You, Cut Outs from Love Bandit collection) BoBunny Press *Color medium:* (red marker) Copic *Accents:* (white pearls) Kaisercraft *Fibers:* (green ribbon) Offray *Tool:* (border punch) Fiskars

Come Fly with Me

Designer: Beatriz Jennings

❶ Make card from cardstock, adhere patterned paper, and ink edges. ❷ Adhere patterned paper and zigzag-stitch edges. ❸ Adhere pearls to chipboard label and adhere. ❹ Layer flowers and adhere to card. Thread button with twine and adhere. ❺ Adhere lace and tie on ribbon.

Finished size: 4½" x 5½"

Elegant Be Mine

Designer: Jessica Witty

❶ Make card from cardstock. ❷ Punch paper, apply glitter, and adhere. ❸ Stamp cupid, text, and sentiment on cardstock. ❹ Trim, adhere ribbon, and adhere using foam tape. ❺ Adhere button.

Finished size: 3½" x 5"

SUPPLIES: *Cardstock:* (Vintage Cream) Papertrey Ink *Patterned paper:* (Birdie Border, Postcard 2 from Artsy Urban collection) GCD Studios *Dye ink:* (Vintage Photo) Ranger Industries *Accents:* (bird chipboard label) GCD Studios; (white flower, white button, white pearls, red crochet flower) *Fibers:* (white stitched ribbon, tan lace, natural twine)

SUPPLIES: *Cardstock:* (white) Papertrey Ink; (gray) Stampin' Up! *Paper:* (white) *Clear stamps:* (cupid from Cupid set) Pink Paislee; (sentiment from Simple Valentine set; text from Background Basics: Hearts set) Papertrey Ink *Dye ink:* (gray) Stampin' Up! *Specialty ink:* (True Black, Scarlet Jewel hybrid) Papertrey Ink *Accents:* (silver filigree button) Making Memories; (iridescent glitter) Papertrey Ink *Fibers:* (white ribbon) Papertrey Ink *Tool:* (border punch) Martha Stewart Crafts

5 From My Heart

Designer: Ellen Hutson

1 Make card from cardstock, and lightly stamp Wavy Heartfelt Messages with Bravo Brown. **2** Apply stripes with alternating colors of watercolor crayons to wet watercolor paper rectangle paper. Stamp sentiment when dry. **3** Embroider French knots on edges, distress paper edges and double mat with cardstock. Adhere to card. **4** Stamp heart on watercolor paper. Stamp flowers on heart; color with watercolor crayons and mat with cardstock. Tie ribbon around heart; adhere to card with pop-up dot. **5** Punch oval from cardstock; stamp and attach to heart with stick pin.

Finished size: 4¼″ x 5½″

SUPPLIES: *Rubber stamps:* (Large Stitched Heart, Wavy Heartfelt Messages, Pop Petals, Fashion Blooms) Hero Arts; (Linen Background) Stampin' Up! *Dye ink:* (Basic Brown, Bravo Burgundy) Stampin' Up! *Cardstock:* (pink, Chocolate) Memory Box; (Wine) Bazzill Basics Paper *Specialty paper:* (watercolor) Strathmore *Color medium:* (watercolor crayons) Stampin' Up! *Accent:* (red stick pin) *Fibers:* (velvet ribbon) May Arts; (embroidery floss) DMC *Adhesive:* (pop-up dots) *Tools:* (oval punch) Stampin' Up!; (water brush)

:5: Just My Type

Designer: Windy Robinson

1. Make card from cardstock. Adhere patterned paper.
2. Punch cardstock strip, wrap with ribbon, and adhere.
3. Stamp typewriter and sentiment on cardstock, color hearts, and mat with cardstock. Stitch edges and adhere. 4. Tie button to ribbon length with string. Adhere heart and adhere to card with foam tape.

Finished size: 4¼" x 5½"

SUPPLIES: *Cardstock:* (Umber, cream) The Paper Company; (kraft) DMD, Inc. *Patterned paper:* (Can Beef Consommé from Grandma's Christmas Soup collection) Jillibean Soup *Rubber stamps:* (typewriter, sentiment from Simply Magical set) Unity Stamp Co. *Dye ink:* (Walnut Stain) Ranger Industries *Color medium:* (red pen) Sakura *Accents:* (white button) Denami Design; (red metal heart) Colorbok *Fibers:* (brown twine) May Arts; (brown polka dot ribbon) Michaels *Tool:* (embossing border punch) EK Success

:5: A Million Little Things

Designer: Laura O'Donnell

1. Make card from cardstock. 2. Punch hearts from patterned papers and adhere. 3. Ink sentiment portion of Love Scrapblock, stamp on cardstock, trim, and adhere using foam tape.

Finished size: 4" x 5¼"

DESIGNER TIP
This design is a great way to use up scraps!

SUPPLIES: *Cardstock:* (Vanilla, Black Linen) Cornish Heritage Farms *Patterned paper:* (green floral, blue paisley, cream floral, brown stripe, orange polka dots, red polka dots, blue mini floral, lattice floral, pink floral from Wild Raspberry pad) K&Company *Rubber stamp:* (Love Scrapblock) Cornish Heritage Farms *Dye ink:* (Tuxedo Black) Tsukineko *Tool:* (heart punch) EK Success

You Take the Cake

Designer: Debbie Olson

❶ Make card from cardstock. Round bottom corners. ❷ Trim patterned paper, round bottom corners, and adhere. ❸ Die-cut border of cardstock and patterned paper; layer and adhere. ❹ Die-cut and emboss circle from cardstock. Stamp cupcake, color, and apply dimensional glaze. Stamp sentiment. ❺ Adhere stamped piece with foam tape. Thread buttons with string and adhere.

Finished size: 2¾" square

Corrugated Heart

Designer: Wendy Price

❶ Make card from cardstock. Adhere cardstock. ❷ Stamp heart on corrugated cardstock; trim. ❸ Thread button with twine, tie around heart, and adhere using foam tape.

Finished size: 2¾" x 3"

DESIGNER TIP

Give your stamps extra use by using them as patterns. When trying this technique, stamp on the back of your paper and trim for a nice, clean look.

SUPPLIES: *Cardstock:* (Hibiscus Burst, white) Papertrey Ink *Patterned paper:* (polka dots, heart stripes from Simple Valentine collection) Papertrey Ink *Clear stamps:* (cupcake, sentiment from Tiny Treats: Valentine set) Papertrey Ink *Dye ink:* (Tuxedo Black) Tsukineko *Color medium:* (assorted markers) Copic *Accents:* (pink buttons) Papertrey Ink *Fibers:* (white string) *Dies:* (scalloped border, circle) Spellbinders *Tools:* (corner rounder punch) Marvy Uchida *Other:* (dimensional glaze) Ranger Industries

SUPPLIES: *Cardstock:* (black) Prism; (kraft) The Paper Company; (corrugated kraft) *Rubber stamp:* (heart from From the Heart set) Lizzie Anne Designs *Dye ink:* (Tuxedo Black) Tsukineko *Accent:* (red button) Autumn Leaves *Fibers:* (natural twine)

You Make My Heart Melt

Designer: Becky Olsen

OUTSIDE

1. Cut card base and pieces, following patterns on p. 283.
2. Adhere pieces to base.
3. Affix sticker.
4. Tie ribbon in bow around card front.

INSIDE

1. Stamp heart inside card and on patterned paper. Trim second image and adhere.
2. Stamp sentiment.

Finished size: 3¼" x 7¼"

SUPPLIES: *Cardstock:* (white) *Patterned paper:* (Delicious, Pleasant from Enchanting collection; Graceful from Captivating collection) Pink Paislee *Rubber stamps:* (sentiment, heart from Heart Warmers set) Cornish Heritage Farms *Dye ink:* (Coffee) Ranger Industries *Sticker:* (chipboard sentiment tile) We R Memory Keepers *Fibers:* (green ribbon) Creative Impressions

Love U

Designer: Kalyn Kepner

OUTSIDE

1 Make card from cardstock; round bottom corners.

2 Trim patterned paper, ink edges, and adhere. Cross-stitch with floss and apply glitter glue.

3 Trim cardstock piece with decorative-edge scissors. Adhere cardstock strip trimmed with decorative-edge scissors; draw stitching.

4 Tie ribbon around cardstock piece; mat with cardstock, using foam tape. Ink mat edges and adhere to card.

5 Spell "Love" with stickers and adhere "U".

INSIDE

1 Adhere patterned paper.

2 Repeat outside step 3. Mat piece with cardstock, ink edges, and adhere.

3 Affix letters to spell "Much" and write "So".

Finished size: 6½" x 5¼"

SUPPLIES: *Cardstock:* (brown, pink, kraft) Bazzill Basics Paper *Patterned paper:* (Cherry Cordial from Bittersweet collection) BasicGrey *Chalk ink:* (Chestnut Roan) Clearsnap *Color medium:* (white gel pen) Sakura *Accents:* (gold glitter glue) Ranger Industries; (pink glitter chipboard letter) K&Company *Stickers:* (Daiquiri alphabet) American Crafts *Fibers:* (pink ribbon, pink floss) *Tools:* (decorative-edge scissors, corner rounder punch)

Happy Heart

Designer: Kimberly Crawford

OUTSIDE

1. Make card from cardstock; lightly ink edges.

2. Stamp Modern Lines on card front.

3. Paint chipboard heart frame; adhere. Cut inside of heart out.

4. Die-cut and emboss tag from cardstock. Punch heart from patterned paper, ink edges, stamp love you, and adhere to tag. Fussy-cut flower from patterned paper and adhere.

5. Tie floss in bow through button; adhere to tag. Adhere tag with foam tape.

INSIDE

1. Cut patterned paper, ink edges, and adhere.

2. Die-cut and emboss tag from cardstock. Stamp heart happy and adhere.

3. Punch heart from patterned paper and ink edges. Adhere with foam tape.

4. Tie floss through button and adhere.

Finished size: 4¼" x 5½"

SUPPLIES: Cardstock: (Vintage Cream) Papertrey Ink Patterned paper: (Apron Strings, Farmers Market from Early Bird collection) Cosmo Cricket Rubber stamp: (Modern Lines) Hero Arts Clear stamps: (love you, heart happy from Anytime Messages set) Hero Arts Chalk ink: (Lime Pastel, Blue Lagoon, Creamy Brown, Blackbird) Clearsnap Paint: (red) Making Memories Accents: (chipboard heart frame) Cosmo Cricket; (green buttons) Making Memories Fibers: (blue twine) Martha Stewart Crafts Dies: (tags) Spellbinders Tool: (medium heart punch) EK Success

There is No Doubt

Designer: Charlene Austin

OUTSIDE

1. Make card from cardstock; ink edges.

2. Punch border on patterned paper piece and adhere; stitch three sides.

3. Cut heart shape from chipboard; cover with patterned paper, sand edges, and adhere.

4. Stamp sentiment on cardstock; trim, ink edges, and adhere with foam tape.

5. Stitch cardstock strip to card and adhere rhinestones.

INSIDE

1. Punch border on patterned paper strip and adhere.

2. Cut heart from patterned paper, adhere, and stitch. Adhere rhinestone.

3. Stamp sentiment on cardstock; trim, ink edges, and adhere with foam tape.

Finished size: 4½" x 6"

SUPPLIES: *Cardstock:* (Vintage Cream, Raspberry Fizz) Papertrey Ink *Patterned paper:* (Girl Vine Dot from Just Chillin collection) Making Memories; (pink heart polka dot from Greenhouse pad) K&Company *Clear stamps:* (sentiments from Loving Words set) Technique Tuesday *Dye ink:* (Peeled Paint, Walnut Stain) Ranger Industries *Accents:* (clear rhinestones) Martha Stewart Crafts *Tool:* (border punch) Fiskars *Other:* (chipboard)

You Hold the Key

Designer: Kim Hughes

OUTSIDE

Sand all edges.

1. Make card from cardstock; trim patterned paper, round corners, and adhere.

2. Tie twill in bow and adhere; thread button with twine and adhere.

3. Punch border from patterned paper strip and adhere; adhere patterned paper strips and stitch.

4. Make key, following pattern on p. 283. Adhere, using foam tape at bottom.

5. Print sentiment on cardstock, trim, and adhere.

INSIDE

Sand all edges.

1. Make heart, following pattern on p.283; adhere.

2. Print sentiment on cardstock and trim; adhere, using foam tape in center. Punch circles from patterned paper and adhere.

3. Punch border from patterned paper strip and adhere; adhere patterned paper strips and stitch.

Finished size: 4¾" square

SUPPLIES: *Cardstock:* (orange) Die Cuts With a View; (ivory) Prism *Patterned paper:* (Teeny Weeny Stripe from All Girl collection, Pretty Rad Polka Dot from Sisters collection, Aqua Fancy from Best Friends Forever collection) My Mind's Eye; (Orange Cream from Lime Rickey collection) BasicGrey *Accent:* (pink button) BasicGrey *Fibers:* (cream twill, brown twine) Creative Impressions *Font:* (AL Landscape) www.twopeasinabucket.com *Tools:* (border punch) Stampin' Up!; (corner rounder punch) Marvy Uchida

Love is in the Air

Designer: Wendy Sue Anderson

OUTSIDE

1. Make card from patterned paper.
2. Trim patterned papers to cover card and stitch.
3. Trim cardstock strip with decorative-edge scissors; adhere. Adhere ribbon and tie on twill.
4. Attach brad to label die cut; adhere. Attach brad to charm and attach to knot with thread.

INSIDE

1. Fold and score a 5½" wide strip of patterned paper at 1½", 3", 3¾", 4½", and 5½" to create pop-up piece; adhere ends inside card.
2. Adhere photos.
3. Cut cardstock strip, stitch edges, and adhere. Cut heart from patterned paper; adhere. Layer and affix stickers to spell "We" and "You".
4. Add brads to tag die cut and adhere.

Finished size: 5½" x 6"

SUPPLIES: All supplies from Making Memories unless otherwise noted. *Cardstock:* (black) American Crafts; (kraft) no source *Patterned paper:* (Battenburg, Hearts Doily, Sampler, Die-Cut Artisan from Love Notes collection) *Accents:* (metal charm, black heart brads, sentiment label, tag die-cuts) *Stickers:* (Love Notes alphabets) *Fibers:* (red striped twill, cream dotted ribbon) *Tool:* (decorative-edge scissors) *Other:* (photographs) no source

the best is yet to be

-Robert Browning

Grow old along with me

Grow Old

Designer: Rae Barthel

OUTSIDE

Ink patterned paper edges.

1. Make card from cardstock. Adhere patterned paper.
2. Print sentiment on patterned paper; trim and adhere to card.
3. Tie ribbon in bow around card.
4. Adhere glitter to chipboard heart; adhere with foam tape.

INSIDE

Ink patterned paper edges.

1. Trim patterned paper, round corners, and adhere.
2. Trim patterned paper strip and adhere.
3. Print sentiment on patterned paper and trim using label die cut as template; adhere with foam tape.
4. Adhere rhinestones.

Finished size: 5" square

DESIGNER TIP

Use accents to pull colors from your patterned paper.

SUPPLIES: *Cardstock:* (kraft) DMD, Inc. *Patterned paper:* (Lovable from Knave of Hearts collection, Naturally Sweet from Sweet Shoppe collection) Collage Press *Chalk ink:* (Olive Pastel) Clearsnap *Accents:* (chipboard heart) Making Memories; (bracketed label die cut) My Mind's Eye; (silver glitter) Martha Stewart Crafts; (aqua rhinestones) Michaels *Fibers:* (blue ribbon) Offray *Font:* (Santa's Sleigh) www.dafont.com *Tools:* (corner rounder punch) EK Success

Followed My Heart

Designer: Betsy Veldman

OUTSIDE

Ink all paper edges.

1. Make card from cardstock and stamp script background.

2. Adhere patterned paper piece. Punch edge of patterned paper strip and adhere.

3. Stamp flourish and sentiment.

4. Stamp swirl heart on cardstock and trim; tie twine through button and adhere. Adhere to card with foam tape.

5. Knot and adhere ribbon.

INSIDE

Ink all paper edges.

1. Stamp script background.

2. Stamp flourish and sentiments.

3. Stamp solid heart on cardstock, trim, adhere rhinestone, and adhere with foam tape.

Finished size: 4¼" x 5½"

Designer Tip

The background of this card is stamped in cream ink on cream cardstock, giving a very subtle and pretty look. Inking the edges with a light brown chalk ink brings out the texture and gives lots of interest.

SUPPLIES: *Cardstock:* (Vintage Cream, Hibiscus Burst) Papertrey Ink *Patterned paper:* (This Little Piggy from Ducks in a Row collection) October Afternoon; (aqua grid from Bitty Box Basics collection) Papertrey Ink *Clear stamps:* (solid heart, swirl heart, sentiments from February Word Puzzle set) Close To My Heart; (flourish from Fancy Flourishes set, script background from Background Basics: Text Style set) Papertrey Ink *Pigment ink:* (Vintage Cream) Papertrey Ink *Chalk ink:* (Creamy Brown) Clearsnap *Specialty ink:* (Pure Poppy, Hibiscus Burst hybrid) Papertrey Ink *Accents:* (aqua button) Papertrey Ink; (blue rhinestone) Kaisercraft *Fibers:* (red ribbon) Papertrey Ink; (jute twine) The Beadery *Tool:* (border punch) Fiskars

Falling for You

Designer: Sherry Wright

Ink all edges.

1 Make card from cardstock. **2** Adhere patterned paper to card. **3** Cut tree top from patterned paper; adhere. **4** Stamp sentiment on sticker and affix. **5** Die-cut tree and adhere. **6** Stamp leaves on patterned paper and cut out; adhere. **7** Attach brad to felt heart; adhere.

Finished size: 5" x 6"

I Love You

Designer: Kim Frantz

1 Make card from cardstock. **2** Stamp Lacy Border. Trim; punch holes. **3** Punch cardstock circle. Ink edges. Draw border. **4** Stamp heart on scrap paper; cut out to make heart stencil. Place stencil over punched circle; apply ink to create red heart on circle. Overstamp heart on circle, slightly off-center. **5** Adhere ribbon. Adhere circle with foam tape. Adhere buttons. **6** Draw borders. **7** Apply rub-ons to spell "Love"; write "I" and "you" with pen.

Finished size: 4¼" x 5¾"

BONUS IDEA

Create a matching envelope and use the same heart as a seal.

SUPPLIES: *Rubber stamps:* (sentiment, leaves from Fall Silhouettes set) Cornish Heritage Farms *Chalk ink:* (Chestnut Roan, Lipstick Red) Clearsnap *Cardstock:* (Sunflower Medium) Prism *Patterned paper:* (Samara, Atelier Toile from Autumn Fall in Love collection) Daisy D's *Accents:* (brown felt heart) Fancy Pants Designs; (red heart brad) Queen & Co. *Sticker:* (kraft circle) Making Memories *Die:* (tree) Ellison *Tool:* (die cut machine) Ellison

SUPPLIES: *Rubber stamps:* (Heart with Flower, Lacy Border) Justjohanna Rubber Stamps *Dye ink:* (black) Tsukineko *Chalk ink:* (red) Clearsnap *Cardstock:* (Fairy Tale Pink, Brown Bag) WorldWin *Color medium:* (black pen) EK Success *Accents:* (red buttons) Jesse James & Co. *Rub-ons:* (Heidi alphabet) Making Memories *Fibers:* (black grosgrain ribbon) Michaels; (red gingham ribbon) American Crafts *Adhesive:* (foam tape) 3L *Tools:* (⅛" circle punch, 1¾" circle punch) Marvy Uchida

5 STEPS XOXO Love U

Designer: Linda Beeson

1 Make card from cardstock.
2 Cut cardstock slightly smaller than card front with decorative scissors.
3 Stamp and emboss xoxo on patterned paper; mat with cardstock and adhere.
4 Paint chipboard letter, apply lacquer, and adhere to card. 5 Stamp love sentiment, punch hole through corner of card; and tie ribbon through hole.

Finished size: 5½" square

SUPPLIES: *Rubber stamps:* (xoxo, love from Love set) Spunky Stamps *Dye ink:* (black) Stewart Superior Corp. *Watermark ink:* Tsukineko *Embossing powder:* (white) *Cardstock:* (Ciliega, Eclipse Black, White Prismatic) Prism *Patterned paper:* (Girl Pretty in Pink from Girl Collectionz) Junkitz *Paint:* (black) Plaid *Finish:* (crystal lacquer) Sakura Hobby and Craft *Accent:* (chipboard letter) Making Memories *Fibers:* (striped ribbon) *Tools:* (decorative-edge scissors) Family Treasures

Hugs & Kisses

Designer: Vicky Nelson

1 Make card from cardstock. 2 Stamp cardstock with Linen; trim slightly smaller than card front and adhere to card. 3 Stamp sentiment on cardstock; trim into strip, tear side, ink edges, and adhere to card. 4 Punch tag from cardstock; stamp and ink edges.
5 Cut strip of cardstock; tear top. Thread tag through cord; tie around cardstock, adhere. 6 Stamp flowers on cardstock; trim and adhere to card with pop-up dots.

Finished size: 5½" x 4¼"

DESIGNER TIP

Spectrum ink pads tend to dry out easily. Make sure your ink pad is always closed tightly and re-ink the pad when the differentiation between the colors begins to fade.

SUPPLIES: All supplies from Stampin' Up! unless otherwise noted. *Rubber stamps:* (flowers from Best Blossoms set, sentiment from Alphabet Soup set, sentiment from Everyday Flexible Phrases, Linen Background) *Dye ink:* (Cotton Candy Spectrum, Rose Red) *Cardstock:* (pink, red) *Fibers:* (pink cord) Sulyn Industries *Tools:* (tag punch) McGill

SUPPLIES: *Rubber stamps:* (The Kiss) The Stampsmith; (Large Stitched Heart) Hero Arts *Acrylic stamp:* (love from Truly, Madly, Deeply set) Technique Tuesday *Dye ink:* (Jet Black, Vermillion Lacquer) Ranger Industries *Cardstock:* (red, black) Provo Craft; (white glossy) Judikins *Patterned paper:* (Text from Ledger collection) Making Memories

Classic Kiss

Designer: Teri Anderson

1 Make card from red cardstock. Trim cardstock slightly smaller than card front; adhere to card. **2** Stamp heart on patterned paper; trim and adhere to card. **3** Stamp The Kiss on glossy cardstock; adhere to card. **4** Stamp sentiment on card front.

Finished size: 5¾" square

DESIGNER TIP

When using photographic stamps, use glossy cardstock rather than traditional cardstock for a cleaner, crisper image.

SUPPLIES: *Acrylic stamps:* (Masterpieces of Paisley, Circle Background) Technique Tuesday *Dye ink:* (Toile Pink, black, burgundy) Stewart Superior Corp. *Cardstock:* (white) Bazzill Basics Paper *Patterned paper:* (True Love Words, Love in Bloom from True Love collection) Flair Designs *Rub-ons:* (sentiments) Flair Designs *Sticker:* (sentiment strip) Flair Designs *Tools:* (1½" circle punch) EK Success

Pink & Black Paisley

Designer: Karen Day

1 Make card from cardstock; cut patterned paper to fit card front and adhere. **2** Stamp white cardstock; ink edges and adhere to card. **3** Cut strip of patterned paper; adhere to card. Apply sticker to seam. **4** Punch cardstock; stamp, apply rub-ons, and adhere to card.

Finished size: 5½" x 4¼"

⁵ Any Excuse to Eat Chocolate

Designer: Alice Golden

1 Cut Candy Stripe paper slightly smaller than large card flap; print sentiment, adhere stickers, and adhere to card. **2** Cut Candy Stripe slightly smaller than small flap; adhere. **3** Cut heart shape. Print sentiment, leaving room for stamps; mat with Red cardstock. **4** Adhere candy wrapper cups along border. Cut second heart shape and adhere to back of original. Adhere entire piece to small card flap. **5** Stamp Chocolat and Chocolates.

Finished size: 4½" x 9¼"

This card is the ideal accompaniment to a box of decadent chocolates for your best girlfriend!

SUPPLIES: **Rubber stamps:** (Chocolat, Chocolates) *Hampton Art* **Dye ink:** (Artprint Brown) *Stewart Superior Corp.* **Textured cardstock:** (Red) *Die Cuts With a View* **Patterned paper:** (Shimmer Glitter Mini Dots, Candy Stripe from Love of My Life collection) *Heidi Grace Designs* **Accent:** (candy wrapper cups) **Stickers:** (girl with chocolates, heart) *Creative Imaginations* **Font:** (Jeana) www.scrapvillage.com **Other:** (red matchbook card) *Making Memories*

Crushin' On You

Designer: Kathleen Paneitz

1 Make card from white textured cardstock. **2** Cut Geometric paper slightly smaller than card front; adhere. **3** Print "For crushin' on you" on white cardstock; cut into rectangle, ink edges, and adhere. **4** Stamp Dressmaker's Delight on rectangle of white; chalk image, and adhere decorative tape and index tab. Ink edges of piece; adhere. **5** Apply rub-ons to spell "Busted" on index tab insert; tuck into tab. **6** Apply do you like me rub-on.

Finished size: 3⅞" x 5¼"

SUPPLIES: **Rubber stamps:** (Dressmaker's Delight) *Stampabilities* **Pigment ink:** (Black) *Tsukineko* **Cardstock:** (white) **Textured cardstock:** (white) **Patterned paper:** (Geometric from Uptown collection) *Cross My Heart* **Color media:** (pink chalk) *Craf-T Products*; (black marker) *EK Success* **Accents:** (plastic index tab, decorative tape) *Heidi Swapp* **Rub-ons:** (do you like me, Portobello alphabet) *7gypsies* **Font:** (Bad Hair Day) www.twopeasinabucket.com **Other:** (dimensional glaze) *Duncan*

:5: Love Always Card

Designer: Celeste Rockwood-Jones

1 Cut two pieces of patterned paper and one piece of vellum to finished size.

2 Cut squares from patterned paper and adhere.

3 Cut out center square.

4 Clip together all three sheets with vellum in center.

5 Apply rub-on to vellum in opening.

Finished size: 4¼" square

SUPPLIES: *Patterned paper:* (Crush, Girlfriend, Devotion, Angelic from Blush collection; Posey from LilyKate collection) BasicGrey *Vellum:* (white) *Accent:* (copper spiral clip) Heidi Swapp *Rub-on:* (love always) BasicGrey

5 STEPS · Be My Valentine Card

Designer: Heather Thompson

1 Make card from cardstock. **2** Crimp patterned paper; wrap ribbon and adhere. Adhere button; adhere patterned paper to card. **3** Adhere cardstock to swirl chipboard; sand edges. Apply rub-ons; adhere swirls. **4** Adhere hearts with foam tape.

Finished size: 6" x 5"

DESIGNER TIP

Using pre-made glitter accents on projects is another quick and easy way to add texture to a design.

SUPPLIES: All supplies from Melissa Frances unless otherwise noted. *Cardstock:* (Mountain Rose metallic, Champagne metallic) Prism *Patterned paper:* (Brian) *Accents:* (chipboard swirl) Deluxe Designs; (ivory button; pink, white chipboard hearts) *Rub-ons:* (be my valentine) *Fibers:* (pink floral ribbon) *Adhesive:* (foam tape) Therm O Web *Tool:* (paper crimper) Fiskars

Love & Cherish Card

Designer: Wendy Johnson

1 Make card from cardstock. **2** Cut heart window from patterned paper. **3** Apply rub-on to cardstock and adhere behind patterned paper. **4** Stitch sequins around heart with floss. Adhere piece to card.

Finished size: 4¼" square

Sweet Valentine's Day Garland

Designer: Betsy Veldman

1 Emboss cardstock; adhere to chipboard. **2** Cover chipboard cherries with patterned paper. **3** Embellish squares with cherries, die cut alphabet, rub-ons, rhinestones, and ribbon. **4** Die-cut scalloped frames from patterned paper and adhere with foam tape. Adhere rhinestones. **5** Punch holes in frames and tie on ribbon. Pin squares to cording. Tie cording ends in bows.

Finished size: each piece 5¼" square

SUPPLIES: *Cardstock:* (Chantilly, Route 66) Bazzill Basics Paper *Patterned paper:* (kraft polka dot) Making Memories *Accents:* (white flower sequins) Doodlebug Design *Rub-on:* (love & cherish) American Crafts *Fibers:* (white floss)

SUPPLIES: *Cardstock:* (white) *Patterned paper:* (Crimson Dots, Elegant, Delightful from Serendipity Blue Boutique collection; Raspberry Ripple, Green Apple from Serendipity Scrumptious collection) Sassafras Lass *Accents:* (red rhinestones) Imaginisce; (chipboard cherries) Creative Imaginations; (pink, green safety pins; clear rhinestones) *Rub-ons:* (be mine, sweetheart, sweet) Junkitz *Fibers:* (pink dotted grosgrain ribbon, pink/red/white cording) Michaels; (red grosgrain ribbon) Offray; (red/pink gingham ribbon) May Arts *Dies:* (scalloped frame, alphabet) Provo Craft *Template:* (swirl embossing) Provo Craft *Adhesive:* (foam tape) *Tool:* (die-cut/embossing machine) Provo Craft *Other:* (chipboard)

Be Mine Card

Designer: Alisa Bangerter

1 Make card from cardstock. **2** Sand edges of patterned paper and attach brads to corners; adhere. **3** Trim cardstock block. Lightly trace heart shape with pencil; stitch ribbon around heart outline. Zigzag-stitch block to card. **4** Fold strip of ribbon; stitch to card. **5** Apply rub-ons to spell "Be mine" to cardstock; trim, ink edges, and adhere with foam tape.

Finished size: 5" x 7"

Missing You Card

Designer: Wendy Sue Anderson

1 Make card from cardstock. **2** Trim patterned paper to fit card front; ink edges and adhere. Adhere patterned paper blocks; stamp stitches around edges. **3** Tie ribbon to tag; adhere tag to card. Stamp circle stitches and affix stickers to spell "I am missing". **4** Cover chipboard letters with patterned paper; adhere. Affix sentiment sticker. **5** Attach clip to tag.

Finished size: 5¾" x 4½"

SUPPLIES: *Cardstock:* (red, white) *Patterned paper:* (Cut-A-Part Cardmaker from Formality collection) One Heart One Mind *Dye ink:* (black) Stewart Superior Corp. *Accents:* (white brads) Making Memories *Rub-ons:* (Simply Stated alphabet) *Fibers:* (red grosgrain ribbon) Offray; (black stitched ribbon) Pebbles Inc. *Adhesive:* (foam tape) Making Memories

SUPPLIES: *Cardstock:* (cream) *Patterned paper:* (Diamond Brocade, Postcard, Journal, Color Block from Travel collection) Making Memories *Clear stamps:* (stitches, circle stitches from Baby set) Doodlebug Design *Pigment ink:* (Chestnut) Clearsnap *Accents:* (chipboard letters, clip, journaling tag) Making Memories *Stickers:* (Tiny alphabet) Making Memories; (wish you were here) 7gypsies *Fibers:* (black/cream gingham ribbon) Creative Impressions

⁵steps XOXO Hearts

Designer: Lori Tecler

❶ Make card from cardstock.

❷ Stamp large heart and xoxo on cardstock. Knot and adhere ribbon. Adhere to card.

❸ Stamp small heart on cardstock. Punch into heart and adhere with foam tape.

Finished size: 5½" x 4¼"

DESIGNER TIP

Make a slit in the heart so you can easily thread the ribbon through the cardstock and tie it on.

⁵steps Sweet Hearts Be Mine

Designer: Anabelle O'Malley

❶ Make card from cardstock; adhere patterned paper.

❷ Adhere rhinestone circle. Tie on ribbon.

❸ Paint frame. Distress edges and adhere with foam tape.

❹ Stamp hearts on cardstock. Cut out and adhere, using foam tape for one. Adhere rhinestones.

❺ Stamp be mine on card. Insert stick pin.

Finished size: 4" x 6"

SUPPLIES: *Clear stamp:* (large, small hearts; xoxo from Heart Prints set) Papertrey Ink *Pigment ink:* (Basic Black) Stampin' Up! *Specialty ink:* Raspberry Fizz hybrid) Papertrey Ink *Cardstock:* (Raspberry Fizz) Papertrey Ink; (black, white) Stampin' Up! *Fibers:* (black ribbon) Target *Tool:* (heart punch) EK Success

SUPPLIES: *Clear stamps:* (swirl, text, floral hearts; be mine from Heart Prints set) Papertrey Ink *Specialty ink:* (Pure Poppy, Hibiscus Burst hybrid) Papertrey Ink *Paint:* (cream) Delta *Cardstock:* (Pure Poppy, Vintage Cream) Papertrey Ink *Patterned paper:* (red scallop from Paperie Rouge collection notebook) Making Memories *Accents:* (red rhinestones, pink rhinestone circle) Zva Creative; (pink pearl stick pin) Caramelos; (chipboard frame) Maya Road *Fibers:* (red ribbon) Papertrey Ink

INSIDE

5 STEPS You Make Life Sweet

Designer: Lisa Johnson

1 Adhere tag to card. **2** Wrap ribbon around card; knot. **3** Stamp You Make Life Sweet on white cardstock with Basic Black; punch out with window punch. Adhere. **4** Stamp Ice Cream Truck on white with Basic Black; stamp rickrack with Bashful Blue. Trim image, round top corners, and adhere. **5** Stamp Ice Cream Truck on white with Basic Black; cut out image and apply ink with water brush as desired. Adhere over original stamped image with foam squares.

Finished size: 4¼" square

Knock Knock

Designer: Teri Anderson

CARD

Cut White textured cardstock to 11¼" x 5"; accordion-fold into five 2¼" x 5" panels.

PANEL 1

1 Cut Tan cardstock to fit panel; ink lightly with Charcoal and adhere. **2** Stamp text heart on White cardstock; cut out, ink edges with Charcoal, and adhere. **3** Stamp "Knock knock" on Red cardstock with Jet Black; cut out and adhere. **4** Stamp zigzag with Vermillion Lacquer. Attach clip.

PANEL 2

1 Cut Red to fit panel; stamp "Who is there" with Jet Black. **2** Knot ribbon around piece; adhere to panel.

PANEL 3

1 Stamp Trio Heart Border three times on panel with Vermillion Lacquer. **2** Stamp "Love" on Tan with Jet Black; trim to fit bookplate and adhere to panel. **3** Attach bookplate with brads.

PANEL 4

1 Stamp "Love who" on Red with Jet Black; trim to fit panel, and adhere. **2** Stamp small heart on strip of White with Vermillion Lacquer; adhere.

PANEL 5

1 Stamp Thin Striped Rectangle on panel with Vermillion Lacquer. **2** Stamp frame on Red with Jet Black; trim and adhere. **3** Stamp "Love you" on Tan; trim and adhere to panel. **4** Punch small heart from White textured cardstock; adhere.

Finished size: 2¼" x 5"

DESIGNER TIP

To keep cardstock from bending or creasing when attaching brads, use a pushpin to make the holes first.

SUPPLIES Rubber stamps: (Ice Cream Truck, You Make Life Sweet) *A Muse Artstamps*; (rickrack) **Dye ink:** (Bashful Blue, Creamy Caramel, Real Red, Basic Black) *Stampin' Up!* **Cardstock:** (white) **Accents:** (red asterisk tag) *A Muse Artstamps*; (glitter) *Stampin' Up!* **Fibers:** (light blue, red gingham ribbon) *May Arts* **Adhesive:** (foam squares) *3M* **Tools:** (corner rounder punch, word window punch, water brush) *Stampin' Up!* **Other:** (Celestial Blue card) *A Muse Artstamps*

SUPPLIES Rubber stamps: (text heart from Be Mine Sentiments) *My Sentiments Exactly!*; (Trio Heart Border; small heart from Classic Lowercase alphabet; zigzag from Ribbons & Stitches set) *Hero Arts*; (Jen alphabet) *Rusty Pickle*; (Thin Striped Rectangle) *Savvy Stamps* **Acrylic stamps:** (Williamsburg Lower Case Letters) *Technique Tuesday* **Dye ink:** (Vermillion Lacquer) *Ranger Industries* **Solvent ink:** (Jet Black) *Tsukineko* **Chalk ink:** (Charcoal) *Clearsnap* **Cardstock:** (Red, Tan, White) *Provo Craft* **Textured cardstock:** (White) *Bazzill Basics Paper* **Accents:** (red brads) *Die Cuts With a View*; (silver bookplate) *Making Memories*; (red metal clip) *Design Originals* **Fibers:** (white polka dot ribbon) *Michaels* **Tools:** (small heart punch) *EK Success*

SWAK

Designer: Wendy Sue Anderson, courtesy of Making Memories

1 Cut Pink Gingham paper to fit inside card; adhere.
2 Cut window in card front; stamp lips on transparency and trim to fit behind window. Adhere and stitch border. **3** Stamp SWAK on Pink Gingham; trim into tag shape. Punch hole and attach charm with jute. Adhere to card. **4** Remove white string from card closures; thread ribbon through and tie closed.

Finished size: 5" square

Kiss a Lot of Frogs

Designer: Stacey Stamitoles, courtesy of Paper Salon

1 Cut Petal cardstock slightly smaller than card front; cut rectangle of Pear cardstock and zigzag-stitch to piece. Adhere to card. **2** Trim Cotton cardstock to fit inside acrylic frame; stamp Frog Prince. Color image with pencils and adhere to frame. **3** Cut square of Lipstick cardstock to fit behind frame; adhere. Adhere frame to card. **4** Print sentiment on Cotton; trim, attach brads, and adhere to card. **5** Tie ribbon bow; adhere to card.

Finished size: 4¼" x 5½"

SUPPLIES *All supplies from Making Memories unless otherwise noted.* **Foam stamps:** (lips, SWAK from Valentines set) **Transparency sheet; Patterned paper:** (Pink Gingham from Bella collection) **Paint:** (Red Wagon) **Accent:** (key charm) **Fibers:** (red stitched ribbon); (white thread, red jute) no source **Tools:** (1⁄16" circle punch) **Other:** (Rose Petal Solid gatefold card)

SUPPLIES **Rubber stamps:** (Frog Prince) *Paper Salon* **Dye ink:** (Licorice) *Paper Salon* **Cardstock:** (Cotton, Petal, Lipstick, Pear) *Paper Salon* **Color medium:** (assorted colored pencils) *Sanford* **Accents:** (polka dot acrylic frame) *Making Memories*; (red heart brads) **Fibers:** (red stitched ribbon) *Fibers by the Yard*; (white thread) **Font:** (CK Journaling) *Creating Keepsakes* **Tools:** (blending stump) **Other:** (Lipstick card) *Paper Salon*; (sandpaper)

5 STEPS You Make My Heart Sing

Designer: Katie Stilwater

1. Cut patterned paper slightly smaller than note card.

2. Die-cut heart from cardstock; adhere to patterned paper piece.

3. Stamp Branch and MB Little Bird on heart. Color with markers and pencils; draw hearts with pencil.

4. Wrap piece with ribbon; adhere to note card. Tie ribbon bow; adhere.

5. Stamp Heart Sings on cardstock; trim, notch end, and adhere with foam tape.

Finished size: 4¼" x 4"

5 STEPS Peacock Love

Designer: Kim Moreno

1. Make card from patterned paper. Adhere patterned paper strip.

2. Cut cardstock to fit card front; cut in curve. Stamp xoxo repeatedly; emboss.

3. Punch scalloped circles from patterned paper; adhere behind edge of embossed piece. Adhere to card.

4. Stamp love. Adhere rhinestone.

5. Ink card edges. Tie with ribbon.

Finished size: 5½" x 4¼"

DESIGNER TIP
Look for fun elements on patterned paper that can serve as focal points on your projects. It saves adding extra bulk and expense with additional embellishments.

SUPPLIES: *Rubber stamps:* (MB Little Bird, Branch, Heart Sings) A Muse Artstamps *Dye ink:* (black) Ranger Industries *Cardstock:* (lavender, white) *Patterned paper:* (Kitchen Chocolate) A Muse Artstamps *Color media:* (tan, green, yellow markers) Copic Marker; (light aqua, dark aqua, lavender pencils) Prismacolor *Fibers:* (aqua stitched ribbon) A Muse Artstamps *Adhesive:* (foam tape) *Die:* (heart) Spellbinders *Tool:* (die cut machine) Spellbinders *Other:* (aqua note card) A Muse Artstamps

SUPPLIES: *Rubber stamps:* (xoxo from Hugs & Kisses set, love from Cute Curls set) Cornish Heritage Farms *Dye ink:* (red, orange) Clearsnap *Watermark ink:* Tsukineko *Embossing powder:* (clear) Hampton Art *Cardstock:* (orange) Core'dinations *Patterned paper:* (Bubbly, Wishes, Zoology from The Menagerie collection) Dream Street Papers *Accent:* (clear rhinestone) Kaisercraft *Fibers:* (blue stitched ribbon) Fancy Pants Designs *Tool:* (scalloped circle punch) Martha Stewart Crafts

Love You Vine

Designer: Dawn McVey

1. Make card from cardstock. Distress bottom edge.
2. Stamp leaf wreath repeatedly on card.
3. Cut strip of cardstock, distress edges, and adhere.
4. Stamp branches on cardstock; cut out and adhere. Stamp love you.
5. Adhere leaf trim. Tie ribbon bow and adhere.

Finished size: 4¼" x 5½"

Floral Love

Designer: Melissa Phillips

1. Make card from cardstock. Cover with patterned paper.
2. Adhere slightly smaller patterned paper piece; stitch edges.
3. Trim long edges of patterned paper strip with decorative-edge scissors. Adhere patterned paper strip. Tie with ribbon and adhere to card. Zigzag-stitch right edge.
4. Stamp butterfly line twice on cardstock; cut out. Apply glitter glue. Attach flowers with brads. Adhere to card.
5. Stamp scroll on tag. Spell "Love" with rub-ons. Tie button and tag to ribbon with twine.

Finished size: 5" x 3¾"

SUPPLIES: All supplies from Papertrey Ink unless otherwise noted. *Clear stamps:* (branches, leaf wreath, love, you from Rustic Branches set) *Dye ink:* (Old Olive) Stampin' Up! *Specialty ink:* (Spring Moss, Plum Pudding hybrid) *Cardstock:* (Spring Moss, Plum Pudding, white) *Fibers:* (green leaf trim, purple ribbon)

SUPPLIES: *Rubber stamps:* (butterfly line, scroll from Little Labels 2 set) Unity Stamp Co. *Pigment ink:* (Opera Pink) Tsukineko *Cardstock:* (Light Coffee Brown, white) WorldWin *Patterned paper:* (Stylish, Fandango, Friar from Sultry collection) BasicGrey; (green polka dot) BasicGrey; (green flowers) Prima; (pink glitter glue) Ranger Industries *Rub-ons:* (Ginger alphabet) American Crafts *Fibers:* (tan ribbon) Martha Stewart Crafts; (hemp twine) Darice *Tool:* (decorative-edge scissors) Provo Craft

DESIGNER TIP

Make this card even more personal by using the wedding couple's colors.

 Love Birds

Designer: Winter Sims

❶ Make card from cardstock; adhere patterned paper. ❷ Stamp branch and birds on cardstock. Trim and adhere, using foam tape for birds. ❸ Cut heart from cardstock and adhere with foam tape. ❹ Adhere lace and tie on ribbon bow.

Finished size: 4¼" x 5½"

 You Are My Heart

Designer: Asela Hopkins

❶ Make card from cardstock; adhere patterned paper. ❷ Stamp sentiment, color heart with marker, and apply dimensional glaze. ❸ Adhere ribbon.

Finished size: 3½" x 5"

SUPPLIES: *Cardstock:* (cream, burgundy) Stampin' Up! *Patterned paper:* (Red Circles from Lush collection) My Mind's Eye *Clear stamps:* (birds, branch from Love Birds collection) Wplus9 Design Studio *Pigment ink:* (Close to Cocoa) Stampin' Up! *Chalk ink:* (Charcoal) Clearsnap *Fibers:* (burgundy ribbon) Offray; (black lace) Hobby Lobby

SUPPLIES: *Cardstock:* (white) Neenah Paper *Patterned paper:* (Vintage Travel from On Holiday collection) The Girls' Paperie *Rubber stamp:* (sentiment from Savor the Journey set) Unity Stamp Co. *Dye ink:* (black) *Color medium:* (red marker) Copic *Fibers:* (red/tan ribbon) BasicGrey *Other:* (dimensional glaze) Aleene's

DESIGNER TIP

The Simple Little Things set is no longer available for purchase. Try using a sentiment from the Wedding Day set from Papertrey Ink as a replacement.

Now & Forever

Designer: Latisha Yoast

1 Make card from cardstock; adhere transparency sheet.
2 Stamp sentiment and adhere rhinestones. 3 Tie on ribbon bow.

Finished size: 3¾" x 5½"

Cherish

Designer: Lucy Abrams

1 Make card from cardstock. 2 Create 4¼" x 5" project in software. Stamp image and resize as desired; print on cardstock. Drop in patterned paper behind image, print on cardstock, stitch edges, and adhere. Trim umbrella from first image and adhere.
3 Stamp cherish. 4 Tie on ribbon bow and adhere pearl.

Finished size: 4½" x 5¼"

SUPPLIES: *Cardstock:* (white) *Transparency sheet:* (Milla) Prima *Clear stamp:* (sentiment from Simple Little Things set) Papertrey Ink *Dye ink:* (Tuxedo Black) Tsukineko *Accents:* (clear rhinestones) BasicGrey *Fibers:* (pink ribbon) Offray

SUPPLIES: *Cardstock:* (Eggshell) Hero Arts *Clear stamp:* (cherish from Best Wishes set) Hero Arts *Dye ink:* (black) *Accent:* (cream pearl) Prima *Digital elements:* (heart patterned paper from Home is Where the Heart Is kit, couple stamp from Vintage Lifestyle set) www.twopeasinabucket.com *Fibers:* (cream ribbon) Creative Impressions *Software:* (photo editing)

⑤ What is Love?

Designer: Lea Lawson

❶ Make card from cardstock. ❷ Mat cardstock rectangle with patterned paper. Border-punch sides. ❸ Affix stickers and apply rub-on to piece. ❹ Adhere ribbon and adhere piece to card with foam tape. ❺ Adhere rhinestones. Tie ribbon bow and adhere.

Finished size: 4¼" x 5½"

⑤ Elegant Love

Designer: Ellie Augustin

❶ Make card from cardstock. Stamp solid diamonds. ❷ Die-cut label from cardstock, stamp love, and adhere with foam tape. ❸ Tie on ribbon bow and adhere pearl and rhinestones.

Finished size: 3¾" x 5½"

SUPPLIES: *Cardstock:* (red, white) Bazzill Basics Paper *Patterned paper:* (Stripe from Distressed Couture collection) Glitz Design *Accents:* (red rhinestones) Glitz Design *Rub-on:* (heart with flourish) Glitz Design *Stickers:* (what is love, you + me labels) Glitz Design *Fibers:* (red polka dot ribbon) Offray *Tool:* (border punch) Fiskars

SUPPLIES: *Cardstock:* (white) Papertrey Ink *Clear stamps:* (love from Urban Grunge set) Stampers Anonymous; (solid diamonds from A Little Argyle set) Papertrey Ink *Specialty ink:* (True Black hybrid) Papertrey Ink *Accents:* (white pearl) Martha Stewart Crafts; (clear rhinestones) Kaisercraft *Fibers:* (red ribbon) Stampin' Up! *Die:* (label) Making Memories

DESIGNER TIP

Printing and trimming letters to look like stickers is an inexpensive way to create sentiments for your cards.

Can't Contain My Love

Designer: Tanis Giesbrecht

① Make card from cardstock. ② Adhere strips of patterned paper together, round corners, and adhere to card. ③ Affix jar and spell "My love" with stickers. ④ Print remainder of sentiment on cardstock, trim, and adhere. ⑤ Cut heart from felt. Stitch with floss and adhere.

Finished size: 4¼" square

Rosy Love You

Designer: Teri Anderson

① Make card from cardstock. ② Adhere cardstock and patterned paper strip. ③ Adhere journaling tag. ④ Loop ribbon and adhere behind love you die cut; adhere to card with foam tape. ⑤ Adhere rhinestones.

Finished size: 3½" x 5½"

SUPPLIES: *Cardstock:* (kraft, white) Stampin' Up! *Patterned paper:* (Strawberry Jam, Sprinklers from Fly a Kite collection) October Afternoon *Stickers:* (jar) American Crafts; (Mini Market alphabet) October Afternoon *Fibers:* (white floss) *Font:* (Small Typewriting) www.fontriver.com *Tool:* (corner rounder punch) We R Memory Keepers *Other:* (red felt)

SUPPLIES: *Cardstock:* (white) Georgia-Pacific; (red embossed) Bazzill Basics Paper *Patterned paper:* (Homespun Diecut Label from Homespun collection) Jenni Bowlin Studio *Accents:* (red rhinestones) Kaisercraft; (rose journaling tag) Jenni Bowlin Studio; (love you die cut) Ormolu *Fibers:* (pink ribbon) Papertrey Ink

⑤ Cupid Wishes

Designer: Vanessa Menhorn

Ink all paper edges.
① Make card from cardstock. ② Stamp best and wishes on patterned paper panel and cupid on cardstock. ③ Die-cut cupid into oval and die-cut scalloped oval from cardstock. Layer and adhere to panel. ④ Tie floss around panel and adhere to card. ⑤ Thread button with floss. Adhere buttons and pearls.

Finished size: 4¼" x 5½"

Celebration of Love

Designer: Beatriz Jennings

① Make card from cardstock; ink edges. ② Adhere patterned paper and stamp post card. ③ Zigzag-stitch patterned paper to card. Trim tag from patterned paper; adhere. ④ Adhere appliqué. Adhere glitter to chipboard and adhere to card. ⑤ Tie ribbon bow and adhere. ⑥ Adhere button, pearl, rhinestones, and flower.

Finished size: 4¼" x 5½"

SUPPLIES: *Cardstock:* (Vintage Cream, Dark Chocolate, white) Papertrey Ink *Patterned paper:* (Dream Big from 365 Degrees collection) Pink Paislee *Clear stamps:* (best, wishes from Giga Guide Lines set) Papertrey Ink; (cupid from Cupid set) Pink Paislee *Dye ink:* (Walnut Stain, Antique Linen) Ranger Industries *Pigment ink:* (Pearlescent Chocolate) Tsukineko *Accents:* (cream pearls) Prima; (cream buttons) Papertrey Ink *Fibers:* (brown floss) *Dies:* (oval, scalloped oval) Spellbinders

SUPPLIES: *Cardstock:* (Rustic Cream) Papertrey Ink *Patterned paper:* (Tender Missives, Tags from Le Romantique collection) Graphic 45 *Clear stamp:* (post card from Timeless Romance set) Tattered Angels *Dye ink:* (Vintage Photo) Ranger Industries *Accents:* (chipboard frame) Tattered Angels; (iridescent glitter) Doodlebug Design; (blue rhinestones, white pearl) Kaisercraft; (pink flower, clear button, pink lace appliqué) Michaels *Fibers:* (blue ribbon) Michaels

Designer Tip

Mixing and matching small squares of patterned paper is a great way to use up your scraps!

:5: My Heart Adores You

Designer: Kim Hughes

❶ Make card from cardstock. Trim ¼" from front flap. ❷ Border-punch patterned paper and adhere to front flap. ❸ Adhere patterned paper squares. *Note: Apply rose rub-on before adhering left squares.* Affix photo corners to one square. ❹ Apply sentiment rub-on and attach flower with brad. ❺ Thread button with floss and adhere. Adhere chipboard heart.

Finished size: 4¾" x 5"

:5: Tic Tac Love

Designer: Tiffany Johnson

❶ Make card from cardstock; adhere patterned paper. ❷ Draw lines with marker. ❸ Stamp heart, X, and O repeatedly on stickers. Affix to card.

Finished size: 4¼" x 5½"

SUPPLIES: *Cardstock:* (String of Pearls shimmer) Bazzill Basics Paper *Patterned paper:* (Front Porch from Fly a Kite collection; Shady Lane RV Park from Road Map collection; Collector's Item, Last One from The Thrift Shop collection) October Afternoon; (Front Porch from Bayberry collection) Pink Paislee; (Hear the Beat from Dan the Record Man collection) Nikki Sivils Scrapbooker; (Big Butterfly from Artsy Urban collection) GCD Studios; (For Him Playful from Ooh La La collection) My Mind's Eye *Accents:* (yellow chipboard heart) American Crafts; (yellow glitter brad) Doodlebug Design; (aqua button) Papertrey Ink; (yellow fabric flower) Little Yellow Bicycle *Rub-ons:* (yellow rose) American Crafts; (sentiment) Creative Imaginations *Stickers:* (white photo corners) Therm O Web *Fibers:* (aqua floss) DMC *Tool:* (border punch) Stampin' Up!

SUPPLIES: *Cardstock:* (Vintage Cream) Papertrey Ink *Patterned paper:* (Blueline from Basics collection) BasicGrey *Clear stamps:* (Harold's ABCs; heart from Just My Type Too set) Lawn Fawn *Dye ink:* (Tuxedo Black, Lady Bug) Tsukineko *Color medium:* (black marker) Sakura *Stickers:* (metal rimmed tags) EK Success

Groovy Love Card

Designer: Latisha Yoast

1. Make card from cardstock.

2. Cut strip of patterned paper; trim to form curve and adhere.

3. Cut strip of patterned paper; punch border and adhere.

4. Die-cut hearts from patterned paper; adhere.

5. Stamp sentiment on cardstock; trim and adhere with foam tape.

6. Thread button with twine; attach stick pin and tie bow. Adhere button.

Finished size: 4¼" x 5¾"

SUPPLIES: *Cardstock:* (white) Flourishes *Patterned paper:* (Birdy Gossip from Animal Bash collection) Prima *Clear stamp:* (groovy love sentiment from Feeling Groovy set) Verve Stamps *Dye ink:* (Tuxedo Black) Tsukineko *Accents:* (red heart stick pin) Making Memories; (yellow button) Autumn Leaves *Fibers:* (white twine) May Arts *Die:* (heart) Spellbinders *Tool:* (border punch) Martha Stewart Crafts

Best Wishes Card

Designer: Rae Barthel

SUPPLIES: *Cardstock:* (black) Hobby Lobby *Patterned paper:* (Tan Floral with Black Flocking, tan textured, small squares, tiny polka dots from La Crème pad) Die Cuts With a View *Chalk ink:* (Blackbird) Clearsnap *Accents:* (chipboard hearts) Making Memories; (white felt flower) Zva Creative; (black rhinestone) Kaisercraft *Font:* (Garton) www.fontstock.net *Tool:* (½" circle punch) EK Success

Finished size: 4¼" x 6¼"

Designer Tip
Keep black, white, and cream patterned paper on hand to create classic wedding and anniversary cards.

Joy Hearts Card

Designer: Beatriz Jennings

SUPPLIES: *Cardstock:* (kraft) DMD, Inc. *Patterned paper:* (Thankful from Thankful collection) Melissa Frances *Dye ink:* (Vintage Photo) Ranger Industries *Specialty ink:* (gold shimmer spray) Tattered Angels *Accents:* (cream chipboard wings) Tattered Angels; (date tag, flower die cut) K&Company; (white glitter chipboard hearts, white button, green-rimmed button, white pearls) *Rub-on:* (joy) Melissa Frances *Fibers:* (aqua ribbon, white lace trim, twine)

Finished size: 3½" x 6"

Two Hearts
Miss You Card

Designer: Maile Belles

SUPPLIES: *Cardstock:* (Melon Berry, Vintage Cream, Dark Chocolate, kraft) Papertrey Ink *Clear stamps:* (miss you from Beyond Basic Borders set) Papertrey Ink; (Houndstooth Block) Studio Calico *Specialty ink:* (Aqua Mist, Dark Chocolate hybrid) Papertrey Ink *Accents:* (brown buttons) Papertrey Ink *Fibers:* (pink floss) DMC *Dies:* (heart, heart frame) Provo Craft *Tools:* (border punch) Stampin' Up!; (circle cutter)

Finished size: 3½" x 7¼"

Designer Tip
Use strong adhesive to attach the scalloped edge to the base—it will have to bear the weight of the card.

5 STEPS You Rock Card

Designer: Ryann Salamon

1. Make card from cardstock.

2. Cut patterned paper and mat with cardstock. Cut photo corners from cardstock and adhere. Adhere to card.

3. Affix stereo and thought bubble. Spell sentiment with stickers.

Finished size: 4¼" square

SUPPLIES: *Cardstock:* (Dark Chocolate) Papertrey Ink; (Classic Red) Prism *Patterned paper:* (Tube Socks from The Boyfriend collection) Cosmo Cricket *Stickers:* (chipboard stereo, thought bubble) Cosmo Cricket; (Wonderful alphabet) My Little Shoebox

Hey Chick Card
Designer: Ashley C. Newell

SUPPLIES: *Cardstock:* (Aqua Mist, Dark Chocolate, Hibiscus Burst, Lavender Moon, Lemon Tart, white) Papertrey Ink *Patterned paper:* (yellow grid from 2008 Bitty Box Basics collection) Papertrey Ink *Clear stamps:* (sentiment from Everyday Button Bits set; birds, legs from Bird Watching Additions set) Papertrey Ink *Dye ink:* (Chocolate Chip) Stampin' Up! *Specialty ink:* (Aqua Mist, Plum Pudding, Summer Sunrise hybrid) Papertrey Ink *Accents:* (pink, yellow, blue rhinestones) Kaisercraft *Other:* (yellow felt) Heather Bailey

Finished size: 5" square

Woof Card
Designer: Angie Tieman

SUPPLIES: *Cardstock:* (kraft) Stampin' Up! *Patterned paper:* (Admiral from June Bug collection) BasicGrey; (Elements from Jolly By Golly) Cosmo Cricket *Stickers:* (chipboard dog) BasicGrey; (Playroom alphabet) American Crafts *Template:* (Houndstooth embossing) Provo Craft

Finished size: 5¼" square

Really Ruff You Card
Designer: Laura O'Donnell

SUPPLIES: *Cardstock:* (white) Cornish Heritage Farms *Rubber stamps:* (sentiment from Doggie Expressions set, The Honeymooners, Vintage Text Scrapblock) Cornish Heritage Farms *Dye ink:* (black, Summer Sky) Tsukineko *Color medium:* (black, red markers) Tsukineko

Finished size: 5" square

Designer Tip
Use dye ink markers when coloring directly on the stamp so that it doesn't permanently stain the rubber.

Love You Anniversary Card

Designer: Kim Hughes

1 Make card from patterned paper. **2** Cut window in card. **3** Trim transparency and attach to card with eyelets. **4** Adhere patterned paper inside card. **5** Apply rub-ons to sticker labels; affix sticker inside card. **6** Tie floss to label tag; affix to button. **7** Wrap trim around card. Adhere flower and button with tag.

Finished size: 4½" x 5½"

5 STEPS Congratulations Gift Bag

Designer: Wendy Sue Anderson

1 Adhere patterned paper to front of bag. Stitch along bottom edge. **2** Cut piece of patterned paper, stitch edges, and attach eyelets to each corner. Adhere. **3** Cover chipboard flower with patterned paper and adhere circle of patterned paper in center. **4** Create tag from tag rim and patterned paper. Apply rub-ons and attach eyelet to tag. **5** Tie ribbon through eyelet and around chipboard flower; adhere.

Finished size: 5" x 7"

SUPPLIES: *Cardstock:* (red) Bazzill Basics Paper *Patterned paper:* (Stamp Shape from Noteworthy collection) Making Memories *Transparency sheet; Accents:* (red flower) Prima; (cream button) Autumn Leaves; (white flower eyelets) Doodlebug Design *Rub-ons:* (sentiments) American Crafts *Stickers:* (label tag, flocked label) Making Memories *Fibers:* (cream waxed floss) Scrapworks; (trim) *Tool:* (heart punch) EK Success

SUPPLIES: *Patterned paper:* (Stamp Shape, Pink Floral, Text from Noteworthy collection) Making Memories *Accents:* (metal tag rim) Making Memories; (chipboard flower) O'Scrap!; (peach eyelet) *Rub-ons:* (sentiments) Making Memories *Fibers:* (teal polka dot ribbon) American Crafts *Tool:* (tag maker) Making Memories *Other:* (white gift bag)

Have a Heart the Whole Year Through

You probably have a variety of heart-shaped scrapbooking supplies—from punches and die cuts to buttons and epoxies. While February seems like the perfect month to pull them out, why not use one of the most pleasing shapes in your creations all year through? Try these creative ways to use hearts in non-traditional ways, including imaginative takes on butterflies, flowers, and fashion accessories. Even the fish is a great way to bring humor to your designs while putting an unconventional twist on a favorite shape.

SPRING

DESIGNER TIP

Let the seasons inspire you—go from bright pastels to fall tones.

DESIGNER TIP

Make texture your theme: combine a showy embossed copper sheet with dimensional stickers.

Colors of Spring

Dee Gallimore-Perry

Finished size: 3¾" x 4¾"

Give Thanks

Alice Golden

Finished size: 3¾" x 4¾"

SUPPLIES: *Textured cardstock:* (Heather, Piñata) Bazzill Basics Paper *Patterned paper:* (Multicolored Diamonds from Chelsea collection) K&Company *Rubber stamps:* (Handwritten alphabet) Hero Arts *Dye ink:* (Basic Black) Stampin' Up! *Accents:* (lavender brad) K&Company; (metal-rimmed vellum tags) Making Memories *Stickers:* (butterfly, dragonfly, flowers) K&Company *Fibers:* (purple organdy ribbon) Embellish It!; (pink ribbon) Making Memories *Adhesive:* foam dots *Other:* sandpaper

SUPPLIES: *Cardstock:* (Honored Sienna) The Crafter's Workshop *Specialty paper:* (Mocha Bling embossed) FiberMark *Dye ink:* (Peeled Paint) Ranger Industries *Accents:* (antique copper brads) Karen Foster Design; (rectangle, square vellum tags) Making Memories *Stickers:* (acorn, leaves, squash) K&Company *Fiber:* (brown satin ribbon) A.C.Moore *Template:* (give thanks) Creative Imaginations *Other:* (bronze metal sheet) Karen Foster Design

Spring Blooms

Designer: Nicole Keller

1 Make card from cardstock. **2** Stamp bottom of card with flower stamp. **3** Adhere ribbon to card. **4** Apply rub-ons, and adhere brads and metal accents. **5** Separate and paint chipboard. **6** Apply Leaf Green paint to Old French Writing stamp using brayer; stamp on white painted chipboard. **7** Apply Wicker White paint to Old French Writing stamp using brayer; stamp on green painted chipboard. Let dry. **8** Assemble chipboard pieces and adhere to card.

Finished size: 5½" x 4¼"

DESIGNER TIPS

- When inking the stamp with the brayer, make a test stamp impression on scrap paper to make sure you have evenly covered the stamp with paint.

- If you don't have a script stamp, try any background stamp with an overall pattern, or stamp a tiny image repeatedly around the paisley.

SUPPLIES: *Rubber stamp:* (Old French Writing) Hero Arts *Foam stamp:* (flower) Making Memories *Chalk ink:* (Cloud White) Tsukineko *Cardstock:* (Leaf Green) Die Cuts With a View *Paint:* (Leaf Green, Wicker White) Plaid *Accents:* (silver brads, metal accents) Hot Off The Press; (paisley chipboard) Maya Road *Rub-ons:* (spring) Die Cuts With a View *Fibers:* (green paisley ribbon) Michaels *Tools:* (brayer) Speedball

Butterfly Wishes

Designer: Lisa Johnson

1 Make card from cardstock.
2 Trim cardstock slightly smaller than card front; mat with cardstock. **3** Stamp circle in selected color, stamp off once; roll edges in same color. Stamp on cardstock. Repeat with various colors. **4** Stamp butterfly over circles. Adhere piece to card. **5** Stamp sentiment; punch. **6** Punch shadow from cardstock; attach brad. Adhere to card.

Finished size: 5½" x 4¼"

DESIGNER TIPS

- Doodle over the circle image for a unique creation.

- For more information on this stamping technique see the Rock and Roll instructions on p. 9.

SUPPLIES: All supplies from Stampin' Up! *Rubber stamps:* (butterfly, circle from Sweet and Sassy set; wish from Small Script set) *Dye ink:* (Apricot Appeal, Basic Black, Certainly Celery, Bashful Blue) *Cardstock:* (Apricot Appeal, Basic Black, Whisper White) *Accent:* (black brad) *Adhesive:* (foam squares) *Tools:* (word window punch)

Happy Spring Card

Designer: Kalyn Kepner

Ink all edges.

1. Make card from cardstock. Adhere patterned paper; stitch edges.

2. Trim cardstock strip using decorative edge scissors; adhere to bottom.

3. Trim patterned paper strips, punch border on one, and adhere. Apply glitter glue.

4. Trim patterned paper into half-circle using template and mat with cardstock. Trim mat with decorative-edge scissors, zigzag-stitch seam, and adhere. Apply glitter glue.

5. Write "Happy" with gel pen. Die-cut "Spring" from cardstock and adhere.

6. Adhere flower and acrylic dot. Thread buttons with floss and adhere.

Finished size: 5½" square

SUPPLIES: *Cardstock:* (green, yellow, cream) Bazzill Basics Paper *Patterned paper:* (Butterfly, Stripe, Floral Stripe from Flower Patch collection) Making Memories *Dye ink:* (pink, blue, yellow) Clearsnap *Color medium:* (green gel pen) Sakura *Accents:* (pink, yellow buttons) Papertrey Ink; (blue flower) Prima; (yellow acrylic dots) The Robin's Nest; (yellow glitter glue) Ranger Industries *Fibers:* (white floss) DMC *Template:* (circle) Provo Craft *Dies:* (Reuse alphabet) QuicKutz *Tools:* (border punch) Fiskars; (decorative-edge scissors)

5 STEPS Spring Card
Designer: Layle Koncar

1 Make card from cardstock.
2 Trim patterned paper pieces and adhere; adhere ribbon.
3 Affix sentiment and adhere flower.
4 Adhere pearls.

Finished size: 5" square

COLOR POP
Layle's use of a variety of textures within the color family takes her simple design to a whole new level.

SUPPLIES: *Cardstock:* (kraft) *Patterned paper:* (Lovey Dovey from Sweet Cakes collection) Pink Paislee; (Frosted from Life at the Pole collection) Sassafras Lass *Accents:* (white flower) Prima; (green pearls) BasicGrey *Stickers:* (Daiquiri alphabet) American Crafts *Fibers:* (teal scalloped ribbon) Creative Imaginations

Easter Blessings

Designer: Julia Stainton

OUTSIDE

1. Make pocket from patterned paper by cutting die cut patterned paper in half. Score vertically 4" from left and right edge; fold in and adhere.

2. Spell "Easter" with stickers.

INSIDE

1. Make insert card from cardstock.

2. Cut patterned paper slightly smaller than insert card; mat with cardstock, stitch border, and adhere.

3. Stamp Bible verse.

4. Adhere flower; thread button with floss and adhere.

5. Stamp blessings on cardstock; trim, punch hole, and attach to button with safety pin.

Finished size: 4" x 6½"

SUPPLIES: *Cardstock:* (white) Cornish Heritage Farms; (Intense Teal) Prism *Patterned paper:* (Die Cut Scallop, Pattern Stripe Floral from Flower Patch collection) Making Memories *Rubber stamps:* (blessings from Christmas Expressions set, Bible verse from Scripture Essentials I set) Cornish Heritage Farms *Dye ink:* (Tuxedo Black) Tsukineko *Accents:* (teal button) Autumn Leaves; (white flower) Prima; (mini safety pin) Creative Impressions *Stickers:* (Addie chipboard alphabet) Making Memories *Fibers:* (pink floss) *Tool:* (1/8" circle punch)

What Sweet Joy

Designer: Beth Opel

OUTSIDE

1. Make card from cardstock; trim one corner to create rounded flap.
2. Adhere ribbon.
3. Print sentiment on photo paper; punch into scalloped circle and adhere flower.
4. Mat with scalloped circle punched from cardstock, using foam tape. Adhere piece with foam tape.

INSIDE

1. Cut patterned paper to fit inside panel; adhere.
2. Print sentiment on photo paper; trim and mat with cardstock. Adhere piece.

Finished size: 7" x 5"

SUPPLIES: *Cardstock:* (blue) American Crafts; (olive) Prism *Patterned paper:* (South Market Street from Ashville collection) Scenic Route *Specialty paper:* (matte photo) Hewlett-Packard *Accent:* (orange rubber flower) KI Memories *Fibers:* (orange gingham ribbon) Making Memories *Fonts:* (Century Gothic) Microsoft; (Caslon Openface BT) www.myfonts.com *Tools:* (scalloped circle punches) Marvy Uchida

⁵Easter Wishes

Designer: Kimberly Crawford

1 Make card from cardstock.

2 Airbrush card front with markers.

3 Die-cut and emboss ovals from cardstock. Stamp flower strip on cardstock, trim, and adhere to ovals.

4 Die-cut label from cardstock; stamp sentiment. Tie label to oval with twine. Adhere ovals to card.

5 Ink paper strip and adhere.

Finished size: 7" x 4"

Easter Blessings Flower

Designer: Lisa Johnson

1 Make card from cardstock. Ink edges.

2 Stamp script on cardstock; trim. Trim bottom with decorative-edge scissors, ink edges, and adhere to card.

3 Stamp medallions and frame sides on patterned paper and trim; ink edges. Adhere ribbon and adhere with foam tape.

4 Stamp script on cardstock, trim into leaves, fold in half, and adhere to card with foam tape.

5 Punch six ovals from cardstock, score, and curl. Adhere ends to cardstock scrap to form flower; adhere to card with foam tape. Adhere button.

6 Stamp sentiment on cardstock and emboss. Punch into oval and adhere. Adhere rhinestones.

Finished size: 4¼" x 5½"

SUPPLIES: *Clear stamps:* (flower strip from Limitless Labels set, sentiment from Just Hatched set) Papertrey Ink *Dye ink:* (Tuxedo Black) Tsukineko *Chalk ink:* (lavender, pink, blue, yellow, green) Clearsnap *Cardstock:* (white) *Color medium:* (green, blue markers) Copic *Accent:* (swirl paper strip) Bazzill Basics Paper *Fibers:* (cream twine) Papertrey Ink *Dies:* (label) Provo Craft; (oval) Spellbinders *Tool:* (airbrush system) Copic

SUPPLIES: *Clear stamps:* (medallions, frame sides from Guide Lines Two set; sentiment from Tags for Spring set; script from Background Basics: Text Style set) Papertrey Ink *Watermark ink:* Tsukineko *Specialty ink:* (Smokey Shadow, Sweet Blush hybrid) Papertrey Ink *Embossing powder:* (white) Stewart Superior Corp. *Cardstock:* (Soft Stone, Sweet Blush) Papertrey Ink *Patterned paper:* (grid from Guide Lines II Grid collection) *Accents:* (white button) Papertrey Ink; (clear rhinestones) *Fibers:* (white ribbon) *Tools:* (small, large oval punches) Stampin' Up!; (decorative-edge scissors) Fiskars

Embrace New Life

Designer: Julia Stainton

OUTSIDE

1. Make card from cardstock; fold back front flap.

2. Adhere specialty paper to transparency sheet; cut square and adhere. *Note: Adhere to folded flap only.*

3. Cut square of patterned paper; stitch border and adhere.

4. Stamp sentiment on patterned paper; trim and adhere.

5. Affix chipboard bird sticker and adhere rhinestone.

INSIDE

1. Cut patterned paper to fit inside panel; adhere and stitch edges.

2. Print sentiment on patterned paper; trim to fit behind chipboard frame sticker. Adhere to frame.

3. Affix frame and ladybug.

Finished size: 5" square

SUPPLIES: *Cardstock:* (kraft) Bazzill Basics Paper *Patterned paper:* (Dandelion, Splash, Saltwater Taffy) BasicGrey *Specialty paper:* (Doilies Tablecloth die cut from Lemonade collection) BasicGrey *Transparency sheet:* Cornish Heritage Farms *Rubber stamp:* (Happy Easter Script) Cornish Heritage Farms *Dye ink:* (Tuxedo Black) Tsukineko *Accents:* (clear rhinestones) Me & My Big Ideas *Stickers:* (chipboard bird, ladybug, circle frame) BasicGrey *Font:* (Maiandra) www.fonts.com

Simple Easter Blessings

Designer: Dawn McVey

1 Make card from cardstock. 2 Cut rectangle of cardstock; punch border. 3 Stamp flowers, leaves, and sentiment on cardstock; trim and adhere to punched piece. 4 Wrap ribbon around piece; tie bow. Adhere piece with foam tape. 5 Thread buttons with twine; adhere.

Finished size: 5½" x 4¼"

Elegant Easter Wishes

Designer: Rae Barthel

1 Make card from cardstock. 2 Cut rectangles of patterned paper; adhere. 3 Cut strip of cardstock; adhere. Tie on ribbon. 4 Paint chipboard frame; let dry and adhere glitter. Cut cardstock to fit behind frame; adhere. 5 Adhere cross; adhere frame with foam tape. 6 Die-cut tag from cardstock; stamp sentiment. Attach with floss; adhere rhinestone.

Finished size: 4" x 6"

DESIGNER TIP

Shop post-holiday clearance sales for unique embellishments. The gorgeous rhinestone cross in this project was found at a major craft retailer—for a whopping 80% off!

SUPPLIES: All supplies from Papertrey Ink unless otherwise noted. *Cardstock:* (Lavender Moon, Plum Pudding, Rustic Cream) *Clear stamps:* (flowers, leaves from Blooming Button Bits set; Easter blessings from Tags For Spring set) *Pigment ink:* (Spring Moss) *Specialty ink:* (Plum Pudding hybrid) *Accents:* (lavender buttons) *Fibers:* (green twill, cream twine) *Tool:* (border punch) Fiskars

SUPPLIES: *Cardstock:* (white) Bazzill Basics Paper *Patterned paper:* (Dandelion, Pink Fizz from Lemonade collection) BasicGrey *Clear stamp:* (Easter wishes from Mega Mixed Messages set) Papertrey Ink *Pigment ink:* (Onyx Black) Tsukineko *Paint:* (white) DecoArt *Accents:* (scalloped chipboard frame) Maya Road; (clear rhinestone cross) Hobby Lobby; (clear rhinestone) The Beadery; (white glitter) Martha Stewart Crafts *Fibers:* (white ribbon) Michaels; (white floss) DMC *Die:* (tag) Spellbinders

Elegant Easter Blessings

Designer: Latisha Yoast

❶ Make card from cardstock, round bottom corners. ❷ Emboss cardstock piece, round bottom corners. Tie ribbon around piece and adhere to card with foam tape. ❸ Print "Easter blessings" on cardstock; die-cut into label. ❹ Stamp label on die cut. Apply rub-ons and adhere rhinestones; adhere to card with foam tape.

Finished size: 5½" x 3¾"

Designer Tip

If you don't have a stamp that fits your sentiment needs, print out a sentiment using a cool font or two.

Friendly Bunny

Designer: Tiffany Johnson

❶ Make card from cardstock. ❷ Cut rectangle of cardstock; emboss. ❸ Stamp carrots on cardstock; color with markers, trim, and adhere to embossed piece. Stitch border. ❹ Stamp bunny on cardstock; cut out and adhere to ribbon charm. ❺ Stamp sentiment on ribbon charm; thread with ribbon. Wrap ribbon around embossed piece and adhere. ❻ Attach pin; adhere entire piece with foam tape.

Finished size: 5½" x 4¼"

SUPPLIES: *Cardstock:* (white) Flourishes *Clear stamp:* (label from Very Vintage Labels No. 1 set) Waltzingmouse Stamps *Dye ink:* (Pumpkin Pie) Stampin' Up! *Accents:* (clear rhinestones) BasicGrey *Rub-ons:* (scrolls) BasicGrey *Fibers:* (purple ribbon) Offray *Fonts:* (American Typewriter) www.fonts.com; (CK Ali) Creating Keepsakes *Template:* (flourish embossing) Spellbinders *Die:* (label) Spellbinders *Tool:* (corner rounder punch) Creative Memories

SUPPLIES: *Cardstock:* (Orange Zest, kraft, white) Papertrey Ink *Clear stamps:* (bunny, carrot from Jelly Beans set) My Cute Stamps; (Easter from Say It in Style set) Close To My Heart *Specialty ink:* (Dark Chocolate hybrid) Papertrey Ink *Color medium:* (green, orange markers) Copic *Accents:* (white chipboard ribbon charm) Close To My Heart; (orange stick pin) *Fibers:* (green ribbon) Papertrey Ink *Template:* (Swiss Dots embossing) Provo Craft

⁵ᵀᵉᵖ Bunny Easter Wishes

Designer: Tina Fussell

① Make card from cardstock. ② Stamp bunnies on cardstock panel; color. Stamp bunnies on patterned paper, trim, and adhere pieces to panel. ③ Mat panel with patterned paper, using foam tape. Adhere to card. ④ Stamp Easter wishes on patterned paper; trim and adhere.

Finished size: 5½" x 4¼"

⁵ᵀᵉᵖ Spiritual Easter

Designer: Jessica Witty

① Make card from cardstock. Cover with patterned paper. ② Stamp cross on cardstock; emboss and adhere. ③ Cut transparency sheet to fit card front. Stamp sentiment and adhere. ④ Pierce corners of card front, lace with twine, and tie bow.

Finished size: 4¼" x 5½"

Designer Tip
Stamping on slick surfaces can be tricky, so to get a clean image: set the stamp down, press gently, and pick it back up very carefully.

SUPPLIES: *Cardstock:* (Rustic Cream, kraft) Papertrey Ink *Patterned paper:* (Daydream, Strawberry Cheesecake, Tea Party from June Bug collection) BasicGrey; (green) *Clear stamps:* (Easter wishes from Mixed Messages set) Papertrey Ink; (bunny from Sending Happy Thoughts set) Hero Arts *Dye ink:* (Chocolate Chip) Stampin' Up! *Color medium:* (white, pink, blue colored pencils) Crayola

SUPPLIES: *Cardstock:* (Soft Stone) Papertrey Ink; (Very Vanilla) Stampin' Up! *Patterned paper:* (Something Old from Everafter collection) Cosmo Cricket *Transparency sheet:* Office Max *Rubber stamps:* (cross, verse, Easter, blessings from Cross of Christ set) Our Daily Bread Designs *Solvent ink:* (Timber Brown) Tsukineko *Watermark ink:* Tsukineko *Embossing powder:* (white) Stampin' Up! *Fibers:* (natural twine) Papertrey Ink

⁙5⁙ Happy Easter Gift Bag

❶ Fold cardstock and combine inks to create color washes. Apply color washes to each folded section.

❷ Stamp flowers, dots, and swirls.

❸ Trim cardstock and adhere to gift bag.

❹ Print "Happy Easter!" on cardstock. Cut into circle using template. Spray with mist and stamp dots.

❺ Tie ribbon to bag, adhere sentiment circle with foam tape; attach spiral clip.

Finished size: 5½" x 8½"

DESIGNER TIP

Make sure not to apply your color washes too quickly. Lightly brush or spray on your washes to prevent your paper from curling. Continue applying additional coats only once the wash is dried until you achieve your desired color.

Bonus Idea

Experiment with dye inks, acrylic paint, mists, and unsweetened drink mixes to create a wide variety of colors and effects for your color-washed projects.

SUPPLIES: *Cardstock:* (white) Bazzill Basics Paper *Clear stamps:* (swirl from BackRounds Medium set) Technique Tuesday; (dot, flower from Friends Always set) My Sentiments Exactly! *Dye ink:* (Bikini Pink, Ocean) Ranger Industries; (Eggplant Envy, Green Galore) Stampin' Up! *Specialty ink:* (Stream, Cranberry color wash) Ranger Industries; (Honey Dew, Spring Violet mist) Tattered Angels *Accent:* (purple spiral clip) Creative Impressions *Fibers:* (sheer purple ribbon) *Font:* (CK Newsprint) Creating Keepsakes *Adhesive:* (foam tape) *Template:* (2" circle) Fiskars *Other:* (purple gift bag) DMD, Inc.

:5: Floral Easter Card

Designer: Courtney Kelley

1 Make card from cardstock; distress and ink edges.
2 Stamp lined background repeatedly on cardstock; trim
and ink edges. **3** Mat stamped piece with cardstock;
distress and ink edges. Adhere. **4** Apply rub-ons. **5** Spell
"Easter" with chipboard letters.

Finished size: 6½" x 3¼"

DESIGNER TIP

When layering different colors of cardstock, inking the
edges helps each color stand out.

SUPPLIES: *Cardstock:* (Fussy, Gumdrop, Buttercream) Bazzill Basics Paper
Rubber stamp: (lined background from Creative Textures set) Stampers
Anonymous *Chalk ink:* (Yellow Citrus, Wisteria, Rouge) Clearsnap *Accents:*
(green chipboard letters) Scenic Route *Rub-ons:* (flowers) KI Memories;
(stitches) Die Cuts With a View

⟨5⟩ Hope Card

Designer: Cary Eldred

❶ Stamp 3 Crosses and hope on card.

❷ Stamp For God So Loved on card and cardstock. Punch center from cardstock image; adhere to card with foam tape.

❸ Stamp butterfly on card; color with marker. Apply glitter glue.

❹ Tie on ribbon; adhere rhinestone.

Finished size: 4½" square

Oh Happy Day Card

Designer: Melissa Phillips

❶ Make card from cardstock; ink edges. Adhere cardstock.

❷ Adhere patterned paper; zigzag-stitch sides.

❸ Adhere patterned paper strip; stitch sides.

❹ Die-cut butterflies from patterned paper and cardstock; apply glitter and adhere butterflies to card.

❺ Thread button with floss and adhere.

❻ Apply rub-ons and affix stickers.

Finished size: 3¾" x 4¾"

SUPPLIES: *Cardstock:* (Whisper White) Stampin' Up! *Rubber stamps:* (For God So Loved) Stampabilities; (3 Crosses) MorningStar Stamps; (butterfly from Basket Full of Fun set) Stampin' Up!; (Faith Hope Love) Hero Arts *Dye ink:* (Summer Sun, More Mustard) Stampin' Up! *Pigment ink:* (Onyx Black) Tsukineko *Color medium:* (purple marker) Stampin' Up! *Accents:* (clear rhinestone) Hero Arts; (iridescent glitter glue) Ranger Industries *Fibers:* (black stitched ribbon) Offray *Adhesive:* (foam tape) *Tool:* (½" circle punch) EK Success *Other:* (white/green notecard) A Muse Artstamps

SUPPLIES: *Cardstock:* (black, white, yellow) Bazzill Basics Paper *Patterned paper:* (Turquoise Tiny Dot, Love Song from Tangerine Dream collection) Jenni Bowlin Studio; (Clown Nose from Cupcake collection, Pooro from Romani collection) BasicGrey *Dye ink:* (Old Paper) Ranger Industries *Accents:* (iridescent glitter) Melissa Frances; (green button) *Rub-ons:* (flourish) Maya Road; (happy) Scenic Route; (oh) Cosmo Cricket *Stickers:* (Bookworks Mini alphabet) EK Success *Fibers:* (red floss) *Dies:* (butterflies) Provo Craft *Tool:* (die cut machine) Provo Craft

5 STEPS Big Bloom

Designer: Terri Davenport

1 Make card from cardstock. Cover with Shelby's Bouquet paper. Cut Blush paper into curved strip; adhere. **2** Adhere flower. **3** Punch circle from coaster; ink edge. Stamp "Happy Easter" on Blush; trim into strip with slightly curved edges; adhere. Ink piece and emboss. Repeat for desired effect. **4** Adhere piece to flower center.

Finished size: 4¼" x 5½"

5 STEPS Easter Hope

Designer: Alice Golden

1 To stamp cross, mask off shape on cardstock with tape; stamp Acanthus Leaf overlapping with Gold ink. **2** Trim piece into rectangle. Cut Lilac paper slightly larger and stamp Acanthus Leaf with Violet Mist around border. Double mat cross piece with stamped Lilac and Gold paper. **3** Print sentiment on transparency sheet; adhere. **4** Set eyelets in hydrangea center; adhere. **5** Adhere piece to card.

Finished size: 5⅝" x 7"

SUPPLIES: **Rubber stamps:** (Printer's Type Alphabet) *Hero Arts* **Watermark ink:** *Tsukineko* **Cardstock:** (olive) **Patterned paper:** (Blush, Shelby's Bouquet from Flowers of Steel collection) *Imagination Project* **Embossing powder:** (clear) **Accents:** (dots chipboard coaster) *Imagination Project*; (silk flower) **Tool:** (1¾" circle punch)

SUPPLIES: **Rubber stamp:** (Acanthus Leaf) *Duncan* **Dye ink:** (Violet Mist) *Clearsnap* **Pigment ink:** (Gold) *Plaid* **Cardstock:** (Natural) *Bazzill Basics Paper* **Patterned paper:** (Gold) *Canford*; (Lilac from Genuine Girl collection) *Reminisce* **Transparency sheet:** *3M* **Accents:** (Amethyst Jeweled Hydrangeas) *Mermaid Tears*; (mini gold eyelets) *HyGlo* **Fonts:** (Aberration, Scriptina) *www.free-font-downloads.com* **Adhesive:** (spray) *Creative Imaginations*; (low-tack tape) **Other:** (ivory card) *Halcraft*

Happy Easter Blocks

Designer: Karen Day

1 Make card from Pebble cardstock. **2** Stamp chocolate bunnies on reverse-side of Bubble Gum cardstock; cut into square. Ink edges; adhere. **3** Stamp bunny on reverse-side of Limeade cardstock; cut into square. Ink edges; adhere. **4** Stamp jar on reverse-side of Swimming Pool cardstock; cut into square. Ink edges; adhere. **5** Stamp jelly beans on reverse-side of Bumble Bee cardstock; cut into square. Ink edges; adhere. **6** Spell "Easter" with stickers and write "Happy" with pen on Pebble. Cut in oval shape; ink edges and adhere with foam squares. Punch holes; wrap and tie with ribbon.

Finished size: 6" square

DESIGNER TIP
Use watermark ink for its hue-harmonizing versatility. It will complement and match any paper color, every time.

Little Yellow Chick

Designer: Teri Anderson

1 Make card from White cardstock. Stamp Criss-Cross with Bubblegum. **2** Trim Pink Wash paper to fit front; tear corner and adhere. **3** Cut slit in fold for ribbon; tie ribbon. **4** Stamp Happy Easter on Honeydew cardstock with Jet Black. Cut out using template; adhere. **5** Stamp Chick with Jet Black; color with pencils. Punch and adhere with foam squares.

Finished size: 4¼" x 5½"

SUPPLIES: Rubber stamps: (bunny, chocolate bunnies, jar, jelly beans from Easter set) *The Angel Company* **Watermark ink:** *Tsukineko* **Textured cardstock:** (Bubble Gum, Bumble Bee, Limeade, Pebble, Swimming Pool) *Bazzill Basics Paper* **Color medium:** (Black pen) *American Crafts* **Stickers:** (white alphabet) *Doodlebug Design* **Fibers:** (white organza ribbon) *Offray* **Adhesive:** (foam squares)

SUPPLIES: Rubber stamps: (Chick) *A Muse Artstamps*; (Happy Easter from Dot Happy Easter Cube) *Northwoods Rubber Stamps*; (Criss-Cross background) *Savvy Stamps* **Dye ink:** (Bubblegum) *Close To My Heart*; (Jet Black) *Ranger Industries* **Cardstock:** (White) *Provo Craft* **Textured cardstock:** (Honeydew) *Bazzill Basics Paper* **Patterned paper:** (Pink Wash from Romance collection) *Creative Imaginations* **Color medium:** (pink, orange, yellow watercolor pencils) *Royal & Langnickel* **Fibers:** (yellow dotted ribbon) *May Arts* **Adhesive:** (foam squares) **Template:** (oval) *Provo Craft* **Tool:** (scalloped oval punch)

Easter Blessings

Designer: Alice Golden

1 Cover label holder with patterned paper. Stamp Diamond Script and Orchid Botanical repeatedly. **2** Position card fold behind top of label holder; trim. Stamp "Easter" and flourish. Apply rub-on. **3** Adhere label holder to card piece. **4** Loop ribbon through top. **5** Adhere flowers.

Finished size: 5½" x 3¾"

Carrot Hug Tag

Designer: Sharon Harnist

1 Stamp image on watercolor paper; color with ink and water brush. Detail with pens. **2** Trim into tag shape and double-mat with cardstock. **3** Attach brads to flowers; adhere.

Finished size: 2¾" x 5¼"

Share your paper crafting skills, and get some great ideas and creations to keep for yourself! Join one of the many unique and fun swaps on our web site at www.PaperCraftsMag.com/swaps.

SUPPLIES: *Acrylic stamps:* (Diamond Script, Formal alphabet) My Sentiments Exactly!; (Orchid Botanical) PSX; (flourish from Flourishes set) Autumn Leaves *Pigment ink:* (Key Lime, purple metallic, Smoke Blue) Tsukineko *Patterned paper:* (Green Paisley from Apple set) Deja Views *Accents:* (lavender, pink flowers) Savvy Stamps; (label holder) Fancy Pants Designs *Rub-on:* (blessings) Deja Views *Fibers:* (striped ribbon) Strano Designs *Other:* (white card) Halcraft

SUPPLIES: *Rubber stamp:* (Huggin' Bunny) Inky Antics *Dye ink:* (Apricot Appeal, Bashful Blue, Blush Blossom, Certainly Celery, Close to Cocoa, Creamy Caramel) Stampin' Up! *Solvent ink:* Tsukineko *Cardstock:* (Apricot Appeal, Certainly Celery) Stampin' Up! *Specialty paper:* (watercolor) Stampin' Up! *Color medium:* (black glaze pen) Sakura; (white pen) Sanford *Accents:* (green flowers) Prima; (green brads) Stampin' Up! *Tools:* (water brush) Stampin' Up!

Chic Chick

Designer: Betsy Veldman

1 Make card from cardstock; adhere patterned paper. **2** Adhere strip of patterned paper and square of cardstock. Stitch all edges. **3** Stamp chick on cardstock square. Stamp twice on patterned paper, cut out pieces, and adhere to chick on cardstock square. **4** Stamp flower on die cut flowers; stamp flourish on card. Adhere flowers and leaves to card, using foam tape under one flower. **5** Stamp sentiment. **6** Tie buttons with thread and adhere.

Finished size: 4¼" x 5½"

Blessings

Designer: Genelle Collins

1 Make card from cardstock. Stamp leaves. **2** Cut oval from scrap paper to create mask. Cover cardstock with mask and sponge on ink. Stamp leaves in oval. Stamp Lord Bless. **3** Remove mask, mat stamped piece with cardstock, attach brads, and adhere.

Finished size: 4¾" x 6¼"

SUPPLIES: *Clear stamps:* (chick, flower, Easter from Bunnies & Chicks set; happy from Mini Easter set; flourish from Petals set) Inque Boutique *Dye ink:* (black) Inque Boutique *Cardstock:* (white scalloped, green) Die Cuts With a View *Patterned paper:* (Savoy, Belford, Oxford, Wellington from Covent Garden collection) Tinkering Ink *Accents:* (flower die cuts) Tinkering Ink; (blue, green buttons) Autumn Leaves *Adhesive:* (foam tape)

SUPPLIES: *Rubber stamps:* (leaves from Stem Silhouettes set) Stampin' Up!; (Lord Bless) Biblical Impressions *Dye ink:* (River Rock, Basic Black, Old Olive) Stampin' Up! *Watermark ink:* Tsukineko *Cardstock:* (Old Olive, Basic Black, Very Vanilla) Stampin' Up! *Accents:* (pearl brads) K&Company *Template:* (oval)

⁙5⁙ Easter Dress

Designer: Summer Ford

1 Punch 16 squares from cardstock. Stamp each with different image. **2** Sand edges of photo; adhere to cardstock. **3** Adhere stamped squares to page. Stitch page. **4** Stamp date on tag. Knot ribbon on pin, stick pin through flower and tag, and adhere to page. **5** Stamp "Easter dress" with paint.

Finished size: 11" x 8½"

SUPPLIES: *Rubber stamps:* (Flourish Pattern, Berryvine Border) Stampabilities; (Hand Scripted Alphabet) Fontwerks; (date) Making Memories; (Monet's Garden) Leave Memories; (Spring from Seasonal Memories set, Italian Poetry Background) Hero Arts; (Espalier Background) Plaid; (Eucalyptus Leaves) Delta; (Scrollie Flower) Limited Edition Rubberstamps *Acrylic stamps:* (thin, double doodled flowers from Make-A-Flower set) Scrappy Cat Creations *Dye ink:* (Peeled Paint) Ranger Industries *Cardstock:* (white) Bazzill Basics Paper; (black) The Paper Company *Paint:* (Spotlight) Making Memories *Accents:* (tag) Rusty Pickle; (olive paper flower) Prima; (stick pin) Heidi Grace Designs *Fibers:* (stitched olive organdy ribbon) Morex *Tools:* (1⅜" square punch) Morex *Other:* (photo)

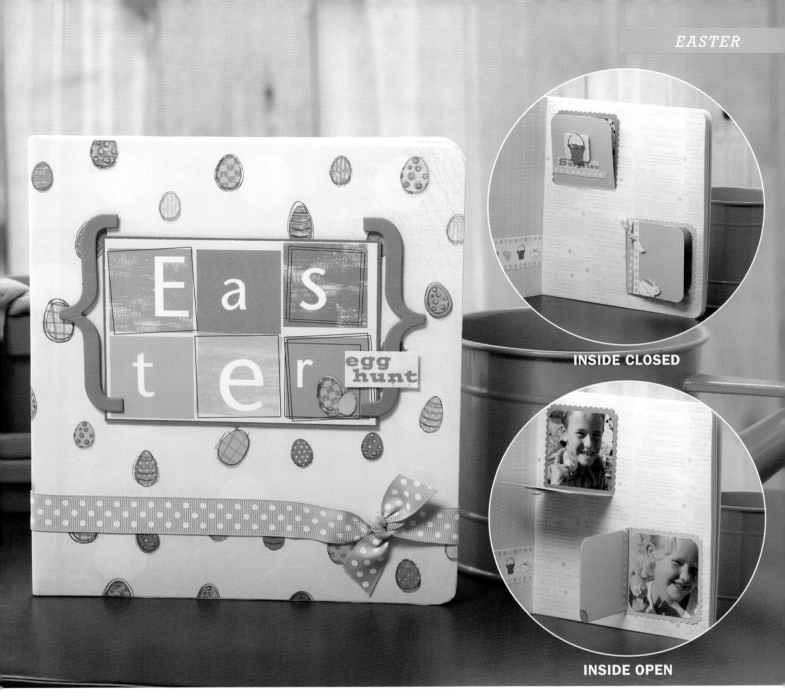

INSIDE CLOSED

INSIDE OPEN

Egg Hunt Book

Designer: Wendy Johnson

❶ Cover book with patterned paper.

❷ Trim Easter from patterned paper, mat with cardstock, and adhere with foam tape.

❸ Paint brackets and adhere.

❹ Trim Egg hunt from patterned paper; adhere. Trim eggs from patterned paper; adhere to Easter.

❺ Adhere knotted ribbon.

❻ Embellish inside pages as desired.

Finished size: 7¾" x 8½"

SUPPLIES: *Cardstock:* (blue) *Patterned paper:* (Easter Egg Fun, Easter Surprise) Adorn It-Carolee's Creations *Paint:* (purple) *Accents:* (chipboard brackets) *Fibers:* (green polka dot ribbon) May Arts *Adhesive:* (foam tape) *Other:* (flap book) Piggy Tales

Simply Irresistible

A resist occurs when a design is created through a coating of ink, heat embossing, wax, or other medium, which creates a barrier. When additional color media are applied, the coating resists the color and the design appears. Using this technique is a great way to create uniquely different projects every time.

5 STEPS Floral Easter Wishes Card

Designer: Emily Call

1 Make card from cardstock. 2 Adhere strips of cardstock and patterned paper; pierce holes. *Note: Distress bottom edge of patterned paper.* 3 Stamp flowers (see "Resisting with Chalk Technique"). Insert brads and adhere with foam tape. 4 Stamp Easter wishes on cardstock; trim into tag shape. Punch hole and tie thread. 5 Staple ribbon and tag to card.

Finished size: 4¼" x 5½"

RESISTING WITH CHALK TECHNIQUE
Stamp image on cardstock with watermark ink.

Apply chalk to stamped image.

SUPPLIES: *Cardstock:* (So Saffron, Whisper White) Stampin' Up! *Patterned paper:* (Sunshine from The Goods collection) American Crafts *Rubber stamps:* (flower from Big Flowers set, Easter wishes from Fundamental Phrases set) Stampin' Up! *Dye ink:* (Close to Cocoa) Stampin' Up! *Watermark ink:* Stampin' Up! *Color media:* (pink, green, purple chalk) *Accents:* (yellow brads) Making Memories; (silver staples) *Fibers:* (green grosgrain ribbon) Stampin' Up! *Adhesive:* (foam tape)

Pink & Green Easter Card

Designer: Melanie Douthit

1 Make card from cardstock. **2** Cut rectangle of patterned paper; trim with decorative-edge scissors. Punch circles, sand edges, and adhere. **3** Adhere rectangle of patterned paper. **4** Adhere rectangle of patterned paper; stitch edges. **5** Cut cardstock rectangle, round corners, stamp sentiment and flowers, and adhere. **6** Punch cardstock circle, stamp chick and sentiment. **7** Paint chipboard circle. Punch circle from reverse side of patterned paper, sand edges, and adhere to chipboard. **8** Adhere stamped circle to chipboard circle; adhere to card. **9** Attach brads to flowers; adhere to card. Tie bow around front flap.

Finished size: 4¼" x 5½"

SUPPLIES: *Cardstock:* (Oxford White) Prism *Patterned paper:* (Stitched Stripe, Posies, Polka Dots from Celebrate collection) Paper Salon *Rubber stamps:* (chick, sentiments from Spring Fling set; small solid flower from Create-a-Flower set) Paper Salon *Dye ink:* (Flamingo, Pineapple, Pear) Paper Salon *Paint:* (white) Plaid *Accents:* (white flower brads) Accent Depot; (scalloped circle chipboard) Deluxe Designs; (pink flowers) Prima *Fibers:* (green striped satin ribbon) Hobby Lobby *Tools:* (decorative-edge scissors) Fiskars; (⅛", 1¼", 1¾" circle punches, corner rounder punch)

Easter Greetings Wall Hanging

Designer: Melissa Phillips

1 Cut six blocks from cardstock. Cut three blocks from each patterned paper; adhere to make pockets. **2** Adhere assorted trims, borders, and ribbon to edges of pockets; straight-stitch pockets to cardstock blocks. **3** Cut six eggs from cardstock and place in pockets. **4** Lay out blocks so patterned paper is alternated. Tape together on reverse side; zigzag-stitch blocks along seams. **5** Hand-stitch felt flowers, leaves, and eggs together. Thread buttons and adhere. **6** Sand edges of chipboard letters; adhere. **7** Set eyelets at top of wall hanging and attach ribbon.

Finished size: 8½" x 12¼"

SUPPLIES: *Cardstock:* (white) Bazzill Basics Paper; (Light Sunshine Yellow, Light Grassy Green, Light Groovy Grape) WorldWin *Patterned paper:* (Flower, Dot from My Baby Girl collection) Pebbles Inc. *Accents:* (chipboard letters) Pressed Petals; (felt flowers, leaves, eggs) American Crafts; (paper borders) Doodlebug Design; (yellow eyelets) We R Memory Keepers; (yellow buttons) SEI; (white buttons) *Fibers:* (white rickrack) Wright's; (white grosgrain ribbon) Offray; (pink gros-grain ribbon, striped ribbon, pink floral trim)

Easter Blessings Bunny Tree Card

Designer: Betsy Veldman

❶ Make card from cardstock; ink edges.

❷ Die-cut scalloped square from cardstock; adhere.

❸ Cut 1" squares from patterned paper; ink edges and adhere.
Cut strip of patterned paper, trim top edge in wave, ink edges,
and adhere. Stamp sentiment and stitch edges.

❹ Die-cut oval from cardstock; ink edges and adhere.

❺ Cut tree shape from cardstock. Cut flowers and punch circles
from patterned paper; adhere to tree and adhere to card.
Adhere rhinestones.

❻ Cut bunny from patterned paper; ink edges and adhere with
foam tape.

Finished size: 4½" square

SUPPLIES: *Cardstock:* (Vintage Cream, kraft) Papertrey Ink *Patterned paper:* (Just Stripes from Bloom & Grow collection, Twirling Circles from Pirouette collection) My Mind's Eye; (Confetti from Celebration collection) Fancy Pants Designs; (pink floral from Razzleberry Lemonade collection) Stampin' Up!; (Cutie Pie from Sweet Cakes collection) Pink Paislee; (Mady from Playful Petals collection) Daisy Bucket Designs; (Thursday from Girl Friday collection) Cosmo Cricket; (Sugar Cone from Sweet Celebration! collection) Bella Blvd; (Animal Stripes from Nana's Nursery-Girl collection) Die Cuts With a View *Clear stamp:* (sentiment from Tags for Spring set) Papertrey Ink *Chalk ink:* (Creamy Brown) Clearsnap *Specialty ink:* (Dark Chocolate hybrid) Papertrey Ink *Accents:* (clear flower rhinestones) Kaisercraft *Dies:* (scalloped square, oval) Provo Craft *Tools:* (½", ¾" circle punches) EK Success

5 STEPS You're on my Mind Card

Designer: Betsy Veldman

1. Die-cut two labels from cardstock; stitch together to form card. Punch and thread with twine; tie bow.
2. Stamp sentiment.
3. Stamp circle and leaves on cardstock. Punch into scalloped circle and ink edges.
4. Punch ½" circles from patterned paper; affix circle stickers. Punch holes to create buttons, thread with twine, and adhere to scalloped circle. Adhere to card.

Finished size: 3¼" square

DESIGNER TIP

Create your own patterned buttons using circles punched from patterned paper and covered with epoxy stickers. Use a heavy-duty punch such as the Crop-a-Dile to easily punch through the epoxies.

Summer Joys Card

Designer: Betsy Veldman

1. Make card from cardstock.
2. Trim patterned paper panel. Adhere patterned paper strip.
3. Die-cut sun from patterned paper; stitch and adhere to panel. Adhere buttons.
4. Cut circle from patterned paper; ink edges and adhere to panel with foam tape.
5. Stamp bikini on cardstock, trim, and adhere with foam tape. Adhere flower and rhinestone.
6. Stamp sentiment on cardstock; ink edges and adhere. Tie on ribbon and adhere panel to card.

Finished size: 4¼" x 5½"

SUPPLIES: *Cardstock:* (Orange Zest, Rustic Cream) Papertrey Ink *Patterned paper:* (blue polka dots from 2008 Bitty Dot Basics collection, orange floral from Autumn Abundance collection, pink floral from Raspberry Fizz Mix collection) Papertrey Ink *Clear stamps:* (sentiment, leaves from Blooming Button Bits set; stitched circle from Borders & Corners {Circle} set) Papertrey Ink *Pigment ink:* (Fresh Snow, Spring Moss, Orange Zest) Papertrey Ink *Chalk ink:* (Creamy Brown) Clearsnap *Stickers:* (clear epoxy circles) EK Success *Fibers:* (cream twine) Papertrey Ink *Die:* (label) Spellbinders *Tools:* (scalloped circle punch, ½" circle punch) EK Success; (⅛" circle punch) We R Memory Keepers

SUPPLIES: *Cardstock:* (Pure Poppy, Vintage Cream, white) Papertrey Ink *Patterned paper:* (orange, yellow polka dot from 2008 Bitty Dot Basics collection) Papertrey Ink; (School's Out, Carbonation from Snorkel collection) Cosmo Cricket *Clear stamps:* (sentiment, bikini from Day at the Beach set) Papertrey Ink *Chalk ink:* (Creamy Brown) Clearsnap *Specialty ink:* (Berry Sorbet, Ocean Tides hybrid) Papertrey Ink *Accents:* (blue flower) Prima; (clear rhinestone) Kaisercraft; (assorted buttons) BasicGrey *Fibers:* (yellow ribbon) Papertrey Ink *Die:* (sun) Provo Craft

Tequila Makes Me Smile Card

Designer: Kim Hughes

Finished size: 4¼" x 7½"

The colors, the umbrella, the glass—these all inspired Kim's cute shaped card.

Pattern on p. 283

SUPPLIES: *Cardstock:* (Papaya Puree Medium) Prism; (Mango) Bazzill Basics Paper; (white) Papertrey Ink *Patterned paper:* (Ocean Dot from Double Dot collection) BoBunny Press; (Dandelions from Fly a Kite collection) October Afternoon; (Uniquely You Special Swirls from Penny Lane collection) My Mind's Eye; (orange floral from Pumpkin Pie Patterns collection) Stampin' Up! *Accents:* (blue buttons) Papertrey Ink; (journaling card) Reminisce *Fibers:* (blue floss) DMC *Tools:* (circle punches) Marvy Uchida *Other:* (wood toothpicks)

5. Endless Summer Card

Designer: Susan Stringfellow

❶ Make 6" x 4" card from cardstock; print sentiment on card.

❷ Cut transparency to size. Paint wave shapes with dry paint brush; let dry. Paint around top of transparency with foam brush; let dry. Sand lightly.

❸ Adhere transparency; zigzag-stitch edges.

❹ Affix stickers. Attach flowers with brads.

Finished size: 7" x 4½"

SUPPLIES: *Cardstock:* (white) *Transparency sheet:* (frame from Island Summer collection) Rusty Pickle *Paint:* (Island Blue, Turquoise, Kiwis, Palm Leaf, white) Synta *Accents:* (orange flowers) Teters; (silver brads) Doodlebug Design *Stickers:* (orange, green rhinestone circles; pink rhinestone) Me & My Big Ideas *Font:* (Buccaneer Swash) www.myfonts.com

Summer Girls Display

Designer: Ana Cabrera

❶ Cut rectangles from transparencies; affix together with tape.

❷ Cut rooftops from patterned paper and cardstock; adhere. *Note: Trim cardstock with decorative-edge scissors before adhering.*

❸ Adhere photos and rhinestones.

❹ Adhere alphabet stickers, chipboard alphabet, and copper alphabet.

❺ Tie silver shell to rooftop with ribbon.

❻ Adhere ribbon and button.

Finished size: 24¼" x 6½"

SUPPLIES: *Cardstock:* (white, brown, orange) *Patterned paper:* (Multi Stripe, Big Dot, Flower from Kraft Paper collection; Scallop Ledger from Noteworthy collection) Making Memories *Transparency sheets:* (2 Dandelions) Hambly Screen Prints; (clear) Hammermill *Accents:* (chipboard alphabet, white button) Making Memories; (orange, clear rhinestones; silver shell) Darice *Stickers:* (Gift Box, Rootbeer Float, Runway alphabets) American Crafts; (copper alphabet; postage, blue floral, pink damask tape) Making Memories *Fibers:* (blue stitched, blue/brown striped grosgrain ribbon) Strano Designs *Tool:* (decorative-edge scissors) *Other:* (photos)

Fourth of July Card

Designer: Mary Bieber

Finished size: 4" x 5½"

SUPPLIES: *Cardstock:* (cream, red, blue)
Accents: (blue buttons) Stampin' Up!
Stickers: (star, sentiment) Me & My Big Ideas
Adhesive: (foam tape)

Let Freedom Ring Card

Designer: Terri Davenport

❶ Make card from cardstock. Adhere cardstock piece.

❷ Print photo on specialty paper; trim, mat with cardstock, and adhere.

❸ Spell sentiment with rub-ons.

❹ Adhere glitter and apply glitter glue to stars; let dry. Adhere.

Finished size: 5½" x 4¼"

DESIGNER TIP

Digital designs don't have to be complicated. Using a digital photo on your project is a fast and easy way to add a digital touch without a lot of effort.

SUPPLIES: *Cardstock:* (Admiral) Bazzill Basics Paper; (white, black) *Specialty paper:* (photo) *Accents:* (chipboard stars) Technique Tuesday; (red glitter) Art Institute Glitter; (red glitter glue) Ranger Industries *Rub-ons:* (All Mixed Up, Simply Sweet alphabets) Doodlebug Design *Other:* (digital photo)

Military Thanks Can

Designer: Anabelle O'Malley

1 Cover can and lid with patterned paper. *Note: Use circle cutter to cut piece for lid.* **2** Stamp notebook paper and attention on cardstock. Affix flag and star stickers. **3** Attach eyelet to stamped piece. Tie around can with cord. **4** Affix duty tags sticker to cardstock, trim, punch and adhere star, and attach eyelet. Attach to cord with safety pin. **5** Punch stars; attach eyelets. Adhere to stamped piece and can. **6** Affix stickers to lid to spell "Thanks".

Finished size: 4¼" diameter x 5" height

SUPPLIES: *Cardstock:* (Bazzill Red) Bazzill Basics Paper *Patterned paper:* (Army from U.S. Military collection) Karen Foster Design *Clear stamps:* (notebook paper, attention from Mini Note-It set) Inque Boutique *Pigment ink:* (Royal Blue) Clearsnap *Accents:* (blue eyelets) Making Memories; (safety pin) *Stickers:* (flag, duty tags, stars) Karen Foster Design; (Road Trip alphabet) Sticker Studio; (Jumbo alphabet) Chatterbox *Fibers:* (blue cord) Making Memories *Tools:* (circle cutter) Provo Craft; (star punch) Marvy Uchida *Other:* (paint can) Lowe's

Military Miss You Card

Designer: Rae Barthel

1. Make card from cardstock; adhere patterned paper panels.
2. Tie on twine.
3. Spell "Miss you" on journaling tag with stickers; adhere with foam tape.

Finished size: 5" x 5½"

SUPPLIES: *Cardstock:* (kraft) DMD, Inc. *Patterned paper:* (Checker, Flocked Camo from Just Chillin collection) Making Memories *Accent:* (kraft journaling tag) Maya Road *Stickers:* (Benny alphabet) American Crafts *Fibers:* (hemp twine)

5 Star-Studded Thanks Card

Designer: Belinda Chang Langner

1. Make card from cardstock.
2. Stamp sentiment; draw frame around card.
3. Trim cardstock block. Adhere twill pieces. Adhere ribbon pieces and adhere rhinestones.
4. Adhere flag to card using foam tape.

Finished size: 5½" x 4¼"

SUPPLIES: *Cardstock:* (white, kraft) Papertrey Ink *Clear stamp:* (sentiment from Celebration of Thanks set) Verve Stamps *Specialty ink:* (Dark Chocolate hybrid) Papertrey Ink *Color medium:* (white gel pen) Sanford *Accents:* (clear heart rhinestones) A Muse Artstamps *Fibers:* (red, white twill; blue ribbon) Papertrey Ink

★5★ A Day to Celebrate Card

Designer: Stephanie Halinski

1. Make card from cardstock.
2. Attach brads to form star. Tie on ribbon.
3. Punch star from cardstock and attach sticker; adhere with foam tape.
4. Stamp sentiment on cardstock; adhere with foam tape.
5. Cut cardstock to fit inside card; adhere.

Finished size: 5½" x 4½"

DESIGNER TIP

The easiest way to make a brad star is to create a star on your computer, print on scrap paper, and trim. Lay the star template against the card front and pierce around the edges, creating guides for the brads.

SUPPLIES: *Cardstock:* (white) Bazzill Basics Paper; (Real Red, Bashful Blue) Stampin' Up! *Clear stamp:* (sentiment from Birthday Messages set) Hero Arts *Dye ink:* (Brocade Blue) Stampin' Up! *Accents:* (silver brads) Making Memories *Sticker:* (4 from Cheeky alphabet) Making Memories *Fibers:* (baby blue gingham ribbon) Stampin' Up! *Tool:* (star punch) Stampin' Up!

5 Patriotic BBQ Caddy

Designer: Alice Golden

1 Cover inside and outside of caddy with patterned paper; ink edges. **2** Adhere ribbon together with ribbon stiffener; let dry. Tie to handle. **3** Mat sticker with cardstock. Tie sticker and charms to handle with floss.

Finished size: 8" x 11" x 7"

SUPPLIES: *Cardstock:* (white) Prism *Patterned paper:* (Star Spangled Sky, Old Glory from Stars & Stripes collection) Karen Foster Design *Dye ink:* (Black Soot) Ranger Industries *Finish:* (ribbon stiffener) Strano Designs *Accents:* (pewter barbecue, spatula charms) Karen Foster Design *Sticker:* (star) Karen Foster Design *Fibers:* (red floss) Karen Foster Design; (red gingham, stars ribbon) *Other:* (wood caddy) IKEA

Patriotic Scrapbook Page

Designer: Alisa Bangerter

Combine a fun photo with an assortment of sentiments. Attach the photo with hinges if you want to include personal journaling.

OPEN VIEW

BONUS IDEA

Mix some vivid reds and oranges with subdued brown for a spectacular fall color spectrum.

Autumn Journal

Designer: Alice Golden

Finished size: 5" square

SUPPLIES *Cardstock:* (Papaya Puree Dark) Prism *Patterned paper:* (Harvest Silly Stripe Chestnut) Scenic Route Paper Co. *Rubber stamp:* (Maple Leaf) A Stamp in the Hand *Dye ink:* (Autumn Leaves) Tsukineko *Accent:* (silver handle) 7gypsies *Rub-on:* (Autumn) Scenic Route Paper Co. *Fibers:* (rust twill ribbon) Scenic Route Paper Co.; (brown polka dot ribbon) SEI; (gold edge organdy ribbon) Mokuba; (brown gingham, gold, brown satin, striped, rust ribbon) May Arts *Other:* (spiral-bound notebook) 7gypsies; canvas squares

BONUS IDEA
The mix-and-match tree design on this card is a great way to use up all those patterned paper scraps you just couldn't toss out!

BONUS IDEA
Turn this snazzy purse into a fruit basket for a Thanksgiving greeting, or a springtime basket filled with colored eggs for Easter.

Autumn Blessings Card

Designer: Kalyn Kepner

1. Make card from cardstock.
2. Cut rectangle of cardstock; print sentiment, ink edges, stitch border, and adhere.
3. Cut leaves from patterned paper and cardstock; adhere. *Note: Adhere front leaves with foam tape.*
4. Die-cut branches from cardstock; adhere.
5. Cut strip of cardstock; punch border and adhere.
6. Adhere lace trim; thread buttons with floss and adhere.

Finished size: 4¼" x 5½"

Purse Full of Thanks Card

Designer: Erin Lincoln

1. Fold cardstock sheet in half; die-cut purse. *Note: Position die so card fold is at top of handle.*
2. Die-cut houndstooth pattern from cardstock; adhere and trim.
3. Cut strip of cardstock; adhere.
4. Die-cut flowers from cardstock; stamp flowers, layer together, and adhere with foam tape.
5. Punch circle from cardstock; adhere.
6. Thread button with twine; tie bow and adhere.
7. Punch tag from cardstock; stamp sentiment and attach with twine.

Finished size: 5½" x 4¼"

SUPPLIES: *Cardstock:* (brown, green, kraft) Bazzill Basics Paper; (orange) Wausau Paper *Patterned paper:* (Goldie, Lightning from Max & Whiskers collection; Vintage Plaid from June Bug collection) BasicGrey; (Elanore Battington from Craft Fair collection) American Crafts *Chalk ink:* (brown) Clearsnap *Accents:* (green buttons) Papertrey Ink *Fibers:* (vintage lace trim) Roberts Crafts; (green floss) DMC *Font:* (Chicago House) www.dafont.com *Die:* (branch) QuicKutz *Tool:* (border punch) Fiskars

SUPPLIES: All supplies from Papertrey Ink unless otherwise noted. *Cardstock:* (Ripe Avocado, Dark Chocolate, Terracotta Tile); (Pineapple Bliss) Bazzill Basics Paper *Clear stamps:* (flowers from Beautiful Blooms II set, sentiment from Mega Mixed Messages set) *Pigment ink:* (Terracotta Tile) *Specialty ink:* (Dark Chocolate, Summer Sunrise hybrid) *Accent:* (red button) *Fibers:* (hemp twine) no source *Dies:* (flowers, purse); (houndstooth pattern) Silhouette America *Tools:* (tag punch) McGill; (circle punch) no source

emboss detail

emboss detail

DESIGNER TIPS

If the chipboard alphabet stickers you're trying to emboss over seem too thick, try peeling up the top layers to make them thinner.

This is a great way to use up leftover chipboard stickers. Since only the paper you emboss will be seen, it doesn't matter what color they are.

Happy Fall Card

Designer: Kelly Marie Alvarez

1. Make card from cardstock; score grid.
2. Trim hills from patterned paper; emboss and adhere with foam tape.
4. Trim trees from patterned paper; adhere, some with foam tape.
5. Spell "Happy fall!" with stickers.

Finished size: 5½" x 4¼"

Scalloped Hello Card

Designer: Heidi Van Laar

1. Make card from cardstock.
2. Spell "Hello" with stickers; cover with cardstock panel and emboss over stickers with stylus. Remove stickers.
3. Score border around panel; lightly sand edges and adhere to card.
4. Trim cardstock panels; emboss two and punch bottom edges. Crimp third panel. Layer and adhere together.
5. Knot ribbon and adhere panels to card.

Finished size: 4¼" x 5½"

SUPPLIES: *Cardstock:* (Desert Storm) Neenah Paper *Patterned paper:* (Falling Down, Maple from Nutmeg collection) Cosmo Cricket *Stickers:* (Origins Micro alphabet) BasicGrey *Tools:* (scoring board, scorer, dot embosser) Scor-Pal Products

SUPPLIES: *Cardstock:* (white) Georgia-Pacific; (yellow) Core'dinations; (kraft) The Paper Company *Stickers:* (Hat Box alphabet) American Crafts *Fibers:* (yellow gingham ribbon) Michaels *Templates:* (Just My Type floral, polka dots embossing) Provo Craft *Tools:* (border punch, paper crimper, embossing stylus) Fiskars; (scorer) Scor-Pal Products

5 STEPS ABC Back to School Card

Designer: Anabelle O'Malley

1. Make card from patterned paper; round top corners and ink edges.
2. Adhere lace and trim.
3. Cut rectangle of felt, using decorative-edge scissors; adhere.
4. Affix stickers to chipboard tile; adhere.
5. Cut heart from felt. Print "Back to school" on cardstock; cut into tag shape and ink edges. Attach tag to heart, using stick pin. Tie twine around pin and adhere.

Finished size: 4½" x 5"

SUPPLIES: *Cardstock:* (cream) Bazzill Basics Paper *Patterned paper:* (Blueberry Grove from Woodland Whimsy collection) Sassafras Lass *Dye ink:* (Antique Linen) Ranger Industries *Accents:* (chipboard journaling tile) Sassafras Lass; (blue star stick pin) Fancy Pants Designs *Stickers:* (Pajamas alphabet) American Crafts *Fibers:* (blue pompom trim, green lace) Webster's Pages; (brown/white twine) Martha Stewart Crafts *Font:* (Bookman Old Style) www.fonts.com *Tools:* (decorative-edge scissors, corner rounder punch) *Other:* (white felt) Michaels

5 STEPS Watch the Leaves Turn Card

Designer: Melissa Phillips

Ink all paper edges.

1. Make card from cardstock.
2. Adhere patterned paper rectangles.
3. Apply rub-on to cardstock, trim, and adhere. Adhere rickrack.
4. Tie on ribbon; adhere leaves.
5. Tie button on with string.

Finished size: 4½" x 5½"

SUPPLIES: *Cardstock:* (Apricot, cream) Bazzill Basics Paper *Patterned paper:* (Chilly Mornings, Cozy Home, Sweater Weather from Weathervane collection) October Afternoon *Dye ink:* (Walnut Stain) Ranger Industries *Accents:* (green, yellow, brown felt leaves) Me & My Big Ideas; (brown button) Michaels *Rub-on:* (sentiment) Pink Paislee *Fibers:* (tan rickrack) May Arts; (green ribbon) Papertrey Ink; (white string)

Batty Boo

Designer: Maren Benedict

OUTSIDE

1. Make card from cardstock.
2. Adhere slightly smaller piece of patterned paper.
3. Die-cut and emboss oval from cardstock, ink edges, and adhere.
4. Adhere rhinestones and tie on ribbon.
5. Affix bat sticker to chipboard and adhere to card with foam tape.

INSIDE

1. Trim journal card from patterned paper and adhere.
2. Adhere rhinestones.

Finished size: 5½" x 4½"

SUPPLIES: *Cardstock:* (Summer Sunrise, kraft) Papertrey Ink *Patterned paper:* (Them Bones, Journal Cards from Haunted collection) Cosmo Cricket *Dye ink:* (Really Rust) Stampin' Up! *Accents:* (clear rhinestones) Me & My Big Ideas; (chipboard bat) Cosmo Cricket *Sticker:* (bat) Cosmo Cricket *Fibers:* (rust ribbon) May Arts *Die:* (oval) Spellbinders

Let's Go a Haunting

Designer: Kalyn Kepner

OUTSIDE

1. Make card from cardstock. Cover front with patterned paper.

2. Cut patterned paper piece and cardstock strip. Punch edges and adhere.

3. Use template to cut patterned paper and cardstock circles; adhere.

4. Adhere stickers with foam tape.

5. Adhere rhinestones.

INSIDE

1. Trim cardstock panel to fit inside card; cut two slits in center on fold to create pop-up. Adhere.

2. Cut patterned paper pieces; punch edge and adhere.

3. Cut tombstone shape from patterned paper, mat with patterned paper using foam tape, and affix skeleton. *Note: Adhere skull with foam tape.* Adhere to pop-up.

4. Print sentiment on patterned paper, trim using circle template, and adhere using foam tape.

Finished size: 6" x 5½"

SUPPLIES: *Cardstock:* (black, orange) Bazzill Basics Paper *Patterned paper:* (Eerie, Gothic, Macabre from Haunted collection) Cosmo Cricket; (Rind from Ambrosia collection) BasicGrey *Dye ink:* (black) K&Company *Accents:* (yellow rhinestones) *Stickers:* (candy corn, moon, stars, haunting sentiment, skeleton) Cosmo Cricket *Font:* (Chipperfield and Bailey) www.dafont.com *Template:* (circle) Provo Craft *Tool:* (border punch) Martha Stewart Crafts

Trick

Designer: Becky Olsen

OUTSIDE

1. Make card from patterned paper. Cut patterned paper panel to fit card front.

2. Cut patterned paper strip and adhere to panel.

3. Cut patterned paper pieces, trim with decorative-edge scissors, and adhere. Adhere patterned paper piece.

4. Tie floss in bow around panel; adhere panel to card.

5. Attach brad and affix stickers to spell "Trick…".

INSIDE

1. Stitch line with floss.

2. Attach brad.

3. Affix stickers to spell "Or treat".

Finished size: 4¼" x 5½"

SUPPLIES: *Patterned paper:* (Witche's Feet, Die-Cut News, Glitter Pumpkins, Icon Stripe from Spook Alley collection) Making Memories *Accents:* (black spider brads) Doodlebug Design *Stickers:* (Diva Shimmer alphabet) Making Memories *Fibers:* (black, cream floss) DMC *Tool:* (decorative-edge scissors) Fiskars

⁙5⁙ Boo!

Designer: Davinie Fiero

OUTSIDE

1. Make card from patterned paper; ink edges.

2. Cut patterned paper panel slightly smaller than card front. Punch edge of cardstock strip and adhere; stitch.

3. Cut patterned paper piece and strip; ink edges and adhere to panel. Stitch edges and adhere to card.

4. Adhere houses and spell "Boo!" with stickers.

INSIDE

Stamp sentiment.

Finished size: 4½" x 5½"

SUPPLIES: Cardstock: (orange) WorldWin *Patterned paper:* (Eclipse, Horizon, and Sunset from Twilight collection) Pink Paislee *Clear stamps:* (happy Halloween from Eerie Alley set) SEI *Solvent ink:* (black) Tsukineko *Accents:* (black, orange chipboard houses) American Crafts *Stickers:* (Fashion Script alphabet) Pink Paislee *Other:* (border punch) Fiskars

Smell My Feet

Designer: Wendy Sue Anderson

OUTSIDE

1. Make card from cardstock.

2. Adhere patterned paper. Punch scalloped circle from patterned paper and adhere.

3. Print sentiment on cardstock, trim, and adhere.

4. Adhere ribbon. Tie ribbon in bow through charm and adhere charm with foam tape.

5. Adhere bat.

INSIDE

1. Adhere patterned paper.

2. Print sentiment on cardstock; trim, draw border, and adhere.

3. Affix bat sticker.

Finished size: 3½" x 7"

SUPPLIES: *Cardstock:* (black damask embossed) American Crafts; (cream) *Patterned paper:* (Foil Brocade, Witche's Feet, scalloped circle notebook page from Spook Alley collection) Making Memories *Color medium:* (black pen) American Crafts *Accents:* (black bat, metal charm) Making Memories *Stickers:* (glitter bat) Making Memories *Fibers:* (black ribbon) American Crafts *Font:* (Rickles Script) www.fontdiner.com *Tool:* (scalloped circle punch) Marvy Uchida

Wicked

Designer: Heidi Van Laar

1 Using pattern on p. 282, make 5" x 5¾" card from cardstock with fold at top. 2 Cut oval from patterned paper for hat brim. Adhere tissue paper strip. 3 Cut hat from patterned paper. Layer ribbon and adhere. Affix flourish sticker and adhere to hat brim. 4 Print sentiment on cardstock; die-cut and emboss into circle. Mat with circle die-cut from cardstock and adhere with foam tape. 5 Adhere hat to card. *Note: Tip of hat should extend ¾" higher than card fold.* Trim card to match hat. 6 Tie ribbon bow, attach brad, and adhere to card.

Finished size: 5" x 7"

DESIGNER TIP

When scrunching or gathering tissue paper, don't worry about being perfect. Use your fingers to gather and adhere as you go.

SUPPLIES: *Cardstock:* (black, white, orange) The Paper Company *Patterned paper:* (Glitter Stripe from Spook Alley collection) Making Memories; (Tombstone from Eerie collection) BasicGrey *Specialty paper:* (green tissue) Accent: (orange rhinestone spider brad) Making Memories *Sticker:* (flourish) BasicGrey *Fibers:* (green ribbon) Michaels; (black ribbon) Offray *Fonts:* (Baldur) www.dafont.com; (Baker Signet) www.fonts.com *Dies:* (circles) Spellbinders

{Boo}

Designer: Sarah Martina Parker

1 Make card from cardstock. 2 Tie on ribbon, thread button with twine, and adhere. 3 Cut label shape from patterned papers, cut in half, and adhere together. Draw stitches. 4 Ink and apply glitter to stickers and affix. 5 Punch cardstock, draw stitches, and adhere using foam tape. 6 Adhere label using foam tape.

Finished size: 4¼" x 5½"

DESIGNER TIP

If your stickers aren't the color you need, consider painting or inking them to make them fit your project.

SUPPLIES: *Cardstock:* (Plum Pudding, white) Papertrey Ink *Patterned paper:* (orange graphic from August 2009 kit) Scarlet Lime; (Black Damask from Andrea Victoria collection) My Mind's Eye *Specialty ink:* (Plum Pudding hybrid) Papertrey Ink *Color medium:* (white pen) Sakura *Accents:* (clear glitter) Martha Stewart Crafts; (black button) Papertrey Ink *Stickers:* (Typo alphabet) American Crafts *Fibers:* (orange ribbon) Michaels; (cream twine) Papertrey Ink *Tool:* (border punch) EK Success

 Eek!

Designer: Teri Anderson

① Make card from cardstock. ② Adhere patterned paper pieces; round corners. ③ Adhere twill and tie on twine. ④ Cut bat label from patterned paper and adhere. Adhere rhinestones. ⑤ Spell "Eek!" with stickers.

Finished size: 4¼" x 5½"

DESIGNER TIP

If you don't have batty patterned paper, use a die cut label and stamp it with a bat, witch, or other Halloween icon.

 Starry Boo!

Designer: Betsy Veldman

① Make card from cardstock. Cover with patterned paper and stitch edges. ② Trim date element from patterned paper, round top corners, and ink edges. Tie on ribbon and adhere to card. ③ Stamp star border on patterned paper; trim, adhere, and zigzag-stitch seam. ④ Stamp boo tag on patterned paper, cut out with decorative-edge scissors, ink edges, and adhere with foam tape.

Finished size: 4½" square

SUPPLIES: *Cardstock:* (white) Georgia-Pacific *Patterned paper:* (Eclipse, Sunset, Dusk, Postcards from Twilight collection) Pink Paislee *Accents:* (orange rhinestones) Kaisercraft *Stickers:* (Glitzmas alphabet) SEI *Fibers:* (olive twill) Papertrey Ink; (jute twine) DCC *Tool:* (corner rounder punch) Zutter

SUPPLIES: *Cardstock:* (cream) *Patterned paper:* (Dusk, Sunset, Postcards from Twilight collection) Pink Paislee *Clear stamps:* (boo tag from 2009 Halloween Tags set, star border from Boo to You set) Papertrey Ink *Chalk ink:* (Creamy Brown) Clearsnap *Specialty ink:* (True Black) Papertrey Ink *Accent:* (purple button) Papertrey Ink *Fibers:* (natural twine, orange ribbon) Papertrey Ink *Tools:* (decorative-edge scissors) Provo Craft; (corner rounder punch) EK Sucess

Halloween No. 31

Designer: Rae Barthel

① Make card from cardstock. Sand edges. ② Adhere patterned paper layers and adhere tag die cut. ③ Tie on ribbon. ④ Adhere flowers and rhinestone.

Finished size: 4½" x 6"

{Trick or Treat}

Designer: Maren Benedict

① Make card from cardstock. ② Stick pin through fabric, distress edges, and adhere. ③ Adhere buttons and rhinestones.

Finished size: 4¼" x 5½"

SUPPLIES: *Cardstock:* (Wizard from Black Magic collection) Core'dinations *Patterned paper:* (Dusk, Eclipse from Twilight collection) Pink Paislee *Accents:* (tag die cut) Pink Paislee; (rust, text flowers; amber rhinestone) Prima *Fibers:* (black ribbon) Hobby Lobby

SUPPLIES: *Cardstock:* (black) Papertrey Ink *Accents:* (black buttons) BasicGrey; (orange rhinestones) Zva Creative; (bat pin) Making Memories *Other:* (spooky fabric patch) Pink Paislee

Pumpkin Trio

Designer: Betsy Veldman

① Make card from cardstock. Cut patterned paper panel to fit; ink edges. ② Stamp stems on cardstock piece; ink edges and adhere to panel. Stamp pumpkin faces on buttons, thread with twine, and adhere. ③ Adhere strips of patterned paper and die cut paper; zigzag-stitch. ④ Tie ribbon on panel; adhere to card. ⑤ Die-cut tag from cardstock, stamp boo!, and ink edges. Tie on ribbon with twine.

Finished size: 4¼" x 5½"

SUPPLIES: *Cardstock:* (Rustic Cream) Papertrey Ink *Patterned paper:* (Eclipse from Twilight collection) Pink Paislee; (orange plaid from Nutmeg collection) Cosmo Cricket *Specialty paper:* (Pink/Brown Doilies die cut from Nook & Pantry collection) BasicGrey *Clear stamps:* (pumpkin face, stem, boo! from Boo to You set) Papertrey Ink *Pigment ink:* (Orange Zest) Papertrey Ink *Chalk ink:* (Creamy Brown) Clearsnap *Specialty ink:* (True Black, Ripe Avocado hybrid) Papertrey Ink *Accents:* (orange buttons) Papertrey Ink *Fibers:* (brown polka dot ribbon; cream, natural twine) Papertrey Ink *Die:* (tag) Provo Craft

Vintage Halloween

Designer: Beatriz Jennings

① Make card from cardstock. Ink edges. ② Emboss cardstock and adhere. Adhere patterned paper and zigzag-stitch edges. ③ Affix sticker. ④ Apply glitter to frame, tie on ribbons, and adhere. Thread button with string and adhere. ⑤ Apply sentiment rub-on, adhere rhinestones, and adhere lace. ⑥ Thread buttons with twine and adhere.

Finished size: 4¼" x 5½"

SUPPLIES: *Cardstock:* (Vintage Cream) Papertrey Ink; (black) *Patterned paper:* (Breigh) Melissa Frances *Dye ink:* (Vintage Photo) Ranger Industries *Accents:* (white frame) Melissa Frances; (black, green, orange, cream buttons; green rhinestones, orange glitter) *Rub-on:* (sentiment) Melissa Frances *Sticker:* (black bird's cider) Melissa Frances *Fibers:* (orange ribbon, green striped ribbon, brown twine, cream lace, cream string) *Template:* (swirls and flowers embossing) Provo Craft

Haunted House
Designer: Rae Barthel

① Make card from cardstock. ② Adhere patterned paper strips and cardstock piece. ③ Affix border stickers. Spell sentiment with stickers. ④ Affix house and witch moon stickers to cardstock; cut out and adhere to card with foam tape.

Finished size: 5" x 6"

Trick or Treat
Designer: Annaka Crockett

① Make card from cardstock. ② Cut cardstock panel. Adhere strips of patterned paper and cardstock, round corners, and tie on ribbon. ③ Adhere chipboard circle. ④ Trim bat from patterned paper and adhere. ⑤ Adhere panel using foam tape.

Finished size: 5½" x 4¼"

SUPPLIES: Cardstock: (Witch) Core'dinations; (Ripe Avocado) Papertrey Ink *Patterned paper:* (Cauldron, Tombstone from Eerie collection) BasicGrey *Stickers:* (house, witch moon, circle border, Eerie alphabet) BasicGrey

SUPPLIES: Cardstock: (black, orange) Bazzill Basics Paper *Patterned paper:* (Venom, Full Moon, Transylvania, Scream from Halloween collection; Up, Up and Away! from Junior collection) American Crafts *Accent:* (chipboard sentiment circle) Creative Imaginations *Fibers:* (black stitched ribbon)

Textured Technique Tags by the Talented Tim Holtz

Designer Tim Holtz created his **Alterations Texture Fades Embossing Folders** to produce deep texture on cardstock, canvas, chipboard, grungeboard, metal, and more. In true grungy Tim-style, he created three ghoulish tags to showcase how totally cool embossing can be!

Designer: Tim Holtz

Add Ink to Emphasize a Pattern
Notice how Tim used the bingo folder very deliberately, placing the number 31 in the bottom right corner and highlighting it with black ink. Add some shimmer spray and heavy metallics to intensify the distressed look.

Combine Embossing & Stamping
Here, Tim inked the background of the tag first, then embossed with a checkerboard folder, and lightly rubbed distress ink over the embossed area. Stamp a spooky spider web, add a skinny skeleton and trendy text paper attached with staples and you've reached the pinnacle of cool.

Create a Debossed Effect
Tim's a genius! This tag was created by inking the wood grain folder itself with distress ink first and then embossing the tag to create a stamped and debossed effect. Enhance the woodgrain with a caged raven and all sorts of dramatic accoutrements.

I Scream, you Scream, We all Scream for Halloween!

Celebrate Halloween with these frightfully fun cards, tags, and treat containers.

DESIGNER TIP

To help prevent embossing powder from sticking to your cardstock where it's not wanted, rub a used dryer sheet or wax paper across your cardstock before applying the ink and embossing powder.

5 STEP Haunted Boo Card

Designer: Kazan Clark

1 Make card from cardstock.
2 Stitch edge of patterned paper panel with floss. Adhere patterned paper piece.
3 Adhere ribbon over seam.
4 Tie on buttons and tag using twine.
5 Adhere panel.

Finished size: 5" x 6"

Happy Haunting Card

Designer: Carrie Lipovich

1 Make card from cardstock.
2 Adhere strip of patterned paper.
3 Punch strip of cardstock; adhere.
4 Stamp crow on cardstock panel and emboss.
5 Stamp sentiment, mat with cardstock, and adhere.
6 Attach brads.

Finished size: 4¼" x 5½"

SUPPLIES: *Cardstock:* (black) Bazzill Basics Paper *Patterned paper:* (Foil Brocade from Spook Alley collection) Making Memories; (Nutcracker from Fruitcake collection) BasicGrey *Accents:* (boo tag) Making Memories; (silver buttons) *Fibers:* (black floss) Prism; (green ribbon, natural twine)

SUPPLIES: *Cardstock:* (River Rock, black) Stampin' Up! *Patterned paper:* (damask from Fall pad) Die Cuts With a View *Clear stamps:* (crow from Scary Night set) Inkadinkado; (happy haunting from Missy's Halloween set) A Muse Artstamps *Solvent ink:* (black) Tsukineko *Watermark ink:* Tsukineko *Embossing powder:* (black) Hampton Art *Accents:* (black brads) Jo-Ann Stores *Tool:* (border punch) Martha Stewart Crafts

DESIGNER TIP
Lay the label die down with the oval in the center to cut and emboss both shapes at the same time.

Halloween Wishes Ghost Card

Designer: Erin Lincoln

① Make card from cardstock. Cover with patterned paper.

② Punch circle from scrap paper. Use negative space to mask off circle on cardstock. Ink to create moon.

③ Stamp tree frame over moon and trim. Mask moon with punched circle and ink.

④ Stamp halloween wishes, emboss, and adhere.

⑤ Adhere ghost buttons. Thread buttons with string and adhere.

⑥ Tie on ribbon.

Finished size: 4¼" x 5½"

⑤ Pumpkin Gift Bag

Designer: Latisha Yoast

① Die-cut and emboss label from cardstock. Die-cut and emboss oval from label center.

② Cut patterned paper panel. Adhere label and tie on ribbon. Adhere to gift bag.

③ Die-cut and emboss oval from cardstock.

④ Stamp pumpkin on oval, color, and adhere using foam tape

Finished size: 4½" x 5"

SUPPLIES: *Cardstock:* (white) Papertrey Ink *Patterned paper:* (Wholesome from Granola collection) BasicGrey *Clear stamps:* (tree frame from Through the Trees set; halloween wishes from Spooky Sweets II set) Papertrey Ink *Dye ink:* (Denim) Close To My Heart *Pigment ink:* (Terracotta Tile) Papertrey Ink *Specialty ink:* (Summer Sunrise, Enchanted Evening hybrid) Papertrey Ink *Embossing powder:* (white) Papertrey Ink *Accents:* (orange, yellow buttons) Papertrey Ink; (ghost buttons) Jesse James & Co. *Fibers:* (orange stitched ribbon) Papertrey Ink; (white string) *Tool:* (1½" circle punch) EK Success

SUPPLIES: *Cardstock:* (white, kraft) Papertrey Ink *Patterned paper:* (Imagine from 365 Degrees collection) Pink Paislee *Clear stamp:* (pumpkin from Peace & Plenty set) Waltzingmouse Stamps *Dye ink:* (Tuxedo Black) Tsukineko *Color medium:* (orange, dark orange, green markers) Copic *Fibers:* (orange stitched ribbon) Papertrey Ink *Dies:* (oval, label) Spellbinders *Other:* (kraft gift bag) Target

Creepy Treats Boxes

Designer: Shelly Watson

1. Stamp polka dots on cardstock; die-cut circle.
2. Stamp decorative circle and sentiment on circle.
3. Die-cut two scalloped circles from cardstock.
4. Trim strip of cardstock, adhere ends together to create ring, and adhere between scalloped circles.
5. Adhere stamped circle to box top.
6. Repeat steps 1-5 to make second box.

Finished size: 3¼" diameter x 1" height

5 STEPS Green Swirl Boo Card

Designer: Alicia Thelin

1. Make card from patterned paper.
2. Adhere patterned paper.
3. Apply rub-on.
4. Affix stickers to spell "Boo!" and affix swirl.

Finished size: 4¼" x 5½"

SUPPLIES: *Cardstock:* (black, green, purple) Hobby Lobby *Clear stamps:* (decorative circle, spooky sweets, creepy treats from Spooky Sweets II set; polka dots from Polka Dot Basics set) Papertrey Ink *Pigment ink:* (black) Tsukineko *Paint:* (white) *Dies:* (circle, scalloped circle) Spellbinders

SUPPLIES: All supplies from Pink Paislee. *Patterned paper:* (Nightfall, Horizon from Twilight collection) *Rub-on:* (bat circle) *Stickers:* (Glitter alphabet)

DESIGNER TIP

Trimming images from patterned paper makes for cute and simple embellishments. Add a little glitter for a fun glitzy look.

Spooky Bats Card

Designer: Becky Olsen

1. Make card from cardstock. Adhere patterned paper.
2. Punch patterned paper, adhere to patterned paper strip, and adhere.
3. Trim bats from patterned paper, apply glitter glue, and adhere using foam tape.
4. Affix stickers to spell "{spooky}".

Finished size: 5½" x 4¼"

Franken-Scars Card

Designer: Windy Robinson

1. Make card from cardstock. Adhere patterned paper rectangles; stitch seams.
2. Stamp Frankensteins and sentiment on cardstock. Mat with cardstock and adhere.
3. Tie bow around front flap. *Note: Cut slit in seam and thread ribbon.*
4. Adhere buttons and dot.

Finished size: 3¾" x 7¼"

SUPPLIES: *Cardstock:* (white) Prism *Patterned paper:* (Eclipse, Dusk from Twilight collection) Pink Paislee; (Bat Newsprint from Spook Alley collection) Making Memories *Accent:* (black glitter glue) Ranger Industries *Stickers:* (Diva Shimmer alphabet) Making Memories *Tool:* (border punch) Stampin' Up!

SUPPLIES: *Cardstock:* (French Vanilla) Bazzill Basics Paper; (kraft) *Patterned paper:* (Tarragon Leaves from Chicken Noodle collection) Jillibean Soup; (Sunset from Twilight collection) Pink Paislee *Clear stamps:* (happy Halloween from Happy Halloween set, Frankenstein from Halloween set) Hero Arts *Dye ink:* (orange, purple) Technique Tuesday *Pigment ink:* (Onyx Black) Tsukineko *Accents:* (orange, yellow buttons) BasicGrey; (orange acrylic dot) Michaels *Fibers:* (orange ribbon) Hobby Lobby

DESIGNER TIP

When stamping with any background-building set, you may find it easier to create perfectly stamped images using a grid lined stamping block.

DESIGNER TIP

For best results either run the black net through a Xyron machine and adhere to the card or use a clear-drying glue.

One Crazy Cat Card

Designer: Melissa Bickford

1. Make card from cardstock. Stamp stripes to create background.
2. Adhere lace.
3. Stamp cat, flourish circle, and sentiment on cardstock. Color circle border.
4. Mat with cardstock, zigzag-stitch, and punch slot.
5. Adhere rhinestones, thread ribbon, and adhere using foam tape.
6. Tie ribbon around card.

Finished size: 4¼" x 5½"

⚡5⚡ Spectacularly Spooky Card

Designer: Carly Robertson

1. Make card from cardstock. Cover with netting.
2. Layer ribbons and adhere.
3. Die-cut label from cardstock and adhere using foam tape.
4. Die-cut smaller label from cardstock. Apply rub-on, stamp spooky, and adhere rhinestones.
5. Adhere label using foam tape.

Finished size: 4¼" x 5½"

SUPPLIES: *Cardstock:* (Aqua Mist, Summer Sunrise, white) Papertrey Ink *Clear stamps:* (cat, flourish circle, sentiment from Spooky Sweets II set; stripes from Background Basics: Retro set) Papertrey Ink *Pigment ink:* (Aqua Mist) Papertrey Ink *Specialty ink:* (Summer Sunrise, True Black hybrid) Papertrey Ink *Color medium:* (mint green marker) Copic *Accents:* (black rhinestones) K&Company *Fibers:* (yellow ribbon) Papertrey Ink; (white lace) Offray *Tool:* (slot punch) Stampin' Up!

SUPPLIES: *Cardstock:* (kraft) Papertrey Ink *Clear stamp:* (spooky from Halloween Party set) Waltzingmouse Stamps *Dye ink:* (Ruby Red) Stampin' Up! *Accents:* (clear rhinestones) BasicGrey *Rub-on:* (swirl) BasicGrey *Fibers:* (black sheer, black velvet ribbon) May Arts *Dies:* (labels) Spellbinders *Other:* (black netting) May Arts

Calendar journal cards make adorable seasonal tags. Just add a few embellishments and you have a simple tag for a gift.

BONUS IDEA

Try making the milk carton from patterned paper instead of solid cardstock or adding texture by embossing the cardstock with an embossing folder before assembling.

happy halloween

Batty October Tag

Designer: Carolyn King

1. Adhere rhinestones to tag.
2. Affix bat sticker.
3. Punch circle, thread ribbon, and knot.

Finished size: 2¼" diameter

SUPPLIES: *Accents:* (October tag) Jillibean Soup; (black, yellow, orange rhinestones) Michaels *Sticker:* (bat) K&Company *Fibers:* (black polka dot ribbon) Michaels *Tool:* (⅛" circle punch)

Full Moon Treat Holder

Designer: Mary Ashby

1. Die-cut milk carton from cardstock, fold, and assemble. Adhere seams.
2. Punch circle from cardstock. Punch bat from cardstock and adhere to circle. Adhere using foam tape.
3. Stamp sentiment on cardstock, trim, and mat with cardstock. Adhere.
4. Attach library clip and tie on ribbon.

Finished size: 1½" x 3¼" x 1½"

SUPPLIES: All supplies from Stampin' Up! unless otherwise noted. *Cardstock:* (Pumpkin Pie, Whisper White, Basic Black) *Rubber stamp:* (happy halloween from Teeny Tiny Wishes set) *Specialty ink:* (Noir hybrid) Stewart Superior Corp. *Accent:* (silver library clip) *Fibers:* (white ribbon) *Die:* (mini milk carton) Stampin' Up! *Tools:* (1⅜" circle punch); (bat punch) Martha Stewart Crafts

BONUS IDEA

By changing the theme, this would make a fun little treat for any holiday or occasion. It would also be perfect to tuck into a lunch bag for a cute first day of school treat.

INSIDE

or TREAT

Witchy Trick Card

Designer: Ivanka Lentle

OUTSIDE

1. Make card from cardstock. Emboss stripes.
2. Punch crepe paper strip and adhere.
3. Emboss bubbles on strip of cardstock and adhere.
4. Apply witch and trick rub-ons.
5. Tie on ribbon.

INSIDE

1. Adhere patterned paper. Apply or treat rub-ons.
2. Emboss cardstock with stripes, tear, and adhere.
3. Wrap chocolate bar in patterned paper.
4. Emboss bubbles on strip of cardstock, trim, and wrap around chocolate bar.
5. Apply pumpkin rub-on to chocolate bar and adhere.

Finished size: 3½" x 2¾"

Pretty Boo Card

5 STEPS

Designer: Heather Pulvirenti

1. Make card from cardstock.
2. Stamp background on cardstock, emboss, and trim.
3. Affix stickers to spell "Boo".
4. Tie on ribbon and adhere panel.

Finished size: 5½" x 4¼"

SUPPLIES: *Cardstock:* (white, black, purple) Bazzill Basics Paper *Patterned paper:* (Little Blossom from Bloom & Grow collection) My Mind's Eye; (Wildflowers from Sophie collection) BoBunny Press *Rub-ons:* (witch, pumpkin, trick or treat) Making Memories *Fibers:* (orange ribbon) Offray *Templates:* (Candy Cane Stripe, Tiny Bubbles embossing) Provo Craft *Tool:* (border punch) Fiskars *Other:* (green crepe paper, mini chocolate bar)

SUPPLIES: *Cardstock:* (white, kraft) Papertrey Ink *Rubber stamp:* (Antique Flower Background) Hero Arts *Watermark ink:* Tsukineko *Embossing powder:* (Cricket) American Crafts *Stickers:* (Playroom alphabet) American Crafts *Fibers:* (purple ribbon) Papertrey Ink

DESIGNER TIP

Crepe paper is really easy to work with. When creating ruffles, it will easily fold into the form you are trying to achieve.

BONUS IDEA

Start collecting your bottles and decorate multiple bottles for your own creepy pharmacy.

Poison Label

Designer: Courtney Baker

1. Trim strip of patterned paper; adhere to crepe paper.
2. Adhere ribbon, wrapping over ends.
3. Wrap piece around bottle neck and adhere ends.
4. Trim poison label from patterned paper; adhere to front of bottle.

Finished sizes: label 4" x 3", neck wrap 1¾" diameter x 2" height

SUPPLIES: *Patterned paper:* (Dusk, Postcards from Twilight collection) Pink Paislee *Fibers:* (black ribbon) May Arts *Other:* (black crepe paper, bottle)

Raffia Trick or Treat Card

Designer: Ashley C. Newell

1. Make card from cardstock.
2. Adhere strip of cardstock. Trim narrow strips of cardstock, sand edges, and adhere.
3. Emboss cardstock, sand, tear bottom edge, and adhere. Zigzag-stitch edges.
4. Stamp pumpkin on cardstock, trim, and adhere using foam tape.
5. Stamp trick or treat on cardstock, trim, and adhere using foam tape.
6. Cut leaves from trim; adhere. Tie on raffia.

Finished size: 4¼" x 5½"

SUPPLIES: *Cardstock:* (Spring Moss) Papertrey Ink; (Dusty Durango) Stampin' Up!; (Shazam) Core'dinations *Clear stamps:* (pumpkin, trick or treat from Thanks2Fall set) The Stamps of Life *Dye ink:* (black) Close To My Heart *Fibers:* (green leaf trim) Creative Imaginations; (natural raffia) DMD, Inc. *Template:* (polka dots embossing) QuicKutz

Something Good to Eat Card

Designer: Dawn Petrick

1. Make card from cardstock. Cut ¾" from card front.
2. Stamp script on cardstock, trim, and adhere. Ink edges.
3. Stamp spider webs on cardstock, trim, and adhere.
4. Punch strip of patterned paper; adhere twill and adhere to card.
5. Die-cut circle from cardstock. Stamp witch, embellished circle, and sentiment.
6. Die-cut scalloped circle from cardstock, adhere stamped circle, and adhere to card.

Finished size: 4¼" x 5½"

Full Moon Haunted House Card

Designer: Mary Jo Johnston

1. Make card from cardstock. Print digital patterned papers on cardstock. *Note: Do not print Ghostly Graffiti paper.*
2. Cover card front with patterned paper.
3. Trim patterned paper to create hill, ink edges, and adhere.
4. Affix word strip and eyes stickers.
5. Punch circle from patterned paper, punch bat from circle, and adhere with foam tape. Print cloud on cardstock, cut out, and adhere.
6. Create 1½" x 3" project in software. Drop in haunted house. Fill with patterned paper and print on cardstock. Trim and adhere using foam tape.

Finished size: 5" square

SUPPLIES: All supplies from Papertrey Ink unless otherwise noted. *Cardstock:* (Summer Sunrise, Dark Chocolate, kraft) *Patterned paper:* (yellow grid from 2008 Bitty Dot Basics collection) *Clear stamps:* (embellished circle, witch, sentiment, spider web from Spooky Sweets II set; script from Background Basics: Text Style set) *Pigment ink:* (Fresh Snow) *Specialty ink:* (Dark Chocolate, Summer Sunrise hybrid) *Fibers:* (brown twill) *Dies:* (scalloped circle, large circle) Spellbinders *Tool:* (border punch) Fiskars

SUPPLIES: *Cardstock:* (brown) Bazzill Basics Paper; (white) *Patterned paper:* *Dye ink:* (Sepia) Ranger Industries *Digital elements:* (Wheat Pudding, Butternut Corn patterned paper from Plumberry Harvest kit; Ghoulish Green, Ghostly Graffiti patterned paper from Kooky Spooky kit; haunted house from Simply Halloween Word Art kit) www.peppermintcreative.com; (gel cloud) *Stickers:* (word strip) 7gypsies; (epoxy eyes) Heidi Grace Designs *Software:* (photo editing) *Tool:* (2" circle punch) EK Success; (bat punch) Martha Stewart Crafts

Tulle is a great embellishment! A little goes a long way and it adds a very special touch. It can make your project "vintage" in a hurry, or just add a special something to your everyday projects!

Shabby Halloween Card

Designer: Jeni Allen

1. Make card from cardstock. Ink edges.
2. Adhere patterned paper and chipboard tag.
3. Tie on ribbon.
4. Adhere tulle under ribbon.
5. Adhere button.

Finished size: 4¼" x 5½"

My Vampire Card

Designer: Jennifer Buck

1. Make card from cardstock. Affix border sticker.
2. Stamp My Vampire on cardstock panel, mat with cardstock, and tie on ribbon.
3. Punch label from cardstock, adhere behind panel, and adhere using foam tape.
4. Adhere rhinestones.

Finished size: 5½" square

SUPPLIES: *Cardstock:* (Very Vanilla) Stampin' Up! *Patterned paper:* (black brocade from 5th Avenue collection notebook) Making Memories *Dye ink:* (Antique Linen) Ranger Industries *Accents:* (chipboard halloween tag) Scenic Route; (black button) Papertrey Ink *Fibers:* (black ribbon, cream tulle)

SUPPLIES: *Cardstock:* (black) Bazzill Basics Paper; (white) Papertrey Ink *Rubber stamp:* (My Vampire) Unity Stamp Co. *Dye ink:* (black) Tsukineko *Accents:* (red square rhinestones) Glitz Design *Sticker:* (black velvet filigree border) Stampendous! *Fibers:* (red ribbon) Papertrey Ink *Tool:* (label punch) Stampin' Up!

Halloween Party Invitation

Designer: Carly Robertson

1. Make card from cardstock.
2. Die-cut label from wood paper.
3. Stamp sentiments on label, adhere spider, and tie on ribbon.
4. Adhere using foam tape.

Finished size: 5½" x 4¼"

SUPPLIES: *Cardstock:* (black) Bazzill Basics Paper *Specialty paper:* (Thin Birch wood from Real Wood collection) Creative Imaginations *Clear stamps:* (sentiments from Halloween Party set) Waltzingmouse Stamps *Specialty ink:* (Noir hybrid) Stewart Superior Corp. *Accent:* (rhinestone spider) BasicGrey *Fibers:* (black striped ribbon) May Arts *Die:* (label) Stampin' Up!

A Bitter Wind Howls Card

Designer: Beatriz Jennings

1. Make card from cardstock.
2. Ink edges of bingo card, spray with ink, and adhere.
3. Adhere patterned paper strip and border; stitch as desired.
4. Cut doily in half and adhere.
5. Affix sticker to patterned paper, trim, and adhere.
6. Apply glitter to chipboard frame, tie on ribbon, and adhere.
7. Thread button with twine and tie on. Adhere rhinestones.

Finished size: 5¾" x 4¼"

SUPPLIES: *Cardstock:* (kraft) *Patterned paper:* (Ramona) Melissa Frances; (blue from Bailey pad) K&Company *Dye ink:* (Vintage Photo) Ranger Industries *Specialty ink:* (Wheat Fields shimmer spray) Tattered Angels *Accents:* (chipboard frame, bingo card) Tattered Angels; (black gingham border) My Mind's Eye; (black glitter) Martha Stewart Crafts; (clear rhinestones, white button) *Sticker:* (howls oval) Melissa Frances *Fibers:* (orange ribbon, twine) *Other:* (white doily)

DESIGNER TIP
Be sure to wipe away any excess ink to allow the base layer to show through.

⁵ Boo to You Card

Designer: Kimberly Crawford

1. Make card from cardstock.
2. Stamp flourishes on patterned paper; emboss. Apply ink and adhere.
3. Adhere lace and trim.
4. Apply rub-on.
5. Stamp bat on cardstock; cut out and adhere.

Finished size: 5½" x 4¼"

⁵ October 31 Card

Designer: Angie Tieman

1. Make card from cardstock; trim ½" from card front.
2. Punch circles from book page; adhere. Zigzag-stitch lines.
3. Cut oval from cardstock; trim sunburst edges and adhere with foam tape.
4. Apply October 31 rub-on to cardstock; punch into oval and adhere with foam tape.
5. Thread button with twine and adhere. Adhere cardstock inside card and apply crow rub-on.

Finished size: 4¼" x 5½"

SUPPLIES: *Cardstock:* (Smokey Shadow) Papertrey Ink *Patterned paper:* (Tea Towel from Cherry Hill pad) October Afternoon *Clear stamps:* (bat from Spooky Sweets set) Papertrey Ink; (flourishes from Rococo set) Technique Tuesday *Dye ink:* (Peeled Paint) Ranger Industries *Watermark ink:* Tsukineko *Specialty ink:* (Noir hybrid) Stewart Superior Corp. *Embossing powder:* (clear) Stampendous! *Rub-on:* (sentiment) Cosmo Cricket *Fibers:* (green pompom trim) Making Memories; (cream lace) Wrights

SUPPLIES: All supplies from Stampin' Up! unless otherwise noted. *Cardstock:* (Very Vanilla, Pumpkin Pie, Basic Black) *Accent:* (orange button) *Rub-ons:* (October 31 image, crow) *Fibers:* (black twine) *Tools:* (oval punch, 1" circle punch) *Other:* (vintage book page) no source

⑤Boo Gift Bag

Designer: Angie Hagist

❶ Trim patterned paper. Trim top edge along scallops and adhere.

❷ Cut ghost from cardstock, using pattern on p. 284. Hand-stitch edge with floss. Cut eyes and mouth from cardstock; adhere. Adhere to bag. Stuff midsection with wadded newspaper.

❸ Ink letters, wipe away excess, and adhere to spell "Boo".

Finished size: 8" x 9¾"

TRENDY TIP

By using offset scalloped paper as the background and pairing it with a fun Halloween icon in a coordinating color, she's able to accomplish two things: Angie's used a trendy patterned paper that otherwise might not have been considered for a Halloween project.

SUPPLIES: *Cardstock:* Butter Cream, Suede Brown Dark) Bazzill Basics Paper *Patterned paper:* (Sprinklers from Fly a Kite collection) October Afternoon *Dye ink:* (Van Dyke Brown) Ranger Industries *Accents:* (white sheer alphabet) Maya Road *Fibers:* (white floss) DMC *Other:* (kraft gift bag) Target; (newspaper)

⑤Open If You Dare Card

Designer: Erin Lincoln

❶ Make card from cardstock.

❷ Trim cardstock panel; stamp sentiment and scallops. Draw line. Mat with cardstock.

❸ Die-cut jars and snake from cardstock. Stamp web and spiders on one jar. Adhere jars, snake, and wiggle eyes.

❹ Die-cut small and medium labels from cardstock. Stamp sentiments on small labels, mat with medium labels, and adhere with foam tape.

❺ Thread button with twine; adhere. Trim ribbon; adhere. Adhere panel to card front.

Finished size: 6½" x 3½"

TRENDY TIP

Erin has taken this offset scallop stamp and made it more functional than decorative. The pattern gives the shelf upon which these spooky jars are sitting some additional depth and texture.

SUPPLIES: *Cardstock:* (green, purple, orange, white) Die Cuts With a View *Clear stamps:* (large spider, sentiments, web from Spooky Sweets II set; scallops from Background Basics: Retro set) Papertrey Ink; (small spider from Happy Halloween set) Hero Arts *Specialty ink:* (True Black hybrid) Papertrey Ink *Color medium:* (black pen) *Accents:* (purple button, wiggle eyes) *Fibers:* (black stitched ribbon) Papertrey Ink; (white twine) *Dies:* (label, jar, snake) Silhouette America

Scalloped Owl Card

Designer: Nina Brackett

1. Using pattern on p. 282, transfer to cardstocks; cut out pieces.

2. Score kraft body below ears. Adhere red body to kraft body above score line to form card.

3. Stamp scallops on white belly. Color centers. Trim some scallops with craft knife; curl upwards. Adhere.

4. Adhere wings; draw stitches with pen. Adhere eyes and beak to head piece. Adhere eyelids with foam tape. Adhere head with foam tape.

5. Tie on ribbon; thread button with string and adhere.

Finished size: 4¼" x 6¼"

TRENDY TIP

Nina has applied this trendy pattern to the owl's belly—and by cutting and fluffing the "feathers," she's also added texture and dimension.

Spooky Halloween Card

Designer: Kim Kesti

1. Make card from cardstock.

2. Punch six circles from each color of cardstock; adhere, starting at top of card. Trim edges.

3. Die-cut house and tree from cardstock. Adhere tree. Adhere house with foam tape.

Finished size: 4¾" x 5¾"

TRENDY TIP

It's easy to create an offset scallop pattern with a circle punch or even a die-cut circle. Here Kim has added a gradient color palette that gives it an extra trendy "punch"!

SUPPLIES: *Cardstock:* (Rocket Red, kraft, white) Gina K Designs *Clear stamp:* (scallops from Wall Flower set) Clear & Simple Stamps *Dye ink:* (Brick Red) Clearsnap *Color media:* (yellow marker) Copic; (white pen) Ranger Industries *Accent:* (red button) *Fibers:* (yellow ribbon) Stampin' Up!; (white string) May Arts

SUPPLIES: *Cardstock:* (Raven, Thunder, Elephant, Dark Burgundy, Dark Scarlet, Maraschino, Apricot) Bazzill Basics Paper; (Amber, Curry, Honeycomb, Desert, Frankincense, Nomad) Couture Cardstock; (cream) *Dies:* (house, tree) QuicKutz *Tool:* (1" circle punch)

Things That Go Bump in the Night

Celebrate Halloween in style—whether it's cutesy, clever, or creepy creations you desire, you'll find something here that'll thrill all the trick-or-treaters and monster-mashers in your life. Liven up a party with clever treat containers, or surprise someone with a festive greeting or cleverly-packaged gift. After all, Halloween is the time for ghoulies and ghosties and fun paper crafts!

⁙5⁙ Starry Gift Bag

Designer: Ashley Harris

❶ Adhere patterned paper to bag.

❷ Adhere journaling page. Ink over part of sentiment. Stamp Boo!

❸ Spell "Treat" with stickers.

❹ Apply ink and glitter glue to star; let dry. Adhere.

❺ Cut slits in bag; tie on ribbon. Adhere rhinestone.

Finished size: 7¾" x 9¾"

Spooky Mug

Designer: Mary Bieber

❶ Apply spooky spider rub-on to mug.

❷ Punch tag from cardstock; mat with cardstock. Apply sentiment rub-on.

❸ Attach grommet to tag.

❹ Fill cellophane bag with treat; tie closed with ribbon.

❺ Cut length of rope. Burn end with match.

❻ Tie rope to tag and attach to ribbon.

Finished size: 3½" diameter x 4¼" height

Designer Tips

Use caution when burning the rope—some burn very quickly. Have a damp paper towel ready to put out the flame.

If you don't want to burn the rope, use a marker to create a similar look.

This mug should be hand-washed only.

SUPPLIES: *Patterned paper:* (Spooktacular Stars) Teresa Collins Designs *Foam stamp:* (Boo!) Making Memories *Solvent ink:* (Jet Black) Tsukineko *Accents:* (acetate star) Scrap Supply; (black glitter glue) Ranger Industries; (journaling page) Teresa Collins Designs; (orange rhinestone) *Stickers:* (Fashion Script alphabet) Pink Paislee *Fibers:* (black ribbon) Hobby Lobby *Other:* (kraft gift bag)

SUPPLIES: All supplies from Stampin' Up! unless otherwise noted. *Cardstock:* (orange, black) Bazzill Basics Paper *Accent:* (pewter grommet) *Rub-ons:* (eat, drink, and be scary; spooky spider) *Fibers:* (white rope, pumpkin ribbon) *Tool:* (tag punch) *Other:* (orange mug, cellophane bag, treat) no source

Trick-or-Treat Owl Card

Designer: Roree Rumph

❶ Make card from cardstock. Adhere patterned paper. Sand edges.

❷ Trim patterned paper rectangles, sand edges, and adhere.

❸ Trim cardstock and adhere over patterned paper.

❹ Cut cardstock circle, adhere, pierce around edges. Stitch with floss.

❺ Adhere owl die cut. Affix stickers to spell out sentiment.

❻ Cut star from cardstock; adhere. Affix heart sticker and attach brad.

❼ Apply rub-ons to brad.

Finished size: 5½" square

Pumpkin October 31st Card

Designer: Kim Moreno

❶ Make card from cardstock; sand edges and punch bottom front edge.

❷ Cut rectangle of black cardstock, sand edges, and adhere.

❸ Adhere rectangle of patterned paper. Adhere piece of scalloped patterned paper and patterned paper strip.

❹ Apply rub-on to cardstock, trim, and adhere rhinestones.

❺ Cut jack o' lantern from patterned paper; adhere.

❻ Tie on ribbon; adhere rub-on piece.

Finished size: 4" x 5¼"

SUPPLIES: *Cardstock:* (Infatuation) Bazzill Basics Paper; (Eyelet Impressions) Doodlebug Design; (Stars Sublime) KI Memories *Patterned paper:* (Reservation from Travel collection) American Crafts; (Orange Notebook from Spirit collection) Creative Café; (Moon Glade from Vintage Moon collection) Pink Paislee *Accents:* (owl die cut) Target; (leaf brad) American Crafts *Rub-ons:* (Simply Sweet alphabet) Doodlebug Design *Stickers:* (Shimmer alphabet) Making Memories; (glitter heart) Target *Fibers:* (white floss) DMC *Tool:* (circle cutter) Fiskars

SUPPLIES: *Cardstock:* (pumpkin, black, white) Core'dinations *Patterned paper:* (Argyle, Polka Dot Stripe from Spellbound collection) Making Memories; (Jack Attack from Eerie Alley collection) SEI; (Blue Moon from Vintage Moon collection) Pink Paislee *Accents:* (orange rhinestones) Kaisercraft *Rub-on:* (October 31st label) Hambly Screen Prints *Fibers:* (orange ribbon) *Tool:* (border punch) Martha Stewart Crafts

Spooky Kitty Gift Bag

Designer: Wendy Johnson

❶ Cut handles off gift bag. Adhere patterned paper to bag front.

❷ Adhere patterned paper to bag back and fold over top.

❸ Adhere ribbon and rickrack to flap. Attach brad. Adhere fastener to close.

❹ Adhere cat die cut with foam tape.

❺ Cut sentiment from patterned paper, mat with cardstock, and adhere to bag.

❻ Attach wire wrapped with ribbon to bag top.

Finished size: 5¼" x 4¾" x 3¼"

⁵ STEPS Monster Mix Jar

Designer: Kim Kesti

❶ Trim cardstock strips; adhere together and adhere around container.

❷ Tie ribbon and twine around container.

❸ Cut monsters from patterned paper, mat with cardstock, and adhere with foam tape.

❹ Write "Monster mix" on cardstock, trim into circle, mat with cardstock, and trim little "monster bites" around edges of circle. Attach with clothespin.

Finished size: 5" diameter x 6" height

SUPPLIES: *Cardstock:* (purple) *Patterned paper:* (Wednesday, Lurch from Halloween collection) We R Memory Keepers; (Spooky Words from Spooktacular collection) Teresa Collins Designs *Accents:* (decorative rhinestone brad) We R Memory Keepers; (black cat die cut) Little Yellow Bicycle *Fibers:* (black polka dot ribbon) Little Yellow Bicycle; (green rickrack) Wrights *Adhesive:* (foam tape) *Other:* (white gift bag, hook and loop fastener, craft wire)

SUPPLIES: *Cardstock:* (Hopi, Parakeet, Blue Calypso, kraft) Bazzill Basics Paper *Patterned paper:* (Louie from Night Light collection) October Afternoon *Color medium:* (black pen) *Accent:* (wood clothespin) Creative Imaginations *Fibers:* (brown dotted ribbon) May Arts; (jute twine) *Adhesive:* (foam tape) *Other:* (clear container)

⟨5 STEPS⟩ Vintage Frame Halloween Card

Designer: Beatriz Jennings

❶ Make card from cardstock; paint edges.

❷ Cut patterned paper slightly smaller than card front; adhere. Stitch edges.

❸ Tie ribbon around card.

❹ Adhere patterned paper, slightly overlapping top edge of card. Stitch edges.

❺ Apply rub-ons; thread button with string and adhere.

Finished size: 3¾" x 6"

SUPPLIES: *Cardstock:* (pumpkin) Bazzill Basics Paper *Patterned paper:* (Family Floral from Cousins collection) My Mind's Eye; (Cream Floral scalloped from Antique Cream collection) Creative Imaginations *Dye ink:* (Old Paper) Ranger Industries *Paint:* (cream) *Accent:* (black/cream button) *Rub-ons:* (sentiment, boo bat) Melissa Frances *Fibers:* (black polka dot ribbon, cream string)

⟨5 STEPS⟩ Merry Scaring Card

Designer: Maren Benedict

❶ Make card from cardstock.

❷ Adhere slightly smaller patterned paper rectangle; stitch edges.

❸ Apply skeleton rub-on to patterned paper; mat with cardstock. Stitch edges.

❹ Tie ribbon around card front. Adhere skeleton with foam tape.

❺ Apply sentiment rub-on.

Finished size: 5½" x 4¼"

SUPPLIES: *Cardstock:* (cream) Papertrey Ink *Patterned paper:* (Nevermore from Haunted collection) Cosmo Cricket *Rub-ons:* (sentiment, skeleton) Cosmo Cricket *Fibers:* (cream ribbon) Stampin' Up! *Adhesive:* (foam tape)

Halloween Lollipop Tags

Designer: Melissa Phillips

❶ Ink edges of label stickers; affix to patterned tags. *Note: Adhere inked flower and affix boo circle sticker to date prompt label.* Adhere crocheted trim.

❷ Tea-stain or ink small tags; let dry. Stamp images on one tag and apply rub-ons to others. Detail rub-ons with pencils.

❸ Thread small tags and buttons with twine; tie to lollipops and adhere to tags.

❹ Tie ribbon through tags. Thread button with twine and tie to one ribbon.

Finished size: 2½" x 4¾"

Skeleton Dance Card

Designer: Leslie Webster

❶ Make card from cardstock.

❷ Adhere slightly smaller patterned paper. Adhere patterned paper strip.

❸ Die-cut tags from cardstock; adhere. Stamp sentiment; adhere to card.

❹ Adhere buttons. Affix stickers. Apply rub-ons.

❺ Tie on ribbon.

Finished size: 5" x 7"

SUPPLIES: *Clear stamp:* (Halloween, bat from Celebrate Baby set) Melissa Frances *Dye ink:* (Walnut Stain) Ranger Industries *Color medium:* (orange, green watercolor pencils) Close To My Heart *Accents:* (olive polka dot, burgundy floral, orange filigree tags; pewter buttons) Melissa Frances; (small tags) Creative Café; (cream flower; gold, black buttons) *Rub-ons:* (pumpkin patch, Halloween) Melissa Frances *Stickers:* (cider, birdseed, date prompt labels; boo circle) *Fibers:* (cream crocheted trim) Melissa Frances; (green wired ribbon) Berwick Industries; (hemp twine) Darice; (brown ribbon) *Other:* (lollipops, tea)

SUPPLIES: *Cardstock:* (Raven, Hazard) Bazzill Basics Paper *Patterned paper:* (Polka Dot Stripe from Spellbound collection) Making Memories *Rubber stamp:* (Happy Halloween) Imaginisce *Pigment ink:* (black) Tsukineko *Accents:* (cream, black buttons) American Crafts *Rub-ons:* (skeletons) Hambly Screen Prints *Stickers:* (epoxy bats, star) Cloud 9 Design *Fibers:* (black ribbon) Offray *Dies:* (tags) Provo Craft *Tool:* (die cut machine) Provo Craft

5 STEPS Trick-or-Treat Kitty Card

Designer: Maren Benedict

❶ Make card from cardstock.

❷ Stamp moon, cat, and sentiment on cardstock; color with markers and pen.

❸ Mat with cardstock; zigzag-stitch edges.

❹ Adhere stamped piece with foam tape. Tie ribbon around card.

Finished size: 4¼" square

5 STEPS Little Trick-or-Treater Card

Designer: Deena Ziegler, courtesy of Ellison

❶ Make card from cardstock.

❷ Die-cut scalloped circle frame from patterned paper and cardstock. Adhere to card.

❸ Die-cut Hello Kitty w/ Bunny Costume from cardstock; assemble. Add detail with pen. Adhere with foam tape.

❹ Tie ribbon around card.

Finished size: 5" square

SUPPLIES: *Cardstock:* (white) Papertrey Ink; (Pumpkin Pie, Basic Black) Stampin' Up! *Rubber stamps:* (cat, moon, sentiment from Trick or Treat Peeps set) Unity Stamp Co. *Dye ink:* (Tuxedo Black) Tsukineko *Color medium:* (markers) Copic Marker; (yellow glitter pen) *Fibers:* (orange gingham ribbon) *Adhesive:* (foam tape)

SUPPLIES: *Cardstock:* (light pink, dark pink, white, black, orange, yellow) Bazzill Basics Paper; (Buttercup glitter) Die Cuts With a View *Patterned paper:* (Salt & Pepper from French Kitchen collection) Reminisce *Color medium:* (black pen) EK Success *Fibers:* (green polka dot ribbon) Offray *Adhesive:* (foam tape) *Dies:* (circle scallop frame; Hello Kitty w/ Bunny Costume) Ellison *Tool:* (die cut machine) Ellison

⁵Batty Card

Designer: Anabelle O'Malley

❶ Make card from cardstock; sand edges.

❷ Adhere strip of patterned paper. Adhere border.

❸ Apply rub-on to die cut. Adhere with foam tape.

❹ Adhere bat sticker with foam tape.

❺ Adhere rhinestones.

Finished size: 7" x 3½"

⁵Witchy Footwear Card

Designer: Kim Hughes

❶ Make boot card, following pattern on p. 284.

❷ Punch holes along front edge of boot.

❸ Lace ribbon through holes; tie.

❹ Thread button with embroidery floss. Adhere.

Finished size: 4½" x 5½"

Designer Tip
Measure and mark the holes on the back of the card before punching them for even spacing.

SUPPLIES: *Cardstock:* (Slime from Eerie Alley collection) SEI *Patterned paper:* (Nightmare Square from Eerie Alley collection) SEI *Accents:* (starburst circle die cut) Scenic Route; (white zigzag paper border) Doodlebug Design; (orange rhinestones) Me & My Big Ideas *Rub-on:* (happy Halloween) Melissa Frances *Sticker:* (bat) Me & My Big Ideas *Adhesive:* (foam tape)

SUPPLIES: *Patterned paper:* (Spectacular from Fascinating collection) Pink Paislee *Accent:* (purple button) Jesse James & Co. *Fibers:* (green ribbon) Creative Impressions; (orange floss) DMC *Tool:* (⅛" circle punch)

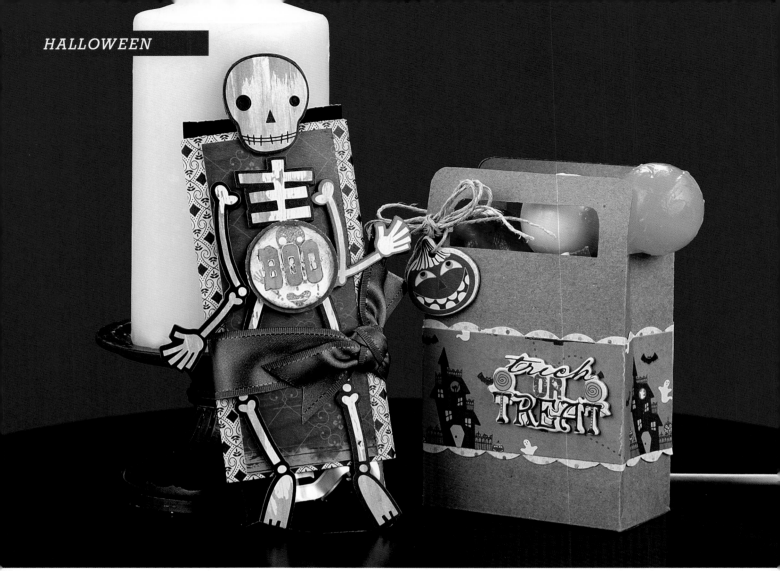

Skeleton Candy Bar Wrap

Designer: Maren Benedict

❶ Wrap candy bar with patterned paper.

❷ Adhere patterned paper rectangle.

❸ Affix skeleton stickers to chipboard pieces. Adhere to wrap.

❹ Punch patterned paper circle; apply rub-on. Stamp skeleton over rub-on. Mat with punched patterned paper circle; ink edges. Adhere.

❺ Tie on ribbon.

Finished size: 2½" x 7"

Haunted House Treat Bag

Designer: Daniela Dobson

❶ Cut strip of patterned paper; trim with decorative-edge scissors. Adhere to bag.

❷ Cut patterned paper strip and adhere.

❸ Adhere chipboard sentiment. Punch hole in chipboard jack o' lantern; tie to box with hemp cord.

Finished size: 3¼" x 5¼" x 1¾"

SUPPLIES: *Patterned paper:* (Nevermore, Ominous from Haunted collection) Cosmo Cricket *Clear stamps:* (small skeleton from Haunted set) Cosmo Cricket *Dye ink:* (Tuxedo Black) Tsukineko; (Pumpkin Pie) Stampin' Up! *Accents:* (chipboard skeleton) Cosmo Cricket *Rub-on:* (boo) Cosmo Cricket *Stickers:* (skeleton parts) Cosmo Cricket *Fibers:* (green ribbon) May Arts *Tools:* (1¼", 1½" circle punches) Stampin' Up! *Other:* (candy bar)

SUPPLIES: *Cardstock:* (kraft) DMD, Inc. *Patterned paper:* (Velcome Inn, Pixie Sticks from Hallowhimsy collection) Imaginisce *Accents:* (chipboard sentiment, jack o' lantern) Imaginisce *Fibers:* (hemp cord) Darice *Tool:* (decorative-edge scissors) *Other:* Kraft gift bag

Fun Trick-or-Treat Card

Designer: Susan Neal

1 Make card from cardstock.

2 Cut strips of patterned paper, sand edges, and adhere.

3 Adhere photo corners.

4 Tie knots in ribbon length; adhere to card.

5 Sand edges of chipboard shapes; adhere. Insert pins.

Finished size: 8½" x 3¾"

Batty Happy Haunting Card

Designer: Kalyn Kepner

1 Make card from patterned paper.

2 Trim cardstock strips with decorative-edge scissors; adhere.

3 Trim patterned paper, ink edges, and adhere.

4 Adhere bat and star stickers with foam tape.

5 Die-cut "Haunting" from cardstock; adhere.

6 Write "Happy" with marker.

Finished size: 5" x 6½"

SUPPLIES: *Cardstock:* (black) Bazzill Basics Paper *Patterned paper:* (Scrap Strip, Briggs Street, Boardman Street from Salem collection) Scenic Route *Accents:* (Halloween chipboard shapes) Scenic Route; (black photo corners, black pins) *Fibers:* (orange/black gingham ribbon)

SUPPLIES: *Cardstock:* (black) Bazzill Basics Paper; (dark gray shimmer) The Paper Company *Patterned paper:* (Gothic, Eerie from Haunted collection) Cosmo Cricket *Dye ink:* (black) K&Company *Color medium:* (black marker) Sanford *Stickers:* (bat, stars) Cosmo Cricket *Adhesive:* (foam tape) *Dies:* (Dragonfly alphabet) QuicKutz *Tools:* (die cut machine) QuicKutz; (decorative-edge scissors) EK Success

Haunted Tree Card

Designer: Mary C. Anderson

❶ Cut Whisper White cardstock rectangle and sponge on More Mustard ink.

❷ Apply Pumpkin Pie ink lightly with brayer.

❸ Punch circle from cardstock to make moon mask. Adhere to inked cardstock with repositionable adhesive. Apply heavy layer of Pumpkin Pie ink over mask and entire rectangle.

❹ Remove mask. Stamp tree, bats, and sentiment. Sponge Bravo Burgundy ink around edges of rectangle. Ink edges with Chocolate Chip.

❺ Mat rectangle with cardstock.

❻ Make card from cardstock; tie on ribbon. Adhere rectangle with foam tape.

Finished size: 5" square

Meow at the Moon Card

Designer: Debbie Tlach, courtesy of Ranger Industries

❶ Squeeze dots of four colors of specialty ink onto applicator felt; tap felt onto cardstock to cover surface.

❷ Repeat step 1 with four different ink colors on another sheet of cardstock.

❸ Punch circle from inked cardstock. Cut linen paper to smaller than finished size; adhere circle with foam tape.

❹ Doodle edges of linen paper piece with pen.

❺ Stamp cat, wing, and meow on cardstock; doodle/color with pens. Cut out and adhere with foam tape.

❻ Make card from inked cardstock. Adhere linen piece.

Finished size: 6½" x 5½"

SUPPLIES: *Cardstock:* (Whisper White, Pumpkin Pie, Basic Black) Stampin' Up! *Rubber stamps:* (tree, bats, sentiment from Spooky Silhouettes set) Gina K. Designs *Dye ink:* (Chocolate Chip, More Mustard, Bravo Burgundy, Pumpkin Pie) Stampin' Up! *Pigment ink:* (Onyx Black) Tsukineko *Fibers:* (black dotted ribbon) Michaels *Adhesive:* (repositionable, foam tape) *Tools:* (1¼" circle punch, brayer)

SUPPLIES: All supplies from Ranger Industries unless otherwise noted. *Cardstock:* (white glossy) *Specialty paper:* (black linen) no source *Clear stamps:* (cat, meow from Cats set) Inkadinkado; (Wings set) Heidi Swapp *Pigment ink:* (Pitch Black) *Specialty ink:* (Aqua, Cool Peri, Willow, Lemonade, Shell Pink, Purple Twilight, Terra Cotta, Pesto, Denim alcohol) *Color media:* (white gel pen; assorted alcohol ink pens) *Adhesive:* (foam tape) *Tools:* (ink applicator felt); (2½" circle punch) no source

HALLOWEEN

emboss detail

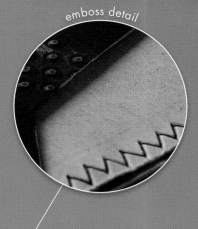

emboss detail

DESIGNER TIPS

When embossing the chipboard alphabet into the card, remove the adhesive with your fingernail, or use a needle tool to peel off adhesive.

When placing letters to emboss, remember to place them mirror-image since you are embossing from behind.

Spooky Boo Card

Designer: Jessica Witty

1. Make card from cardstock.
2. Remove adhesive from back of alphabet stickers.
3. Open card, place letters face-down inside card front; emboss.
4. Flip card over; ink letters, place on card front to spell "Boo", and emboss.
5. Punch bats from cardstock; score wings and adhere to card.

Finished size: 4¼" x 5½"

SUPPLIES: *Cardstock:* (Smokey Shadow, white) Papertrey Ink; (Going Gray) Stampin' Up! *Specialty ink:* (Smokey Shadow hybrid) Papertrey Ink *Stickers:* (Gift Box alphabet) American Crafts *Tool:* (bat punch) Martha Stewart Crafts

Bewitched Hat Card

Designer: Maren Benedict

1. Make card from cardstock; distress edges.
2. Cut cardstock panel, emboss zigzag along edges. Color with gel pen.
3. Cut witch hat following pattern on p. 284; emboss polka dots. Ink edges and embossing. Adhere to panel with foam tape.
4. Distress panel edges, tie on ribbon, and adhere to card.

Finished size: 4¼" x 5½"

SUPPLIES: *Cardstock:* (True Black, Plum Pudding, kraft) Papertrey Ink *Rubber stamp:* (sentiment from Trick or Treat Peeps collection) Unity Stamp Co. *Dye ink:* (Tuxedo Black) Tsukineko *Pigment ink:* (white) Stampin' Up! *Color medium:* (black gel pen) Sakura *Fibers:* (lavender ribbon) Papertrey Ink *Templates:* (Just My Type zigzag, polka dots embossing) Provo Craft

Perfect Paper Pleating

Punch up your projects and add tons of dimension by pleating your cardstock and patterned paper. These nine amazing ways to use pleated paper will inspire you to add fun folds to your next project!

Stamp on tightly pleated paper to add dimension to an image.

Create ruffles by layering loosely pleated paper strips.

Dimensional landscapes are easy with large pleats cut on a curve.

Brooms and skirts stand out with accordion folds gathered at the top.

Make flowers by folding and gathering paper.

Frame a focal point with scored and folded paper strips.

Dress up a die cut shape by adhering pleated paper.

Pleat background paper for instant visual interest.

Create faux ribbon with a pleated paper strip and a folded bow.

DESIGNER TIP

Be sure to use different colored paper if you're using more than one type of pleating technique on a project. This gives your card visual interest.

DESIGNER TIP

Cover die cut shapes with pleated paper, then turn over to trim so you don't accidentally cut into the shape.

Pleated Flower For You Card

Designer: Maren Benedict

❶ Make card from cardstock.

❷ Cut border strips from patterned paper; adhere. *Note: Bend edge up for dimension.* Trim card front to match border.

❸ Pleat patterned paper strip; gather in circle and attach brad.

❹ Die-cut and emboss oval from cardstock; ink edges. Cut stem and leaf from patterned paper; adhere to oval. Adhere flower.

❺ Pleat patterned paper strip and adhere behind oval.

❻ Tie on ribbon. Spell "For you" with stickers. Adhere oval with foam tape.

Finished size: 4¼" x 5½"

Spider EEK! Card

Designer: Maren Benedict

❶ Make card from cardstock; round one corner.

❷ Die-cut circle from cardstock. Pleat patterned paper and adhere to circle; trim to fit.

❸ Punch circles from cardstock; adhere to make eyes. Cut cardstock strip, pleat, and adhere. Adhere lengths of twine.

❹ Cut patterned paper, notch end, and adhere to card. Spell "Eek!" with stickers.

❺ Pleat cardstock strip, ink folds, and adhere to card. Adhere spider.

❻ Fold cardstock strip into bow, ink edges, and adhere. Thread button with twine and adhere.

Finished size: 4¼" x 5½"

SUPPLIES: *Cardstock:* (Orange Zest, Vintage Cream) Papertrey Ink *Patterned paper:* (Horizon, Dusk from Twilight collection) Pink Paislee *Dye ink:* (Black Soot) Ranger Industries *Accent:* (green polka dot epoxy brad) KI Memories *Stickers:* (Handmade Embossed Mini alphabet) K&Company *Fibers:* (orange ribbon) Papertrey Ink *Die:* (oval) Spellbinders

SUPPLIES: *Cardstock:* (New Leaf, True Black, Plum Pudding) Papertrey Ink *Patterned paper:* (Licorice Dot from Double Dot collection) BoBunny Press; (Eclipse from Twilight collection) Pink Paislee *Pigment ink:* (white) Stampin' Up! *Accent:* (purple button) BasicGrey *Stickers:* (Nutmeg alphabet) American Crafts *Fibers:* (black twine) Canvas Corp. *Die:* (circle) Spellbinders *Tools:* (circle punch) Stampin' Up!; (corner rounder punch) Creative Memories

⁙⁙⁵ Batty 4 U Gift Bag

Designer: Maren Benedict

❶ Cut cardstock panel. Cut bat shapes from cardstock; adhere to panel, using foam tape under wing tips as desired.

❷ Loosely fold patterned paper strips; adhere to panel. Tie on ribbon and adhere panel to gift bag.

❸ Adhere patterned paper strip and spell sentiment with stickers.

❹ Pleat cardstock; cut inverted curves along ends. Tie in center with twine. Punch circle from cardstock, adhere, and attach pin. Adhere to gift bag.

Finished size: 8" x 10¼"

SUPPLIES: *Cardstock:* (Orange Zest, True Black) Papertrey Ink *Patterned paper:* (Clover Dot from Double Dot collection) BoBunny Press *Accent:* (black bat stick pin) Making Memories *Stickers:* (Flat alphabet) American Crafts *Fibers:* (black ribbon) Papertrey Ink; (black twine) *Tool:* (circle punch) Stampin' Up! *Other:* (black gift bag)

CREATE A UNIQUE IMAGE OR DESIGN

Cut rub-ons into shapes to create your own image, or apply a variety of rub-ons to build a unique design.

5 STEPS Halloween Treat Can & Card

Designer: Michele Boyer

❶ Make card from transparency sheet; apply rub-ons.

❷ Cut vellum to fit inside card; apply rub-on stitches along fold. Apply adhesive behind fold; adhere inside card.

❸ Decorate can with rub-ons.

Finished sizes: card 3" square, can 3½" diameter x 4½" height

5 STEPS Hello Pumpkin Card

Designer: Kim Hughes

❶ Make card from cardstock.

❷ Adhere patterned paper square.

❸ Cut cardstock square.

❹ Apply flower rub-on for pumpkin.

❺ Cut ampersand rub-on to resemble vine; apply. Cut black flower to resemble stem; apply to pumpkin. Apply brackets for grass.

❻ Stamp sentiment; attach brad.

❼ Adhere to card; outline with pen.

Finished size: 4" square

SUPPLIES: *Vellum:* Stampin' Up! *Transparency sheet; Rub-ons:* (Halloween motifs) Daisy D's; (stitches) Doodlebug Design *Other:* (clear paint can) Papertrey Ink

SUPPLIES: *Cardstock:* (cream) *Patterned paper:* (Wild Child from About a Boy collection) Fancy Pants Designs *Rubber stamp:* (hello pumpkin from Fall Silhouettes set) Cornish Heritage Farms *Solvent ink:* (Jet Black) Tsukineko *Color medium:* (black pen) Sakura *Accent:* (orange brad) Creative Impressions *Rub-ons:* (flowers, alphabet) Tinkering Ink

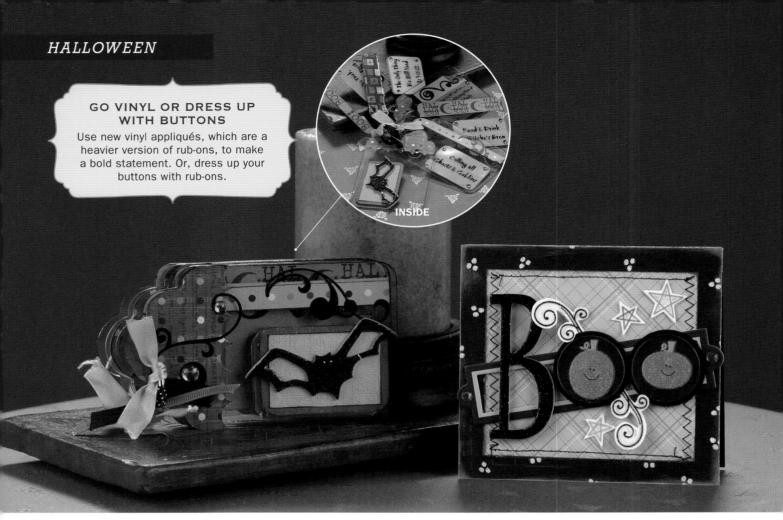

GO VINYL OR DRESS UP WITH BUTTONS

Use new vinyl appliqués, which are a heavier version of rub-ons, to make a bold statement. Or, dress up your buttons with rub-ons.

INSIDE

Batty Tag Invitation

Designer: Emily Holverson, courtesy of Scrapworks

❶ Ink edges of tags.

❷ Decorate with patterned paper pieces.

❸ Apply rub-ons.

❹ Print party details on transparency sheet. Trim and adhere.

❺ Adhere bats and rhinestones.

❻ Tie ribbon on ring.

Finished size: 5" x 3"

DESIGNER TIPS

- To hide the adhesive on the back of each paper piece, adhere a matching paper piece to the back of the tag.

- Apply more pressure when applying the appliqués on an acrylic surface, and less pressure on paper to avoid tearing.

⑤ Curly Boo Card

Designer: Melissa Phillips

❶ Make card from cardstock; cover with patterned paper. Ink edges.

❷ Cut patterned paper; ink and stitch edges. Adhere.

❸ Adhere bookplate and rhinestones.

❹ Apply flourish and star rub-ons to cardstock; color with pencils. Cut out and adhere.

❺ Punch circles from cardstock and adhere behind buttons. Apply pumpkin rub-ons to top. Adhere. Adhere chipboard "b".

Finished size: 4¾" x 4¼"

SUPPLIES: *Patterned paper:* (Bewitched, Deadly Dots, Gone Batty, Haunted Forest, Witches Brew from Spellbound collection) Scrapworks *Transparency sheet:* 3M *Solvent ink:* (Jet Black) Tsukineko *Accents:* (chipboard bats) Scrapworks; (assorted rhinestones) Doodlebug Design *Rub-ons:* (vinyl swirls) Scrapworks *Fibers:* (assorted ribbon) *Font:* (Signboard) Microsoft *Tools:* (corner rounder, notch cutter) BasicGrey *Other:* (acrylic tag album) Scrapworks

SUPPLIES: *Cardstock:* (black, white) *Patterned paper:* (Salem Briggs Street) Scenic Route; (Halloween Witch Boots from Jeepers Creepers collection) Heidi Grace Designs *Dye ink:* (Walnut Stain) Ranger Industries *Chalk ink:* (Frost White) Clearsnap *Color medium:* (watercolor pencils) Close To My Heart *Accents:* (chipboard bookplate) Heidi Grace Designs; (Upper West Side chipboard alphabet) Scrapworks; (clear buttons) 7gypsies; (orange rhinestones) My Mind's Eye *Rub-ons:* (pumpkins, stars, flourish) Doodlebug Design *Tool:* (1 ⅜" circle punch)

ENHANCE TRANSPARENCY SHEETS OR PHOTOS

Rub-ons make classy accents on transparency sheets as the images appear to be printed directly on the surface. And, they also make great captions or accent images for photos.

Spider Card

Designer: Courtney Kelley

1 Cut cardstock to finished size.

2 To make front card flap, cut 6¼" x 4¾" piece of transparency sheet. Fold over cardstock piece and adhere.

3 Apply spider web and Halloween rub-ons.

4 Adhere spider and rhinestones.

5 Cut patterned paper to fit inside card; ink edges and adhere. Apply rub-on stitches.

Finished size: 6¼" x 4¼"

Halloween Memories Album

Designer: Kim Kesti

1 Double-mat photo with cardstock and patterned paper. Adhere to book.

2 Apply rub-ons.

3 Affix sticker inside slide mount; adhere. Write album title.

4 Staple ribbon tabs to divider pages.

Finished size: 8¼" x 6¼"

SUPPLIES: *Cardstock:* (Blackbird) Bazzill Basics Paper *Patterned paper:* (Salem Briggs Street) Scenic Route *Transparency sheet:* 3M *Pigment ink:* (black) Clearsnap *Accents:* (metal spider) Adornit-Carolee's Creations; (black rhinestones) *Rub-ons:* (Halloween, spider web) Hambly Screen Prints; (stitches) Daisy D's

SUPPLIES: *Cardstock:* (Limeade) Bazzill Basics Paper *Patterned paper:* (Halloween Spooky Stripe) Doodlebug Design *Color medium:* (black pen) *Accent:* (black slide mount) Maya Road *Rub-ons:* (candy, trick-or-treat) Karen Foster Design *Sticker:* (green tab) Jenni Bowlin Studio *Fibers:* (black polka dot ribbon) Bo-Bunny Press; (orange patterned ribbon) Scrapworks; (green stitched ribbon) Fancy Pants Designs *Other:* (book) Fancy Pants Designs; (photo, staples)

MASK YOUR PHOTOS

Add a little mystery to your haunting photo projects with masks. Just like a Halloween mask covers all or a portion of your face, a stamping mask covers all or a portion of your design. So, mask your photos and create eerie projects that'll make goblins of all ages "eek" with delight.

SUPPLIES: *Patterned paper:* (Licorice Dot from Double Dot collection) Bo-Bunny Press *Paint:* (Licorice) Plaid *Accent:* (ghouls tag) Making Memories *Stickers:* (All About Alphas alphabet) Making Memories *Fibers:* (orange polka dot ribbon) May Arts *Other:* (wood frame, photo)

SUPPLIES: *Patterned paper:* (Vivid from About a Boy collection, Groovy from Kewl collection) Fancy Pants Designs *Specialty paper:* (photo) Epson *Dye ink:* (Kiwi, black) Close To My Heart *Accent:* (lime green wire) Making Memories *Sticker:* (trick or treat bag) Me & My Big Ideas *Fibers:* (black printed, orange stitched ribbon) Fancy Pants Designs *Die:* (oval) Provo Craft *Tool:* (die cut machine) Provo Craft *Other:* (chipboard cone) Lockhart Stamp Company; (digital photo)

5 Trick or Treat Wall Hanging

Designer: Jessica Witty

❶ Adhere patterned paper to frame. Paint edges.

❷ Tie ribbon and tag to frame.

❸ Affix stickers to photo to spell "Trick or Treat".

❹ Paint over stickers. Remove stickers to reveal masked sentiment.

❺ Insert photo into frame.

Finished size: 11¼" x 9¼"

Original Photo

DESIGNER TIP
Sticker masks are ideal for photos because the glossy surface of the picture is perfect for applying and removing stickers after the masking is complete.

Witch Treat Cone

Designer: Alice Golden

❶ Cover cone with patterned paper. Note: Adhere patterned paper inside cone. Ink top edge and tie on wire to create handle.

❷ Adhere ribbon.

❸ Print photo on photo paper twice. Cut out witch face on one photo to create mask.

❹ Place mask over original photo; ink with Kiwi.

❺ Remove mask, die-cut photo into oval, and adhere.

❻ Tie sticker to handle with ribbon.

Finished size: 3" diameter x 7"

Original Photo

DESIGNER TIP
Trimming portions of a photo to create a mask is a fun way to add subtle coloring and emphasis to an image. By masking the witch photo and inking it with bright green, Alice achieves an eerie look in no time at all.

SUPPLIES: *Cardstock:* (white, kraft, green) Bazzill Basics Paper *Patterned paper:* (Linens from Jack + Abby collection) KI Memories *Specialty paper:* (photo) *Accents:* (brown brads) *Font:* (CK Elegant) Creating Keepsakes *Tool:* (corner rounder punch) *Other:* (digital photo)

SUPPLIES: *Cardstock:* (Dark Peaches & Cream) WorldWin; (Lily White) Bazzill Basics Paper *Paint:* (Chartreuse) Making Memories *Accents:* (green brads) Doodlebug Design; (copper wire) *Font:* (Butterfinger) www.myfonts.com *Adhesive:* (temporary) *Other:* (photo)

5 STEPS Eek Photo Card

Designer: Teri Anderson

1. Make card from cardstock; cover front with cardstock.
2. Print photo on photo paper; trim. Adhere patterned paper strips.
3. Print sentiment on cardstock, trim, and adhere.
4. Insert brads and round bottom corners of piece. Mat with cardstock and adhere.

Finished size: 6½" x 6"

SIMPLE SENTIMENT

Because it's Halloween, a night when wind howls and the dead come alive.

Original Photo

DESIGNER TIP
Instead of masking the actual photo, Teri placed Heidi Swapp alphabet masks on an acrylic block and held them in front of a tree as she took her picture. This creative image makes a stunning focal point for her card and is a great out-of-the-box approach to using masks on your projects.

5 STEPS Good Times Card

Designer: Kim Kesti

1. Make card from cardstock.
2. Draw pumpkin on cardstock, trim, and adhere to photo with temporary adhesive; paint. Remove mask and trim.
3. Mat piece with cardstock and adhere to card.
4. Print sentiment on cardstock; trim. Attach to card with brads.
5. Poke wire through front flap and curl ends.

Finished size: 5¾" x 5¼"

For additional masking projects check out the "Mask-erade" feature on p. 138.

Original Photo

DESIGNER TIP
Kim's photo had a distracting basket in the top left-hand corner. By creating her own shaped mask she was able to highlight the portion of the image she wanted while still creating a unique and well-balanced design.

Mask~erade

Halloween is a time to don creative masks and transform into something completely new. Well, your paper projects shouldn't miss out on the masking fun! Just as a mask covers all or part of a person's face, using a mask when stamping covers all or a portion of the stamp or stamped design. Masks also allow you to create a layered look without showing where the designs overlap, which is ideal for transforming your creations into something exciting and new.

Happy Halloween Pumpkins Card

Designer: Michele Boyer

1. Make card from cardstock.
2. Adhere slightly smaller piece of patterned paper. Pierce holes and draw lines with marker.
3. Mask cardstock, following step-outs.
4. Draw grass and shading with markers; stamp sentiment.
5. Mat piece with cardstock. Attach patterned paper strip with brads.
6. Adhere to card with foam tape.

Finished size: 5½" x 4½"

SUPPLIES: *Cardstock:* (Very Vanilla, Chocolate Chip) Stampin' Up! *Patterned paper:* (Equinox, Cultured from Mellow collection) BasicGrey *Rubber stamps:* (pumpkins, acorn, face from Autumn Harvest set) Stampin' Up!; (happy Halloween from Celebration Sayings set) Lizzie Anne Designs *Pigment ink:* (Graphite Black) Tsukineko *Color medium:* (Golden Yellow, Honey, Chamois, Grayish Olive, Warm Gray markers) Copic Marker; (Chocolate Chip, Basic Black markers) Stampin' Up! *Accents:* (copper brads) Making Memories *Adhesive:* (foam tape)

a. Stamp small pumpkin on cardstock and scrap paper. Trim image from scrap paper and place over cardstock image.

b. Stamp large pumpkin and acorn on cardstock and on scrap paper. Trim images from scrap paper and place over cardstock images.

c. Stamp large pumpkin. Remove masks and stamp faces.

⑤ Spooky Happy Haunting Card

Designer: Alisa Bangerter

❶ Make card from cardstock; adhere patterned paper strip.

❷ Make masked piece, following step-outs. Adhere masked piece and trim.

❸ Sand sticker and adhere with foam tape.

❹ Spray cardstock with specialty ink. Let dry. Punch circles from piece and attach to card with brads.

Finished size: 5½" square

DESIGNER TIP

Let each application of the shimmer spray dry before adding the next. This will help prevent the mask from becoming too wet and allowing the sprayed ink to run under the mask.

SUPPLIES: *Cardstock:* (green, white) *Patterned paper:* (Large Dot from Halloween collection) Making Memories *Dye ink:* (Graphite, Silver) Tattered Angels *Specialty ink:* (Key Lime shimmer spray) Tattered Angels *Accents:* (silver brads) *Sticker:* (happy haunting) Scenic Route *Fibers:* (black trim) *Adhesive:* (foam tape) *Tool:* (½" circle punch) Carl Manufacturing *Other:* (medallion mask) Tattered Angels

a. Spray cardstock with specialty ink. Once dry, place the mask over the card-stock and spray again.

b. Remove mask.

c. Lightly spray masked image.

Trick or Treat Container

Designer: Jessica Witty

❶ Remove handle from take-out box. Trace box sides on cardstock; trim.

❷ Mask trimmed cardstock, following step-outs.

❸ Trace masked design with glitter pen. Adhere pieces to box and reattach handle.

❹ Cover chipboard stars with cardstock, ink edges, and adhere.

❺ Cover wood star with cardstock, stamp Dotted Background, and paint edges. Adhere.

❻ Paint chipboard T, apply glitter, and adhere. Affix stickers to spell sentiment.

❼ Tie ribbon to handle.

Finished size: 6½" x 6½" x 5½"

DESIGNER TIP

Mask vellum instead of cardstock and place a candle inside for a hauntingly fun luminary.

SUPPLIES: *Cardstock:* (Elegant Eggplant) Stampin' Up!; (orange) Stampin' Up! *Rubber stamp:* (Dotted Background) Stampin' Up! *Pigment ink:* (Graphite Black) Tsukineko *Watermark ink:* Tsukineko *Color medium:* (glitter pen) Sakura *Paint:* (Licorice) Plaid *Accents:* (small chipboard stars) Heidi Swapp; (chipboard T) Maya Road; (large wood star) Michaels; (iridescent glitter) Stampin' Up! *Stickers:* (Cheeky Shimmer alphabet) Making Memories *Fibers:* (black gingham ribbon) Offray *Other:* (plastic take-out box) Michaels; (sheer star sheet) Maya Road

a. Place sheer star sheet on cardstock.

b. Apply ink using sponge. Let dry.

c. Remove star sheet.

5 Scary Spider Tag Pocket

Designer: Melissa Phillips

POCKET

❶ Mask bag, following step-outs.

❷ Attach brad to chipboard tag.

❸ Tie tag to bag with ribbon.

TAG

❶ Cut cardstock to fit inside pocket.

❷ Thread button with floss and adhere.

Finished sizes: pocket 4" x 5", tag 3½" x 4½"

SUPPLIES: *Cardstock:* (black) *Clear stamps:* (spider, web from Fall Frolic set) Paper Salon *Solvent ink:* (Jet Black) Tsukineko *Paint:* (Light Ivory) Delta *Accents:* (white glitter, silver glitter brad) Doodlebug Design; (orange button) Creative Café; (eek! chipboard tag) Heidi Grace Designs *Fibers:* (black/white striped ribbon) Imaginisce; (white floss) *Die:* (bookplate) Provo Craft *Tool:* (die cut machine) Provo Craft *Other:* (clear wax bag)

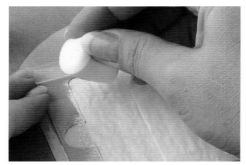

a. Die-cut bookplate from cardstock. Place on bag and paint.

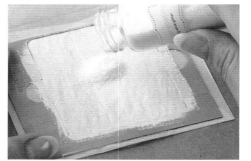

b. While paint is still wet, apply glitter. Let dry.

c. Stamp webs and spiders. Remove mask.

Boo! Ensemble

Designer: Wendy Johnson

INVITATION

❶ Make invitation from cardstock.

❷ Mask slightly smaller piece of cardstock, following step-outs.

❸ Adhere masked piece to card.

❹ Adhere wiggle eyes and adhere stickers to spell "Boo!" using foam tape.

CUPCAKE PICK

❶ Mask cardstock, following step-outs.

❷ Mat masked piece with cardstock.

❸ Adhere wiggle eyes.

❹ Paint wood dowel, adhere to masked piece, and tie with ribbon.

❺ Repeat steps for additional picks.

CENTERPIECE POTS

❶ Mask cardstock, following step-outs; repeat. Adhere wiggle eyes.

❷ Cut letters to spell "Boo!" from cardstock; adhere to cardstock. Note: Adhere some letters to masked pieces.

❸ Mat all pieces with cardstock.

❹ Spray paint metal buckets, adhere ribbon, and fill with floral foam and Spanish moss.

❺ Paint wood dowels, adhere to paper pieces, and insert into buckets.

a. Trim ghost shape

b. Place trimmed cardstock over cardstock and apply paint.

c. Remove trimmed cardstock.

SUPPLIES: *Cardstock:* (orange, black, white, lime green) *Paint:* (Asphalt) Making Memories; (black spray) Krylon *Accents:* (wiggle eyes) *Stickers:* (Sorbet alphabet) Paper Salon *Fibers:* (orange polka dot ribbon) Michaels *Adhesive:* (foam tape) *Other:* (wood dowels, metal buckets, Spanish moss, floral foam)

Finished sizes: invitation 4¼" square, cupcake pick 2¼" x 6½", centerpiece pots 3¾" x 12"

Treat Tricks

Halloween is here again, bringing with it tricks and treats, spells and potions, witches and mummies, and lots of fun. Break out your creepiest cardstock and your spookiest stamps, and get ready to brew up some tricks and treats of your own this season with this fun assortment of Halloween treat containers.

Editor: Bethany Moore

Happy Halloween Window Tin

Designer: Lisa Dorsey

❶ Cover sides of tin with patterned paper.

❷ Trim cardstock; ink edges. Adhere around lip of lid.

❸ Trim cardstock; adhere to lid. Adhere cardstock strips to make window panes; streak with pen.

❹ Cut monster face and spider web from patterned paper; adhere.

❺ Die-cut "Happy Halloween"; adhere.

❻ Cut patterned paper and cardstock to fit around candy bars; ink edges and adhere. Place candy bars inside tin.

Finished size: 6½" x 4½" x 1¼"

🔟 Batty Treat Can

Designer: Alisa Bangerter

❶ Cover can with patterned paper.

❷ Adhere ribbon to can.

❸ Punch ovals and circles from cardstock; adhere to create eyes.

❹ Curl wire; tie ribbon to wire.

❺ Cut bats, following pattern on p. 284; adhere to wire.

Finished size: 4" diameter x 4¾" height

SUPPLIES: *Cardstock:* (green, orange, black) *Patterned paper:* (polka dot, eyes and dots, spider web, monster faces from Halloween Glitter stack) Die Cuts With a View *Pigment ink:* (black) *Color medium:* (white pen) *Dies:* (CK Typist alphabet) QuicKutz *Tools:* (die cut machine) QuicKutz *Other:* (metal window tin) Maya Road; (mini candy bars) Hershey's

SUPPLIES: *Cardstock:* (black, cream) *Patterned paper:* (Scrap Strip from Salem collection) Scenic Route *Accent:* (green wire) Fibre-Craft *Fibers:* (black fringe ribbon) Novtex; (black polka dot ribbon) May Arts; (orange scalloped ribbon) Maya Road *Tools:* (⅛" circle punch, oval punch) *Other:* (can)

⁵⁵ₛₜₑₚₛ Funny Felt Pumpkin Bag

Designer: Melissa Phillips

❶ Cut felt to 5" x 12"; fold and adhere sides. Adhere rickrack.

❷ Trim cardstock pocket; stitch bottom and sides. Adhere three sides to bag.

❸ Die-cut pumpkin twice from cardstock; cut stem from one and adhere together. Trace mouth and eyes with pen; draw dotted border around pumpkin. Adhere to bag.

❹ Attach eyelets to bag.

❺ Apply rub-on to tag; tie ribbon through eyelets and tag.

Finished size: 5" x 6"

⁵⁵ₛₜₑₚₛ Pumpkin Treat Bag

Designer: Donna Polley

❶ Die-cut bag from cardstock; assemble.

❷ Adhere patterned paper to bag; ink edges.

❸ Trim pumpkin from patterned paper; adhere to bag with foam tape.

❹ Trim strips of patterned paper; adhere to candy.

Finished size: 2" x 3¼" x 1"

DESIGNER TIP

To keep your candy tasty and safe, try adhering patterned paper to the candy with tape instead of glue.

SUPPLIES: *Cardstock:* (Green Tea) Bazzill Basics Paper; (Terra-Cotta Medium) WorldWin; (black) *Color medium:* (white pen) Sakura; (black pen) *Accents:* (black felt rickrack, cardstock tag) Creative Café; (large black eyelets) We R Memory Keepers *Rub-on:* (trick or treat) Creative Café *Fibers:* (green polka dot ribbon) *Die:* (pumpkin) Provo Craft *Tool:* (die cut machine) Provo Craft *Other:* (orange polka dot felt) Creative Café

SUPPLIES: *Cardstock:* (black) *Patterned paper:* (Icons, Decor Stripe from Jeepers Creepers collection) Heidi Grace Designs *Dye ink:* (black) *Adhesive:* (foam tape) *Die:* (bag) AccuCut *Tool:* (die cut machine) AccuCut *Other:* (candy)

5 STEPS Haunted Forest Gift Bag

Designer: Stefanie Hamilton

❶ Create 5" x 4" project in software. Open digital elements.

❷ Cut and paste patterned paper strips. Drop in ribbon, branches, tag, and sentiment.

❸ Print on photo paper; trim and adhere to gift bag.

Finished size: 5½" square

5 STEPS Trick or Treat Candy Can

Designer: Wendy Johnson

❶ Adhere paper trim around top of can.

❷ Adhere patterned paper to can.

❸ Mat trick or treat sticker with cardstock; adhere to can.

❹ Affix bat sticker.

Finished size: 2¾" diameter x 4¼" height

SUPPLIES: *Specialty paper:* (photo) *Digital elements:* (red, orange checkered patterned paper; branches from Bats and Potions kit) www.designerdigitals.com; (black ribbon, antique tag) www.jenwilsondesigns.com; (Halloween sentiment) www.heraldsplace.blogspot.com *Software:* (photo editing) *Other:* (gift bag) Target

SUPPLIES: *Cardstock:* (white) *Patterned paper:* (Doodle Madness from Tangerine Dream collection) Sandylion *Accents:* (orange scalloped paper trim) Doodlebug Design *Stickers:* (bat, trick or treat) Heidi Grace Designs *Other:* (tin can)

⁙5⁙ Bucket of Trick or Treats

Designer: Layle Koncar, courtesy of Scenic Route

❶ Trim patterned paper strips; ink edges and adhere to pail.

❷ Affix sticker strips to pail.

❸ Punch chipboard circle; attach to handle with chain.

❹ Trim patterned paper; adhere to pail lid.

❺ Adhere chipboard square to circle sticker. Affix sticker to die cut; adhere die cut to lid.

Finished size: 4½" diameter x 5" height

Monster Beans Carrier

Designer: Betsy Veldman

❶ Die-cut box from patterned paper; assemble. Adhere cardstock strip. Adhere patterned paper strip.

❷ Spell "Monster beans" with rub-ons.

❸ Adhere plastic shape to box. Adhere wiggle eye and plastic shape to pompom; adhere to box.

❹ Adhere patterned paper around vials. Punch circle from patterned paper; adhere to lids.

❺ Adhere plastic shapes to lids. Adhere wiggle eyes and plastic shapes to pompoms; adhere to lids.

❻ Fill vials with candy; place vials inside box.

Finished size: 3" x 7½" x 1"

SUPPLIES: All supplies from Scenic Route unless otherwise noted. *Patterned paper:* (Scrap Strip, Briggs Street from Salem collection) *Chalk ink:* (black) no source *Accents:* (journaling circle die cut, ghost chipboard square, pumpkin chipboard circle, black ball chain) *Stickers:* (orange strip, black strip, circle trick or treat) *Tool:* (⅛" circle punch) no source *Other:* (pail) Stampendous!

SUPPLIES: *Cardstock:* (orange) *Patterned paper:* (little monsters, striped from Halloween Glitter stack) Die Cuts With a View *Accents:* (green, purple, orange pompoms) Fibre-Craft; (plastic shapes) American Crafts; (wiggle eyes) *Rub-ons:* (Simply Sweet alphabet) Doodlebug Design *Die:* (box) Provo Craft *Tools:* (die cut machine) Provo Craft; (¾" circle punch) *Other:* (vials) SKS Bottle & Packaging; (candy)

Treats Only Bucket

Designer: Rae Barthel

❶ Adhere patterned paper to container; adhere cardstock strip.

❷ Print sentiment; stamp frame around sentiment. Trim and adhere to container with foam tape.

❸ Adhere trim and ribbon to container.

❹ String beads on pipe cleaner to create handle; adhere to container.

❺ Trim cardstock strip; adhere inside container.

Finished size: 3½" diameter x 3¾" height

Skull Candy Cover

Designer: Emily Gunnell

❶ Cut cardstock 2¾" x 9". Fold bottom up 1½" and top down 2½" to create cover.

❷ Punch large circle; punch out sides of circle to create top of skull.

❸ Trim cardstock strip with decorative-edge scissors to create teeth; adhere to skull. Adhere to cover.

❹ Punch oval; adhere to cover to create jaw. Outline skull and jaw with pen.

❺ Mat wiggle eyes with cardstock; adhere. Cut nose from cardstock; adhere to skull.

❻ Punch tag from cardstock; stamp sentiment. Write "Or" with pen.

❼ Knot ribbon; adhere to tag. Place candy inside cover.

Finished size: 3" x 4"

SUPPLIES: *Cardstock:* (orange, black) *Patterned paper:* (polka dot from Formal Affair collection) Scrapworks *Clear stamp:* (dotted frame from Mirror Mirror set) Urban Lily *Dye ink:* (black) *Accents:* (orange tinsel pipe cleaner) Hobby Lobby; (black beads) *Fibers:* (black-stitched orange ribbon, beaded black trim) Hobby Lobby *Font:* (Pharmacy) www.dafont.com *Adhesive:* (foam tape) *Other:* (frosting container)

SUPPLIES: *Cardstock:* (black, orange, white) *Rubber stamps:* (trick, treat) JustJohanna Rubber Stamps *Color medium:* (black pen) Sakura *Accents:* (wiggle eyes) *Fibers:* (orange/black ribbon) *Tools:* (3" circle punch, oval punch) Marvy Uchida; (assorted circle punches, tag punch) Stampin' Up!; (decorative-edge scissors) *Other:* (candy)

Candy Bag

Designer: Dawn McVey

1 Stamp bag.

2 Trim cardstock strip with decorative-edge scissors; mat one edge with cardstock and adhere to bag.

3 Spell "Candy" with stickers

Finished size: 4¾" x 8"

Goblin Goodies Bag

Designer: Sherry Wright

1 Adhere patterned paper to bag. Distress window edge. Ink outside edges.

2 Adhere sticker to bag with foam tape.

Finished size: 4¾" x 9½"

SUPPLIES: *Cardstock:* (Basic Black, Really Rust) Stampin' Up! *Clear stamps:* (solid circle, outline circle from Polka Dot Basics set) Papertrey Ink *Dye ink:* (Basic Black, Really Rust) Stampin' Up! *Stickers:* (Sprinkles alphabet) American Crafts *Tool:* (decorative-edge scissors) *Other:* (kraft window bag) Papertrey Ink

SUPPLIES: *Patterned paper:* (Brown Ink on Kraft from Woodgrain collection) Hambly Screen Prints *Chalk ink:* (black) *Sticker:* (ghosts & goblins tile) Making Memories *Adhesive:* (foam tape) *Other:* (kraft window bag) Emma's Paperie

5 STEPS Batty For You Tin

Designer: Lisa Nichols

❶ Fill tin with candy. Tie ribbon around tin.

❷ Stamp image on cardstock; punch into circle. Mat with punched cardstock circle.

❸ Punch scalloped circle from cardstock; adhere to tin with foam tape. Adhere matted circle with foam tape.

Finished size: 3¾″ diameter x 1½″ height

5 STEPS Witch's Brew Candy Box

Designer: Pat Sergeant

❶ Paint wood bag black.

❷ Adhere patterned paper.

❸ Affix stickers.

❹ Tie ribbon to handle.

Finished size: 4¼″ x 5¾″ x 2″

SUPPLIES: *Cardstock:* (black, orange, white) *Rubber stamp:* (bat sentiment from Batty For You set) Stampin' Up! *Solvent ink:* (Jet Black) Tsukineko *Fibers:* (orange stitched ribbon) Michaels *Adhesive:* (foam tape) *Tools:* (1¼", 1⅜" circle punches, scalloped circle punch) Stampin' Up! *Other:* (black tin) Target; (candy)

SUPPLIES: *Patterned paper:* (Halloween Stripe) The Paper Studio *Paint:* (black) *Stickers:* (witch, cauldron) Westrim Crafts *Fibers:* (black printed ribbon) Michaels; (orange polka dot organdy ribbon) Offray *Other:* (wood gift bag) Michaels

Window Treat Pouch

Designer: Carolyn King

❶ Cut cardstock to 4¼" x 9¼"; score and fold at 4" from each end to form pouch. Adhere patterned paper to front.

❷ Die-cut circle from front of pouch. Die-cut scalloped circle from cardstock; adhere.

❸ Fill bag with candy; staple bag inside of pouch.

❹ Trim edge of cardstock strip with slit punch to make scallops. Pierce holes and adhere. Tie with ribbon.

❺ Punch tag from cardstock; pierce holes. Stamp sentiment and ink edges.

❻ Mat tag with cardstock; attach eyelet. Tie to ribbon with twine and adhere with foam tape.

❼ Stamp jack-o-lantern on cardstock; color, trim, and adhere to tag with foam tape.

Finished size: 4¼" x 4"

BONUS IDEA

Use this same design to create a fun piggy bank card, where the bag is full of coins instead of candy.

SUPPLIES: *Cardstock:* (orange, white) *Patterned paper:* (Acorn from The Goods collection) American Crafts *Rubber stamp:* (happy Halloween from All Year Cheer III set) Stampin' Up! *Clear stamp:* (jack-o-lantern from Fright Night set) My Favorite Things *Dye ink:* (Chocolate Chip) Stampin' Up! *Color medium:* (orange, yellow, brown pencils) Prismacolor *Accent:* (brass eyelet) *Fibers:* (brown grosgrain ribbon) Stampin' Up!; (hemp twine) *Adhesive:* (foam tape) Stampin' Up! *Dies:* (circle, scalloped circle) Spellbinders *Tools:* (tag, slit punch) Stampin' Up!; (die cut machine) Provo Craft *Other:* (bag) Clearbags; (candy)

Matchbox Treat Drawers

Designer: Cheryl Baase

❶ Cover matchboxes with patterned paper.

❷ Affix stickers to front of boxes; adhere beads.

❸ Tie boxes together with ribbon.

❹ Affix boo sticker to cardstock; trim. Adhere to wire. Curl wire and wrap around ribbon.

❺ Fill boxes with candy.

Finished size: 2¾" x 4½" x 4¾"

SUPPLIES: *Patterned paper:* (Fossils of Kenya from Out of Africa collection; Tinge Orange from Got Nuance? collection) Zsiage *Accents:* (red bead, black/white swirl beads; wire) *Stickers:* (spider web, spider, trick or treat, boo) The Paper Studio *Fibers:* (white polka dot ribbon) *Other:* (matchboxes, assorted candy)

⑤ Witch's Brew Treat Bag

Designer: Patricia Anderson

❶ Trim patterned paper with decorative-edge scissors. Fold and adhere to top of bag.

❷ Trim patterned paper strip with decorative-edge scissors; adhere.

❸ Cut witch die cut in half. Adhere witch and spider die cuts to bag.

❹ Affix sticker; attach brads.

Finished size: 4¾" x 6¼"

⑤ Lollipop Holder

Designer: Melissa Phillips

❶ Die-cut stars from patterned paper; adhere together. Accent with glitter glue.

❷ Wrap lollipops in cellophane; tie with ribbon. Insert lollipop sticks through stars.

❸ Paint flower pot; tie ribbon around pot.

❹ Place foam in pot; insert lollipops.

❺ Place gift shred around lollipops.

Finished size: 3" diameter x 5" height

SUPPLIES: *Patterned paper:* (Orange Swirl from Halloween collection) K&Company *Accents:* (witch, spider die cuts) K&Company; (black brads) American Crafts *Sticker:* (witch's brew epoxy) K&Company *Tool:* (decorative-edge scissors) Provo Craft *Other:* (clear treat bag)

SUPPLIES: *Patterned paper:* (Main Street from Cape Town collection) Scenic Route; (Haunted Magic, Haunted Sky) KI Memories *Paint:* (black) *Accent:* (black glitter glue) Ranger Industries *Fibers:* (black polka dot ribbon) May Arts; (black grosgrain ribbon) *Dies:* (stars) Provo Craft *Tool:* (die cut machine) Provo Craft *Other:* (mini flower pot, gift shred, foam, cellophane, lollipops)

5 STEPS Trick-or-Treat Doorbell Sign

Designer: Jessica Witty

❶ Cut sign to fit over doorbell; ink edges. Stamp jack-o'-lanterns and candy corns.

❷ Stamp sentiment and trick or treat on cardstock. Trim, round corners, and ink edges. Mat with cardstock piece. Punch notches along bottom. Adhere to sign.

❸ Punch hole for doorbell. Punch ring from cardstock; ink edges and adhere over hole.

❹ Stamp we want candy on cardstock; punch out and ink edges. Attach to sign with clip. Tie with ribbon.

Finished size: 2¾" x 5"

BONUS IDEA

Make a doorbell sign for a party that says, "Ring the bell and come on in, fun and games will soon begin!"

SUPPLIES: *Cardstock:* (Black Tie Bling, Mardi Gras) Bazzill Basics Paper; (Pumpkin Pie) Stampin' Up! *Acrylic stamps:* (jack-o'-lantern, candy corn, we want candy, trick or treat, sentiment from Halloween Turtle set) Inky Antics *Pigment ink:* (Frost White) Clearsnap *Chalk ink:* (Charcoal) Clearsnap *Accent:* (pewter spiral clip) Creative Impressions *Fibers:* (white polka dot ribbon) Crafts Etc. *Tools:* (1¼", 1", ¾", ⅜" circle punches) Marvy Uchida; (corner rounder punch)

Halloween Hoopla

How do you treat yourself to a frightfully fun Halloween? Host a spooky soiree, give out ghostly greeting cards, make luminarias to light up the night, and decorate treat containers that are as sweet as the goodies inside. Create these unique projects to treat yourself and those you love this Halloween. For added thrills, we've included lines from scary movies to help inspire you.

A Chocolatey Treat Card
Designer: Lisa Strahl

CHOCOLATE SPIDER WEB

1 Melt chocolate in double boiler.

2 Once melted, pour into flat-bottomed pan and smooth. Tap pan to remove air bubbles.

3 Press chocolate evenly into texture plate. Refrigerate until chocolate appears frosty. *Note: This usually takes at least 30 minutes.* Remove from texture plate.

4 Heat cookie cutter under hot water. Dry and cut chocolate web into circle.

CARD

1 Make card from reverse side of patterned paper. Trim with decorative-edge scissors.

2 Adhere slightly smaller piece of cardstock.

3 Stamp Spider and sentiment on transparency.

4 Place chocolate web on card.

5 Place transparency over chocolate web and fasten with brads.

Finished size: 5½" square

5 STEPS Witchy Treat Bucket
Designer: Davinie Fiero

1 Remove handle from bucket. Cover bucket with patterned paper. *Note: Punch holes to allow for handles.*

2 Cut wavy strip of patterned paper to fit around bucket. *Note: Trim wave to resemble wavy border on Whimsical Halloween Witch paper.* Adhere.

3 Distress top edge of patterned paper strip; adhere.

4 Adhere buttons.

5 Replace handle and tie with ribbon.

Finished size: 6½" diameter x 7½" height

SUPPLIES: *Patterned paper:* (Orange and Black Stripes, Orange Swirls from Spooky collection) Memory Box *Transparency sheet:* Staples *Rubber stamps:* (Spider, Treat for You) A Muse Artstamps *Solvent ink:* (Jet Black) Tsukineko *Accents:* (black brads) *Template:* (webbing texture plate) Fiskars *Tool:* (decorative-edge scissors) *Other:* (white chocolate wafers, 4½" round metal cookie cutter)

SUPPLIES: *Patterned paper:* (Whimsical Halloween Stripes, Whimsical Halloween Witch, Whimsical Halloween Words) Junkitz *Accents:* (assorted buttons) *Fibers:* (black, orange patterned ribbon) *Tool:* (1" circle punch) EK Success *Other:* (paint bucket)

:5: Jack-O'-Lantern Luminaria Set
Designer: Susan Neal

❶ Cut or punch jack-o'-lantern face pieces from cardstock; adhere to jar.

❷ Wrap tissue paper up around bottle and adhere in place.

❸ Tie ribbon around lip. Place candles in jars.

Finished sizes: large 3½" diameter x 7" height,

small 3" diameter x 5½" height

:5: Iron Gate Jar
Designer: Nichole Heady

❶ Wash and dry jar.

❷ Punch circle from cardstock; ink edges and adhere.

❸ Affix stickers.

❹ Wrap ribbon around lip of jar; attach ends together with brads.

❺ Curl wire and wrap around jar; twist ends together. Form handle from wire; attach to wire on jar.

Finished size: 4¼" diameter x 6½" height

DESIGNER TIP

When the popcorn is finished, insert a candle for an instant spooky lantern.

SUPPLIES: *Cardstock:* (black) Bazzill Basics Paper *Fibers:* (black curling ribbon) *Tools:* (circle punches) EK Success *Other:* (jars, candles, orange tissue)

SUPPLIES: *Cardstock:* (orange) Bazzill Basics Paper *Dye ink:* (Really Rust) Stampin' Up! *Accents:* (black brads) The Paper Studio; (black wire) Crafts Etc. *Stickers:* (gate, bats) Heidi Swapp *Fibers:* (orange ribbon) American Crafts *Tool:* (1½" circle punch) EK Success *Other:* (jar, candle)

⟨5⟩ Gingham Trick or Treat Card

Designer: Dee Gallimore-Perry

❶ Make card from cardstock.

❷ Adhere patterned paper pieces; one reverse side up. Sand edges.

❸ Apply rub-on to patterned paper; trim and adhere.

❹ Tie ribbon around front flap.

❺ Adhere sticker with foam dots.

Finished size: 5¾" x 4¼"

⟨5⟩ Spooky Music CD Envelope

Designer: Kathleen Paneitz

❶ Print envelope template on reverse side of patterned paper; assemble.

❷ Cut piece of cardstock; ink edges and adhere. Affix sticker, apply spooky rub-on, and adhere Halloween image.

❸ Punch holes through top of envelope; affix hole reinforcers on each side.

❹ Thread floss through envelope and tag holes; tie ends together.

❺ Spell "Music" with rub-ons.

Finished size: 5" square

SUPPLIES: *Cardstock:* (Raven) Bazzill Basics Paper *Patterned paper:* (Yellow Geode from Color Theory collection) KI Memories; (Midnight Diamonds) Bo-Bunny Press *Rub-on:* (trick or treat) Bo-Bunny Press *Sticker:* (jack-o-lantern) K&Company *Fibers:* (orange gingham ribbon) Michaels *Adhesive:* (foam dots) Plaid

SUPPLIES: *Cardstock:* (cream) *Patterned paper:* (Lauren Tweed from Holiday collection) Making Memories *Dye ink:* (Antique Linen) Ranger Industries *Accents:* (Halloween image) Crafty Secrets Publications; (eek tag) Making Memories; (fabric hole reinforcers) 7gypsies *Rub-ons:* (Aloha alphabet) Rusty Pickle; (spooky) Royal & Langnickel *Sticker:* (haunting) Rusty Pickle *Fibers:* (cream floss) Karen Foster Design *Template:* (CD envelope) www.ruthannzaroff.com

Scary Scavenger Hunt
Designer: Susan Neal

INVITATION

❶ Make invitation from cardstock; ink edges. ❷ Adhere cardstock strip. Cut patterned paper; ink edges and mat with cardstock. Adhere. ❸ Die-cut 3" letter H from cardstock; adhere. ❹ Print text on cardstock; cut out. Ink and distress edges. Attach brads. Adhere.

CLIPBOARD

❶ Cover clipboard with patterned paper and cardstock; sand and ink edges.
❷ Print scavenger list on cardstock. Trim, ink edges, and clip in place.
❸ Tie pen to clipboard with ribbon.

PRIZE BUCKET

❶ Wrap patterned paper around bucket.
❷ Cut strip of cardstock; ink edges and mat with cardstock. Wrap around top of bucket. ❸ Print text on cardstock. Cut into circle and mat with cardstock. Adhere parentheses with foam tape. Punch hole and tie with ribbon. Tie tag to ribbon with thread. Adhere. ❹ Cover lid with patterned paper. Fill can with black tissue.

DESIGNER TIP

Record spooky music and a clue for one of the scavenger hunt items on a CD. Decorate the case to match the party ensemble.

Finished sizes: invitation 8½" x 3¾", clipboard 6" x 9", prize bucket 6¾" diameter x 7¾" height

---

SUPPLIES: *Cardstock:* (black, Natural, Yam) Bazzill Basics Paper *Patterned paper:* (Cobwebs, Dots, Halloween Words from Halloween collection) Making Memories *Dye ink:* (Brushed Corduroy) Ranger Industries *Accents:* (Halloween brads, trick or treat tag, glitter parentheses) Making Memories *Fibers:* (black, orange grosgrain ribbon) Offray; (black crochet thread) *Fonts:* (Wishmaster Credits) www.norfok.com; (Twylite Zone) www.fontmaster.com *Dies:* (George and Basic Shapes cartridge) Provo Craft *Adhesive:* (foam tape) *Tool:* (die cut machine) Provo Craft *Other:* (clipboard) Wal-Mart; (paint bucket, pen, black tissue)

Good to Eat Card & Treat Box

Designer: Michele Boyer

CARD

❶ Make card from cardstock. ❷ Cut patterned paper; mat with cardstock. Cut cardstock strip; attach brads and adhere. ❸ Cut sentiment from patterned paper; double-mat with cardstock. Adhere. ❹ Die-cut bat from Basic Black and Gable Green cardstock. Remove eyes from black bat; adhere to green bat. Adhere with foam dots. ❺ Adhere to card.

TREAT BOX

❶ Prepare box, following pattern on p. 283. ❷ Adhere matted patterned paper piece to each side of box. ❸ Cut cardstock strip; attach brads and adhere. ❹ Die-cut bat and spider from Basic Black and Gable Green cardstock. Remove eyes from black pieces; adhere to green pieces. Adhere with foam dots. Adhere strip of cardstock for spider web. ❺ Die-cut boo from cardstock. Punch circles from cardstock and adhere behind Os to resemble eyes. Adhere to cardstock. Double-mat with cardstock and adhere. ❻ Attach brads to top.

Finished sizes: card 3" square, treat box 2¾" x 4¼" x 1½"

Happy Pumpkin Treat Box

Designer: Wendy Johnson

❶ Die-cut box from cardstock. ❷ Punch two circles from cardstock; adhere one to accent and adhere. ❸ Wrap ribbon around box; thread ends through tag sticker and knot. ❹ Color dowel with marker; adhere sticker and second punched circle.

Finished size: 3" x 2¾" x 3"

SUPPLIES: *Cardstock:* (Basic Black, Gable Green, Lovely Lilac, Whisper White) Stampin' Up! *Patterned paper:* (Spooky Doodles) Doodlebug Design *Accents:* (green brads) Stampin' Up! *Dies:* (bat, boo, spider) Provo Craft *Adhesive:* (foam dots) *Tool:* (die cut machine) Provo Craft

SUPPLIES: *Cardstock:* (Tangerine) Doodlebug Design *Color medium:* (green permanent marker) *Accent:* (chipboard square) Doodlebug Design *Stickers:* (treats tag, pumpkin) Doodlebug Design *Fibers:* (purple gingham ribbon) Offray *Die:* (box) Provo Craft *Tools:* (die cut machine) Provo Craft; (1" circle punch) *Other:* (wood dowel, green paper shred)

Witch's Brew Card

Designer: Alisa Bangerter

❶ Cut pieces, following pattern on p. 283.

❷ Cut slit in top of cauldron card.

❸ Open card and lay flat. Mix together lime green and texture paint; apply to cauldron and heat-set.

❹ Chalk edges of bones; adhere inside slit.

❺ Adhere wire ends to bats and button. Curl wire and adhere ends inside slit.

❻ Apply rub-on to cardstock. Cut out, ink edges, and adhere with foam squares.

Finished size: 4½" x 6"

Frankenstein's Monster Card

Designer: Kim Hughes

❶ Make card from cardstock.

❷ Trace decorative-edged cardstock on purple cardstock. Cut out and adhere.

❸ Cut eyes, eyelids, and nose from cardstock; adhere.

❹ Attach brads.

❺ Detail with pen.

Finished size: 4¼" x 5½"

SUPPLIES: *Cardstock:* (black, white) *Color medium:* (black chalk) Craf-T Products *Paint:* (white texture) DecoArt; (lime green) Delta *Accents:* (green floral wire) Fibre-Craft; (frog button) Jesse James & Co. *Rub-on:* (happy halloween) Making Memories *Adhesive:* (foam squares) Making Memories

SUPPLIES: *Cardstock:* (black, olive, purple, white) Prism; (decorative-edged) Bazzill Basics Paper *Accents:* (arrow brads) Around The Block *Color medium:* (black pen) Sakura

🖐5 STEPS Halloween Garland

Designers: Catherine Myers, Debbie Ikert

❶ Make each letter panel from cardstock.

❷ Embellish as desired.

❸ Attach eyelets to each panel's sides, tie together with ribbon.

❹ Adhere hook and loop fastener to end panels and attach to wall.

Finished size: 55" x 6½"

SUPPLIES: *Cardstock:* (cream, black, purple, orange, green, lime green) *Patterned paper:* (assorted) Doodlebug Designs, Rusty Pickle, Junkitz, Bo-Bunny Press, Reminisce, Making Memories, Daisy D's, Debbie Mumm, KI Memories, My Mind's Eye, Die Cuts With a View *Specialty paper:* (black corrugated) Michaels; (web) Magenta *Transparency sheet:* (bats) *Rubber stamps:* (Medium Harlequin Background, Zig Zag) Hero Arts; (Geometric Swirl Background) Rubber Stampede *Clear stamps:* (Eiffel Tower alphabet) Technique Tuesday *Foam stamps:* (Center of Attention, New Orleans French Quarter alphabet; spider, bat from Spooks set) Heidi Swapp; (Printer's Block alphabet) Li'l Davis Designs; (witches hat, diamond border from Halloween set) Making Memories *Dye ink:* (black) Stampin' Up! *Chalk ink:* (Charcoal, Alabaster, Wisteria, Tangerine, Creamy Brown) Clearsnap *Color medium:* (black, white marker) Sakura *Paint:* (black) Delta; (Honey Dew) Making Memories; (Antique White) Plaid *Finish:* (crackle) Delta *Accents:* (green, black safety pin; pumpkin charm; green brad) Making Memories; (cat bottle caps, black pocket) Li'l Davis Designs; (cream, orange button; black spider; orange, purple netting; star brad; orange, black, green, eyelets) Jo-Ann Stores; (metal rimmed tag, grey hole reinforcer) Office Max; (black label tape) Dymo; (candy corn) Oriental Trading; (purple flowers) Wal-Mart; (orange plaid, black photo turns; black brads) Queen & Co.; (manila library pocket, tickets, staples, skeleton beads, purple bat charm) *Rub-ons:* (alphabet) Making Memories *Fibers:* (assorted ribbon, tulle, rickrack, waxed string, elastic string) May Arts, Jo-Ann Stores, Wal-Mart, Creative Impressions; (pompom trim) *Font:* (Celtic Hand, Adistillers) www.dafont.com; (Matisse) wwwmyfonts.com *Adhesive:* (foam squares) Therm O Web *Template:* (3" alphabet stencils) Office Max *Tools:* (¾" circle punch) EK Success; (tag punch) Marvy Urchida; (label maker) Dymo *Other:* (white craft foam, plastic spiders, transparent skeleton, mini broom, wood stick, cheesecloth, hook and loop fastener)

Come as You Aargh! Party
Designer: Tresa Black

INVITATION

❶ Make invitation from black cardstock.

❷ Cut strip of Indian Corn Blue cardstock; sand edges and adhere.

❸ Cut two pieces of patterned paper; ink edges and adhere.

❹ Stamp and emboss "Come as you".

❺ Stamp "Aargh!" on cardstock. Cut out, ink edges, and adhere.

❻ Punch skull from patterned paper; mat with cardstock and sand edges. Attach to hinge with brads; attach to invitation.

PIRATE BOOTY BOX

❶ Make pillow box from cardstock, using template.

❷ Cover with patterned paper.

❸ Stamp "Ye pirate booty" and anchor on patterned paper. Trim, ink edges, and wrap around box.

❹ Tie with twine.

YO HO HO TREAT BOX

❶ Cut popcorn box from cardstock, using template.

❷ Cover with patterned paper.

❸ Stamp "Yo ho ho" on patterned paper. Trim, mat with cardstock, and sand edges. Attach to box with brads.

❹ Fill with gift shred.

Finished sizes: invitation 7" x 5", pirate booty box 5¾" x 4½" x 1¼", treat box 2½" x 4½" x 2½"

SUPPLIES: *Cardstock:* (black, Cranberry, Goldrush, Indian Corn Blue) Close To My Heart *Patterned paper:* (Doubloons, Pirate Bandana, Pirate Flag, Pirate Stripes, Treasure Map from Pirates collection) Sandylion *Acrylic stamps:* (anchor from New Horizons set; Rustic, Storytime, Woodcut alphabets) Close To My Heart *Dye ink:* (black, Chocolate, Goldrush) Close To My Heart *Watermark ink:* Tsukineko *Embossing powder:* (white) Close To My Heart *Accents:* (pewter brads, hinge) Close To My Heart *Fibers:* (twine) *Templates:* (pillow box) Close To My Heart; (popcorn box) Provo Craft *Tools:* (1½", 2" circle punches) Marvy Uchida *Other:* (tan gift shred)

Pumpkin Wall Hanging
Designer: Wendy Johnson

BACKGROUND PIECE

❶ Trim cardstock; mat with cardstock and stitch edges. Adhere to chipboard backing. ❷ Punch holes in top and adhere washers. Thread ribbon through washers and knot ends in front. ❸ Affix stickers to cardstock; stitch edges. Stitch floss through buttons. Spell "Happy Halloween" with stickers and buttons.

PUMPKIN

❶ Cut pieces, following pattern on p. 283. Ink edges of pumpkin sections. Stitch middle section to side sections. Stitch to cardstock pumpkin piece along edges, leaving top open. Adhere to background piece. ❷ Stitch and ink edges of stem and top piece. Adhere stem behind top piece; adhere to cardstock for reinforcement. Attach to pumpkin with hook-and-loop fastener. Curl wire and adhere behind front piece. ❸ Stitch edges of face pieces; attach to pumpkin with hook-and-loop fastener.

Finished size: 12" square

DESIGNER TIP

Use a variety of pumpkin face pieces to give your pumpkin different personalities. Store the unused face pieces inside the pumpkin.

SUPPLIES: *Cardstock:* (Chantilly, Hazard, Route 66) Bazzill Basics Paper *Patterned paper:* (Cinnamon Gingham) Frances Meyer; (green gingham) *Dye ink:* (Scattered Straw) Ranger Industries *Accents:* (orange washers) Bazzill Basics Paper; (green wire) Making Memories; (black polka dot buttons) Doodlebug Design *Stickers:* (Simply Sweet alphabet) Doodlebug Design *Fibers:* (white floss) DMC; (black polka dot ribbon) Wrights *Other:* (hook-and-loop fastener) Velcro; (chipboard)

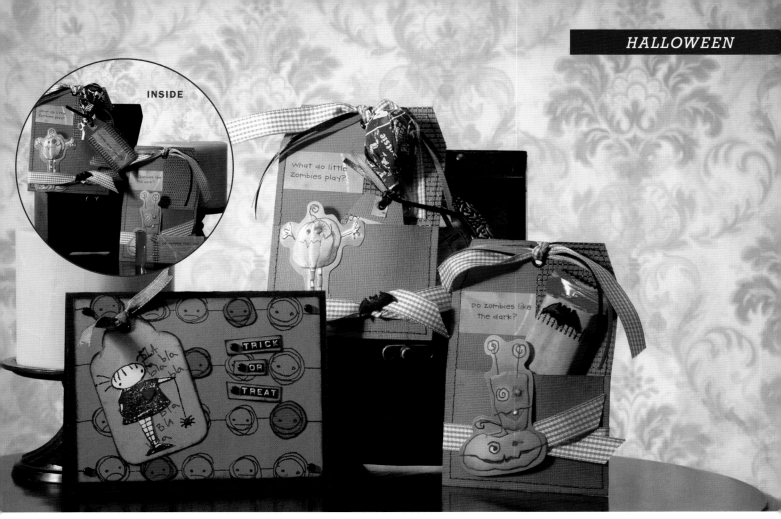

INSIDE

Spider Girl Card

Designer: Josie Cirincione, courtesy of Stampotique Originals

CARD

❶ Make card from cardstock.

❷ Stamp Row Faces repeatedly on blue and rust cardstock. Cut rust faces and randomly adhere to blue piece. Trim, ink edges, and attach brads.

❸ Create "Trick or treat" label; trim and mat with cardstock. Ink edges and attach with brads.

❹ Adhere.

TAG

❶ Punch tag from cardstock; stamp Spider Girl and Bla Bla Bla. Ink edges.

❷ Stamp Spider Girl on cardstock; cut out and adhere over image on tag.

❸ Punch heart from cardstock; ink edges and adhere.

❹ Set eyelet, tie with ribbon, and adhere.

Finished size: 5¾" x 4¼"

Zombie Riddle Tags

Designer: Joan Heaps

❶ Cut tag and pocket from cardstock. Place pocket over tag; stitch and ink edges.

❷ Print riddle question on patterned paper; trim and adhere. Adhere mesh.

❸ Set eyelet and tie with ribbon.

❹ Wrap ribbon around pocket; adhere die cut.

❺ Print riddle answer on patterned paper; trim to create tag or candy bar wrap.

❻ Decorate candy. Cut bat from ribbon and adhere. Tuck in pocket.

Finished size: 3¾" x 5½"

HALLOWEEN RIDDLES

Q: Where do ghosts go swimming?

A: In the Dead Sea

Q: What was the skeleton rock band called?

A: The Strolling Bones

Q: What's the first thing ghosts do when they get in a car?

A: They boo-kle their seatbelts.

Q: Why wasn't there any food left after the monster party?

A: Because everyone was a goblin.

SUPPLIES: *Cardstock:* (black, blue, mustard, rust, tan, red, white) *Rubber stamps:* (Bla Bla Bla, Row Faces, Spider Girl) Stampotique *Dye ink:* (black) Stewart Superior Corp. *Solvent ink:* (Rusty Brown) Tsukineko *Accents:* (black brads, eyelet) Making Memories; (black label tape) Dymo *Fibers:* (olive ribbon) May Arts *Tools:* (label maker) Dymo; (heart punch) Provo Craft; (tag punch) Emagination Crafts

SUPPLIES: *Cardstock:* (orange) *Patterned paper:* (Orange Web) Karen Foster Design *Dye ink:* (black) Hero Arts *Accents:* (Halloween die cuts) Carol Wilson Fine Arts; (black mesh) Magic Mesh; (black eyelets) Jo-Ann Stores *Fibers:* (bat ribbon) May Arts; (black, orange assorted ribbon) Offray *Other:* (candy)

The Pathway Home

Designer: Courtney Kelley

OUTSIDE

1. Make card from cardstock.
2. Stamp trees on patterned paper, trim, and adhere.
3. Adhere strip of patterned paper, folding up bottom edge for dimension.
4. Print sentiment on cardstock, trim, fold up edges, and adhere.
5. Adhere rhinestone.

INSIDE

1. Adhere rectangles of patterned paper, folding up edges for dimension.
2. Stamp house on patterned paper, trim, assemble, and adhere.
3. Adhere strip of patterned paper, folding up bottom edge.
4. Print sentiment on cardstock, trim, fold up edges, and adhere.

Finished size: 5½" x 4¼"

SUPPLIES: *Cardstock:* (brown) Die Cuts With a View; (Butter Cream) Prism *Patterned paper:* (Handsome Henry from Lil' Man collection) Cosmo Cricket; (Lime from Lemon Grass collection) Crate Paper; (brown polka dot, cream/orange grid from Friendly Forest pad) Colorbok; (Oak Lane from Sonoma collection, Scrap Strip from Liberty collection) Scenic Route *Rubber stamps:* (trees from Giggle Grove set, house from ...Another Sweet Day! set) Unity Stamp Co. *Dye ink:* (Walnut Stain) Ranger Industries *Accent:* (orange rhinestone) Art Beads *Font:* (Fancy Free) www.twopeasinabucket.com

Giving Thanks

Designer: Julia Stainton

OUTSIDE

1. Make card from cardstock.
2. Create 4¾" square project in software. Add photos and text, leaving spaces for patterned paper. Print on photo paper, trim, and adhere to card.
3. Adhere squares of patterned paper.
4. Spell "Thanks" with stickers.

INSIDE

1. Create 4" square project in software. Add photo and text.
2. Print on photo paper, mat with cardstock, and adhere.

Finished size: 5¼" square

Designer Tips

Save your digital template for future use.

Repeat a photo from the front in a larger size on the inside to tie the design together.

SUPPLIES: *Cardstock:* (Lizard, kraft) Bazzill Basics Paper *Patterned paper:* (Cookie Jar from Cherry Hill collection) October Afternoon; (Perfumeries from Fashionista collection; Botanical News, Ode to Butterfly from Botanicabella collection) Graphic 45; (Crazy Quilt, Apron from June Bug collection) BasicGrey *Specialty paper:* (glossy photo) Hewlett-Packard *Stickers:* (Darling alphabet) American Crafts *Fonts:* (Embassy BT, Castellar) www.myfonts.com *Software:* (photo editing) Adobe *Other:* (digital photos)

Blessings in Our Lives

Designer: Teri Anderson

OUTSIDE

1. Make card from cardstock; ink edges.

2. Cut panel of patterned paper slightly smaller than card front. Adhere strip of patterned paper.

3. Print sentiment on cardstock, trim, and adhere to panel. Ink panel edges.

4. Tie ribbon around panel; adhere to card.

5. Adhere flower and pearls.

INSIDE

1. Cut patterned paper panel and adhere strips of patterned paper.

2. Print sentiment on cardstock; trim and adhere.

3. Ink panel edges, adhere, and adhere pearls.

Finished size: 8¼" x 4½"

SUPPLIES: *Cardstock:* (cream, white) WorldWin *Patterned paper:* (Ads, Artisan Die-Cut Dot from Vintage Findings collection) Making Memories *Dye ink:* (Old Paper) Ranger Industries *Accents:* (white pearls) Zva Creative; (cream newsprint flower) *Fibers:* (white ribbon) May Arts *Fonts:* (CK Elegant) Creating Keepsakes

Thankful

Designer: Lisa Johnson

OUTSIDE

Ink all paper edges.

1. Make card from cardstock, round top with circle cutter.

2. Cut patterned paper pieces slightly smaller than card front. Trim one piece with border punch; adhere together.

3. Stitch edges. Adhere ribbon around panel and adhere panel to card.

4. Stamp wreath on cardstock; color with markers and pen. Punch into scalloped circle, sew on button with twine, and adhere with foam tape.

5. Stamp thankful on cardstock, trim, and adhere.

6. Stitch buttons with twine; adhere. Tie ribbon bow and adhere.

INSIDE

1. Cut cardstock slightly smaller than card flap and stamp leaves; color with markers and pen.

2. Adhere strip of patterned paper.

3. Stamp for you and draw dots with marker.

Finished size: 4" x 8"

SUPPLIES: *Cardstock:* (Dark Chocolate, Vintage Cream, Summer Sunrise) Papertrey Ink *Patterned paper:* (gratitude from First Fruits collection, brown leaves from Green Tea Leaves collection) Papertrey Ink *Clear stamps:* (wreath, leaves from Rustic Branches set; thankful, for you from First Fruits set) Papertrey Ink *Dye ink:* (Creamy Caramel) Stampin' Up! *Specialty ink:* (Dark Chocolate hybrid) Papertrey Ink *Color media:* (assorted markers) Copic; (gold gel pen) Sakura *Accents:* (dark brown buttons) *Fibers:* (natural twine, green ribbon) Papertrey Ink *Tools:* (circle cutter) Provo Craft; (scalloped circle punch) Marvy Uchida; (border punch) Fiskars

⑤ With Gratitude

Designer: Julie Cameron

① Make card from cardstock. ② Cut cardstock to fit card front; stamp open polka dots and adhere. ③ Cut patterned paper, mat with cardstock, and trim mat bottom with decorative-edge scissors; adhere. ④ Cut cardstock panel. Border punch cardstock strip; adhere behind panel. Punch leaves from cardstock and adhere. Adhere panel to card. ⑤ Punch circle from cardstock, stamp sentiment, and adhere; stitch.

Finished size: 3½" x 5"

SUPPLIES: *Cardstock:* (Ripe Avocado, Vintage Cream, kraft) Papertrey Ink; (Perfect Baby Boy Light, Suede Brown Dark) Prism; (Dark Scarlet) Bazzill Basics Paper; (white) *Patterned paper:* (Silver Birch from Porcelain collection) BasicGrey *Clear stamps:* (sentiment from Thankful Accents set) Verve Stamps; (open polka dots from Polka Dot Basics set) Papertrey Ink *Specialty ink:* (Burnt Sienna hybrid) Stewart Superior Corp. *Tools:* (1" circle punch) Plaid; (fern punch) EK Success; (border punch, decorative-edge scissors) Fiskars

⑤ Thankful For You

Designer: Kim Hughes

① Make card from cardstock. ② Trim cardstock panel to fit front. ③ Write sentiment on cardstock, trim pieces, and adhere to panel. Stitch lines. ④ Trim heart from cardstock and adhere. Trim leaves from patterned paper and adhere. ⑤ Adhere flower and attach brads. Tie on ribbon and adhere panel to card.

Finished size: 4¾" x 4"

SUPPLIES: *Cardstock:* (String of Pearls shimmer, Sun Coral, white) Bazzill Basics Paper *Patterned paper:* (Repeat from Earth Love collection) Cosmo Cricket *Color media:* (black pen) Sakura; (brown marker) Copic *Accents:* (yellow, green glitter brads) We R Memory Keepers; (orange flower) Making Memories *Fibers:* (brown gingham ribbon) May Arts

Grateful for You
Designer: Rae Barthel

① Make card from cardstock. ② Trim patterned paper pieces and adhere. Trim scalloped border from patterned paper and adhere. ③ Tie on ribbon. ④ Stamp sentiment on journaling card, trim, round corners, and ink edges; adhere. ⑤ Adhere rhinestones.

Finished size: 6" x 4¼"

Thankful Hearts
Designer: Rae Barthel

① Make card from cardstock; round corners. ② Cut patterned paper strip and adhere. Cut patterned paper, round corners, and adhere. Adhere patterned paper strip over seam. ③ Cut sentiment label from patterned paper. Double-mat with labels die-cut from patterned paper and cardstock; adhere glitter. ④ Thread buttons with cord, adhere to label, and adhere label to card with foam tape.

Finished size: 6" x 4¼"

DESIGNER TIP
When outlining with glitter, use a glue bottle with a very thin tip applicator.

SUPPLIES: *Cardstock:* (Vintage Cream) Papertrey Ink *Patterned paper:* (Sesame from Kitchen Spice collection) BoBunny Press; (Root Beer from Sweet Shoppe collection) Collage Press *Clear stamp:* (sentiment from Signature Greetings collection) Papertrey Ink *Chalk ink:* (Chestnut Roan) Clearsnap *Solvent ink:* (Timber Brown) Tsukineko *Accents:* (small gold rhinestones) Michaels; (large yellow rhinestone) Prima; (ledger journaling card) Jenni Bowlin Studio *Fibers:* (copper ribbon) Hobby Lobby *Tool:* (corner rounder punch)

SUPPLIES: *Cardstock:* (Bitter Chocolate) Bazzill Basics Paper *Patterned paper:* (Acorn, Falling Down, Cinnamon, Elements, cream floral from Nutmeg collection) Cosmo Cricket *Accents:* (copper glitter) Martha Stewart Crafts; (vintage wood buttons) *Fibers:* (tan cord) Sulyn Industries *Dies:* (labels) Spellbinders *Tool:* (corner rounder punch) EK Success

Thanksgiving Wall Hanging

Designer: Julia Stainton

1 Adhere patterned paper to wall hanging. Sand and ink edges. **2** Adhere patterned paper layers together. Stitch edges of smallest strip. **3** Apply rub-on. Adhere to wall hanging. **4** Sponge leaves with ink; adhere. **5** Tie buttons with fibers; adhere. **6** Tie on cord.

Finished size: 6" square

SUPPLIES: *Patterned paper:* (Autumn, Hansel from Gretel collection) Cosmo Cricket *Dye ink:* (Chocolate Chip) Stampin' Up! *Accents:* (assorted buttons) Daisy D's; (foam leaves) American Crafts *Rub-on:* (giving thanks) Daisy D's *Fibers:* (green gingham ribbon, olive ribbon) Making Memories; (linen thread, lace trim) Stampin' Up!; (faux suede cord) *Other:* (paper mache wall hanging) Michaels

Rustic Thanksgiving Place Card

Designer: Jessica Witty

❶ Trim two patterned papers and ink edges; adhere together and distress edges.

❷ Adhere photo and twill.

❸ Stamp sentiment on cardstock; trim and adhere.

❹ Fussy-cut leaves from patterned paper and adhere; fussy-cut acorn and adhere with foam tape.

❺ Stamp name on cardstock; trim and adhere; adhere button.

❻ Adhere sticks together, placing adhesive only at ends. Insert card.

Finished size: 4½" x 4"

Count Your Blessings Place Card

Designer: Betsy Veldman

❶ Die-cut large scalloped tag from patterned paper; ink edges.

❷ Trim strip of patterned paper to encircle napkin and adhere to tag; fussy-cut patterned paper strip and adhere.

❸ Cut photo in circle, mat with patterned paper, and adhere.

❹ Stamp name on cardstock; trim and attach with brads.

❺ Tie ribbon through tag.

❻ Die-cut small tag and ink edges; stamp sentiment and attach with twine.

Finished size: 7" x 3½"

DESIGNER TIP

Don't have a picture of every person coming to your party? Email them ahead of time and ask them to send a photograph of themselves, no questions asked!

DESIGNER TIP

Place card holders don't have to be expensive. Design your own out of seasonal items such as fruits, vegetables, foliage, or flowers.

DESIGNER TIP

Create an elegant photo napkin ring to grace your Thanksgiving table. Even the youngest family member will be able to spot her face at the kids' table!

SUPPLIES: *Cardstock:* (white) *Patterned paper:* (Flannel, Skipping Stones, Strip Tease from Mr. Campy collection) Cosmo Cricket *Clear stamps:* (Simple Alphabet set) Papertrey Ink *Dye ink:* (Chocolate Chip, Old Olive) Stampin' Up!; (Tea Dye) Ranger Industries *Accent:* (orange button) Autumn Leaves *Fibers:* (brown twill) Martha Stewart Crafts *Other:* (photo, sticks)

SUPPLIES: *Cardstock:* (Vintage Cream) Papertrey Ink *Patterned paper:* (Bohemian Vines, Vines, Candy Stripes from Bloom collection) My Mind's Eye *Clear stamps:* (count your, blessings from Year-Round Puns set; Simple Alphabet set) Papertrey Ink *Dye ink:* (More Mustard, Rose Red, Taken with Teal) Stampin' Up! *Chalk ink:* (Creamy Brown) Clearsnap *Accents:* (bronze brads) Creative Impressions *Fibers:* (brown ribbon) Papertrey Ink; (twine) The Beadery *Dies:* (tags) Provo Craft *Tool:* (circle cutter) Creative Memories *Other:* (cream linen napkin, photo)

⬡5⬡ Thanksgiving Card

Designer: Dee Gallimore-Perry

1 Make card from patterned paper. Crumple patterned paper piece; adhere. **2** Affix border sticker. Adhere cardstock piece. **3** Adhere quote sticker with foam tape. **4** Punch leaves from patterned paper. Crumple and adhere with foam tape. *Note: Crumple leaves gently to avoid tearing.*

Finished size: 4½" x 8"

DESIGNER TIP

To heavily distress paper when crumpling, spray it with water first.

SUPPLIES: *Cardstock:* (natural) *Patterned paper:* (Falling, Cute Dot, Wheat, Small Dotty, Skinny Stripe from Grateful collection) KI Memories *Stickers:* (quote, dotted border) KI Memories *Adhesive:* (foam tape) Therm O Web *Tool:* (leaf punch) Family Treasures

Happy Pumpkin Day Card

Designer: Lisa Dorsey

Ink all edges.

1 Make card from cardstock. Trim edges of patterned paper strips with decorative-edge scissors; adhere.

2 Trim cardstock into pumpkin shape and mask, following step-outs. Color leaves with markers.

3 Trim stem, leaf, and vines from cardstock; adhere to masked pumpkin piece.

4 Adhere pumpkin to card with foam tape.

5 Print "Happy pumpkin day!" on cardstock. Trim and attach to card with brads.

Finished size: 5½" x 4½"

SUPPLIES: *Cardstock:* (Very Vanilla, Chocolate Chip) Stampin' Up! *Patterned paper:* (Equinox, Cultured from Mellow collection) BasicGrey *Rubber stamps:* (pumpkins, acorn, face from Autumn Harvest set) Stampin' Up!; (happy Halloween from Celebration Sayings set) Lizzie Anne Designs *Pigment ink:* (Graphite Black) Tsukineko *Color medium:* (Golden Yellow, Honey, Chamois, Grayish Olive, Warm Gray markers) Copic Marker; (Chocolate Chip, Basic Black markers) Stampin' Up! *Accents:* (copper brads) Making Memories *Adhesive:* (foam tape)

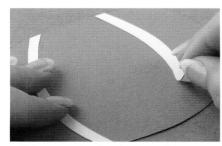

a. Trim curved strips from cardstock. Place on cardstock pumpkin.

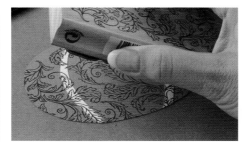

b. Stamp Leaf Pattern Background.

c. Remove cardstock strips. Color with pencils.

Simple Joy

Designer: Becky Olsen

❶ Make card from cardstock; stitch border. ❷ Adhere snowflake and affix stickers.

Finished size: 5½" x 4¼"

Retro Christmas

Designer: Lisa Johnson

❶ Make card from cardstock. ❷ Stamp ornaments and merry Christmas on cardstock; apply glitter. ❸ Adhere panel with foam tape. ❹ Tie ribbon bow and adhere.

Finished size: 4¼" x 5½"

SUPPLIES: *Cardstock:* (white) Prism *Accent:* (clear rhinestone snowflake) Zva Creative *Stickers:* (Glitter alphabet) Pink Paislee

SUPPLIES: All supplies from Papertrey Ink unless otherwise noted. *Cardstock:* (kraft, white) *Clear stamps:* (ornaments, merry Christmas from Christmas Friends set) *Pigment ink:* (Hibiscus Burst, Orange Zest) *Specialty ink:* (Ripe Avocado, True Black hybrid) *Accents:* (iridescent glitter) Stewart Superior Corp. *Fibers:* (orange stitched ribbon)

⁵⁵ₜₑₚₛ Oh Christmas Tree

Designer: Cindy Coutts

① Make card from cardstock. ② Stamp tree on card.
③ Emboss card. ④ Apply rub-on and adhere pearls.

Finished size: 4¼" x 5½"

DESIGNER TIPS

Use the "rock 'n roll" technique when stamping the tree.

Be sure to allow the stamped image to dry completely before embossing or adding embellishments

SUPPLIES: *Cardstock:* (Pearl Metallic) CTI Paper USA *Rubber stamp:* (tree from Forest of Trees set) Flourishes *Solvent ink:* (Forest Green, Olive Green) Tsukineko *Accents:* (white pearls) Michaels *Rub-on:* (sentiment) Imaginisce *Template:* (label embossing) Spellbinders

December 25th

Designer: Leslie Webster

① Make card from cardstock. ② Emboss cardstock and adhere. Adhere lace. ③ Round corners of cardstock and adhere. ④ Trim patterned paper pieces, round outside corners, and adhere. ⑤ Punch circles from cardstock, layer, and adhere. Apply rub-ons. ⑥ Adhere rhinestone tree. Cut tree from patterned paper and adhere with foam tape.

Finished size: 7" x 5"

SUPPLIES: *Cardstock:* (white, burgundy, dark green) Bazzill Basics Paper *Patterned paper:* (Trees from Mistletoe collection) Making Memories; (Reindeer Games, tree stripes, red wreaths from Enchanted Christmas collection) Melissa Frances *Accent:* (green rhinestone tree) BasicGrey *Rub-on:* (date, sentiment) K&Company *Template:* (Textile Texture embossing) Provo Craft *Fibers:* (white lace) *Tools:* (corner rounder punch) Stampin' Up!; (circle punches) EK Success

Home for Christmas

Designer: Charlene Cundy

❶ Make card from cardstock; round bottom corners. ❷ Adhere patterned paper strips. ❸ Punch cardstock strip; ink edges and adhere. ❹ Punch patterned paper strip and adhere. ❺ Punch cardstock strip and ink edges; thread twine through piece and adhere. ❻ Thread button with twine and tie on. Affix sticker.

Finished size: 4¼" x 4¾"

SUPPLIES: *Cardstock:* (Vintage Cream) Papertrey Ink; (kraft) *Patterned paper:* (Sing the Carols, Trim the Tree from Very Merry collection) October Afternoon *Dye ink:* (Frayed Burlap) Ranger Industries *Accent:* (red button) Papertrey Ink *Sticker:* (sentiment banner) October Afternoon *Fibers:* (red striped twine) Martha Stewart Crafts *Tools:* (border punches) Martha Stewart Crafts; (corner rounder punch)

Noel Tree

Designer: Debbie Olson

❶ Make card from cardstock. ❷ Adhere patterned paper pieces to cardstock panel. Stitch edges and zigzag-stitch seam. ❸ Stamp tree, trunk, and star on cardstock; trim and adhere with foam tape. ❹ Thread buttons with twine and adhere. Apply glitter glue. ❺ Trim ribbon with decorative-edge scissors; tie on ribbon. ❻ Stamp noel on cardstock; die-cut and emboss into tag. Tie on tag with twine. ❼ Adhere panel and ink card edges.

Finished size: 4¼" x 5½"

SUPPLIES: *Cardstock:* (Aqua Mist, Vintage Cream) Papertrey Ink *Patterned paper:* (Merry Berry from Jolly by Golly collection) Cosmo Cricket *Clear stamps:* (noel, star, tree, tree trunk from Tree Trimming Trio set) Papertrey Ink *Dye ink:* (Chamomile) Papertrey Ink *Pigment ink:* (Lemon Tart) Papertrey Ink; (Oasis Green, Gingerbread) Tsukineko *Specialty ink:* (Pure Poppy hybrid) Papertrey Ink *Accents:* (clear glitter glue) Ranger Industries; (red buttons) Papertrey Ink *Fibers:* (aqua stitched ribbon) Papertrey Ink; (white twine) *Die:* (tag) Spellbinders *Tool:* (decorative-edge scissors)

Let It Snow

Designer: Gretchen McElveen

❶ Make card from cardstock. ❷ Adhere patterned paper, trim, and rhinestones. ❸ Trim snowflakes from die cut paper, attach brad to one, and adhere. Adhere rhinestones. ❹ Spell "Let it snow" with stickers.

Finished size: 4¼" x 5½"

Ding-Dongs

Designer: Rae Barthel

❶ Make card from cardstock. ❷ Adhere patterned paper panel and tie on ribbon. ❸ Trim sentiment block from patterned paper; round corners, and mat with cardstock. Round mat corners and adhere. ❹ Adhere pearls.

Finished size: 6" x 4"

SUPPLIES: *Cardstock:* (white) Die Cuts With a View *Patterned paper:* (Bombshell from Pop Culture collection) KI Memories *Specialty paper:* (Flurry Bubble die cut from Festive collection) KI Memories *Accents:* (burgundy brad) American Crafts; (clear rhinestones) Heidi Swapp *Stickers:* (Cookie Cutter alphabet) KI Memories *Fibers:* (white scalloped trim) KI Memories

SUPPLIES: *Cardstock:* (Avalanche) Bazzill Basics Paper *Patterned paper:* (Elements, stripes from Jolly by Golly collection) Cosmo Cricket *Accents:* (silver pearls) Michaels *Fibers:* (white rhinestone ribbon) Hobby Lobby *Tool:* (corner rounder punch) EK Success

⭐5 Graphic Ornaments

Designer: Tina Fussell

❶ Make card from cardstock.

❷ Punch circles from patterned paper and adhere.

❸ Draw hooks.

❹ Stamp sentiment on cardstock; trim into tag and punch end.

❺ Thread tag with cord and tie.

Finished size: 5½" x 4¼"

⭐5 Peace on Earth

Designer: Laura O'Donnell

❶ Make card from cardstock.

❷ Stamp Peace On Earth on cardstock; tear and adhere to cardstock panel.

❸ Stamp gnome and bird on cardstock. Color, cut out, and adhere.

❹ Tear top layer from cardboard; adhere to card.

❺ Adhere cardstock panel.

Finished size: 4" square

SUPPLIES: *Clear stamp:* (merry Christmas from Mega Mixed Messages set) Papertrey Ink *Dye ink:* (Riding Hood Red) Stampin' Up! *Cardstock:* (white) Papertrey Ink *Patterned paper:* (Red Rover from Kids collection) American Crafts; (zebra from Black & White Simple collection) Creative Memories; (Laurel Landings Way) Scenic Route *Color medium:* (black marker) Sanford *Fibers:* (silver cord) Stampin' Up! *Tool:* (1" circle punch) Creative Memories; (1/16" circle punch)

SUPPLIES: *Rubber stamps:* (Kelly's Gnome with Birds, Peace On Earth, Kelly's Tiny Bird) Just Johanna Rubber Stamps *Dye ink:* (Tuxedo Black) Tsukineko *Color media:* (assorted markers) Copic; (white gel pen) Sanford *Cardstock:* (blue, green, kraft) Bazzill Basics Paper; (white) Neenah Paper *Other:* (cardboard)

Button Wreath Joy

Designer: Belinda Chang Langner

① Make card from cardstock. ② Stamp joy on cardstock. Mat with cardstock and adhere. ③ Thread buttons on twine; adhere to form wreath. ④ Tie twill bow and adhere.

Finished size: 4¼" x 5½"

Peas on Earth

Designer: Kelly Landers

① Make card from cardstock; adhere ribbon. ② Die-cut and emboss label from patterned paper and adhere. ③ Print image on cardstock; die-cut and emboss into label. Color image. ④ Print image on patterned paper; trim and adhere. ⑤ Tie ribbon bow and adhere.

Finished size: 5½" x 4¼"

DESIGNER TIP

To keep the image from smudging, heat-set the ink before coloring.

SUPPLIES: All supplies from Papertrey Ink unless otherwise noted. *Cardstock:* (Pure Poppy, white) *Clear stamp:* (joy from Seasons of Love set) Waltzingmouse Stamps *Specialty ink:* (Pure Poppy hybrid) *Accents:* (green buttons) *Fibers:* (red twill); (hemp twine) no source

SUPPLIES: *Cardstock:* (white) Georgia-Pacific; (red) *Patterned paper:* (green dots, green stripes from Christmas pad) Die Cuts With a View *Color medium:* (assorted markers) Copic *Digital elements:* (Peas on Earth stamp) www.whimsiedoodles.com *Fibers:* (red/green striped ribbon) American Crafts *Dies:* (labels) Spellbinders

Spirit of Christmas

Designer: Lisa Dorsey

① Make card from cardstock. ② Cut patterned paper panel; adhere patterned paper strip. Trim panel edges with decorative-edge scissors. Adhere trim and tie on ribbon. ③ Adhere panel. Thread button with twine and adhere. Attach pins. ④ Stitch fabric image to card.

Finished size: 4¾" x 6"

SUPPLIES: *Cardstock:* (red) Bazzill Basics Paper *Patterned paper:* (Gold Vines, Gold Flurry from Georgette Holiday collection) Anna Griffin *Accents:* (green leaf stick pins) Maya Road; (red button) *Fibers:* (cream ribbon) Michaels; (cream lace) Jo-Ann Stores; (jute twine) May Arts *Tool:* (decorative-edge scissors) Fiskars *Other:* (fabric image) Crafty Secrets

Christmas Blessings

Designer: Sherry Wright

① Make card from cardstock. Ink edges of patterned paper and adhere. ② Adhere wallpaper and patterned paper strips. ③ Trim ribbon with decorative-edge scissors and adhere. Tie ribbon bow and adhere; trim ribbon ends with decorative-edge scissors. ④ Stamp sentiment on cardstock; trim to fit behind chipboard frame. Ink and emboss frame and adhere to stamped piece. Adhere to card. ⑤ Adhere poinsettia.

Finished size: 4¾" x 6¼"

SUPPLIES: *Patterned paper:* (Wild Berry Dot from Double Dot collection) BoBunny Press; (Winterberry from Wassail collection) BasicGrey *Clear stamp:* (Christmas blessings from Signature Christmas set) Papertrey Ink *Pigment ink:* (gold) Clearsnap *Chalk ink:* (Lipstick Red) Clearsnap; (light brown) *Embossing powder:* (gold) Clearsnap *Accents:* (red fabric poinsettia) Prima; (chipboard frame) Tattered Angels *Fibers:* (gold ribbon) SEI *Tool:* (decorative-edge scissors) *Other:* (vintage wallpaper)

⭐5 Homespun Christmas

Designer: Windy Robinson

❶ Make card from cardstock; ink edges. ❷ Trim edges of fabric image with decorative-edge scissors and mat with patterned paper. Tie knots with floss. ❸ Adhere panel and zigzag-stitch edges. ❹ Stamp merry Christmas on cardstock. Trim, ink edges, and adhere. Thread button with ribbon and adhere.

Finished size: 4¼" x 6"

SUPPLIES: *Cardstock:* (kraft) DMD, Inc. *Patterned paper:* (Postcards from Cupid collection) Pink Paislee *Rubber stamp:* (merry Christmas from Christmas Bough set) Unity Stamp Co. *Chalk ink:* (Chestnut Roan) Clearsnap *Specialty ink:* (Burnt Umber hybrid) Stewart Superior Corp. *Accents:* (brown button) Jillibean Soup *Fibers:* (brown gingham ribbon) Bazzill Basics Paper; (brown floss) DMC *Tool:* (decorative-edge scissors) *Other:* (fabric image) Pink Paislee

⭐5 Winter Wonderland

Designer: Jessica Witty

❶ Make card from cardstock; emboss and apply ink. ❷ Adhere label; tie on twill. ❸ Affix holly sticker and apply glitter.

Finished size: 5" x 3½"

SUPPLIES: *Cardstock:* (kraft) Papertrey Ink *Pigment ink:* (Vintage Cream) Papertrey Ink *Accents:* (cream sentiment label) Cosmo Cricket; (red glitter) Martha Stewart Crafts *Sticker:* (chipboard holly) Cosmo Cricket *Fibers:* (red twill) Papertrey Ink *Template:* (Swiss Dots embossing) Provo Craft

Bright Merry Christmas

Designer: Latisha Yoast

① Make card from cardstock. ② Punch patterned paper and adhere. ③ Tie on ribbon. ④ Adhere tag with foam tape. ⑤ Apply glitter glue.

Finished size: 4¼" square

Merry & Bright

Designer: Kalyn Kepner

① Make card from cardstock; stitch edges and apply glitter glue. ② Punch circles from cardstock and adhere inside card front. ③ Stamp flourishes on card; emboss. ④ Adhere rickrack and ribbon. ⑤ Thread buttons with floss and adhere. ⑥ Spell "Merry" with stickers. Write "& bright".

Finished size: 5½" x 3¼"

SUPPLIES: *Cardstock:* (white) Papertrey Ink *Patterned paper:* (Plaid from Holiday Cheer collection) BoBunny Press *Accents:* (iridescent glitter glue) Ranger Industries; (holiday tag) Kaisercraft *Fibers:* (red polka dot ribbon) Papertrey Ink *Tool:* (border punch) Fiskars

SUPPLIES: *Cardstock:* (cream) Bazzill Basics Paper; (pink) Wausau Paper *Clear stamp:* (flourish from Fancy Flourishes set) Autumn Leaves *Watermark ink:* Tsukineko *Embossing powder:* (white) Hampton Art *Color medium:* (pink pen) *Accents:* (white, pink buttons) Papertrey Ink; (pink glitter glue) Ranger Industries *Stickers:* (Jolly by Golly alphabet) Cosmo Cricket *Fibers:* (pink floss) DMC; (blue rickrack, pink ribbon) *Tool:* (½" circle punch) Provo Craft

⁵ Fa La La

Designer: Tanisha Long

❶ Make card from cardstock. Cover with patterned paper and punch bottom edge. ❷ Emboss cardstock panel; spray with paint. Ink edges. ❸ Spell "Fa la la" with stickers. Apply glitter glue. ❹ Tie on twine. Adhere pearls. ❺ Adhere panel.

Finished size: 4½" x 6½"

SUPPLIES: *Cardstock:* (white) American Crafts *Patterned Paper:* (Sugar Cookies from Good Cheer collection) October Afternoon *Chalk ink:* (Rouge) Clearsnap *Paint:* (Treasured Hymn spray) Shimmering Products *Accents:* (gold pearls) Prima; (white glitter glue) Ranger Industries *Stickers:* (Darling alphabet) American Crafts *Fibers:* (jute twine) *Template:* (Allegro embossing) Provo Craft *Tool:* (border punch) EK Success

Warm Winter Wishes

Designer: Debbie Olson

❶ Make card from cardstock. ❷ Adhere patterned paper and cardstock strips to cardstock panel. Zigzag-stitch seams. ❸ Tie on ribbon. ❹ Stamp snowman on cardstock; color. Die-cut and emboss into circle. Airbrush image. Stamp sentiment, ink edges, and adhere with foam tape. ❺ Apply glitter glue. Thread button with string and adhere. ❻ Adhere panel to card.

Finished size: 4¼" x 5½"

SUPPLIES: *Cardstock:* (Vintage Cream, Ocean Tides) Papertrey Ink *Patterned paper:* (Play Day from Jolly By Golly collection) Cosmo Cricket *Clear stamps:* (snowman, sentiment from Holiday Button Bits set) Papertrey Ink *Dye ink:* (Tuxedo Black) Tsukineko; (Chamomile) Papertrey Ink *Specialty ink:* (Ocean Tides hybrid) Papertrey Ink *Color media:* (assorted markers, glitter pens) Copic *Accents:* (white button) Papertrey Ink; (iridescent glitter glue) Ranger Industries *Fibers:* (pink stitched ribbon) Papertrey Ink; (white string) Coats & Clark *Die:* (circle) Spellbinders *Tool:* (airbrush system) Copic

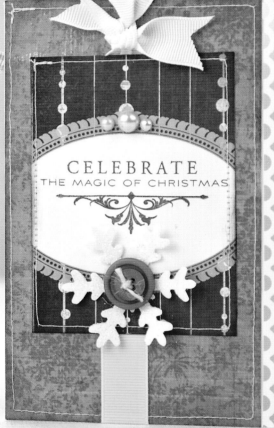

Noel

Designer: Annaka Crockett

1 Make card from cardstock. Trim cardstock panel and adhere. 2 Apply glitter. 3 Trim trees from patterned paper and adhere, using foam tape on center tree. Adhere rhinestone. 4 Tie on ribbon. 5 Apply rub-on to tag; tie on with twine. 6 Paint star; adhere glitter. Adhere to tag.

Finished size: 5½" x 4¼"

5 Magic of Christmas

Designer: Betsy Veldman

1 Make card from cardstock. Punch front flap. 2 Adhere patterned paper and stitch edges. Tie on ribbon. 3 Cut journaling card from patterned paper; adhere and stitch edges. 4 Stamp sentiment and scroll. 5 Punch snowflake from cardstock; adhere glitter and adhere to card. Thread buttons with twine; adhere. Adhere pearls.

Finished size: 4" x 6"

SUPPLIES: *Cardstock:* (white, blue) Bazzill Basics Paper *Patterned paper:* (White Christmas from Tinsel Town collection) Pink Paislee *Paint:* (Capri) Making Memories *Accents:* (silver tag) Office Max; (acrylic star) Heidi Swapp; (iridescent crystal glitter) Floracraft Corp.; (pink rhinestone) *Rub-on:* (noel) Royal & Langnickel *Fibers:* (white twine, pink gingham ribbon)

SUPPLIES: *Cardstock:* (white) Papertrey Ink *Patterned paper:* (Colored Winter, Cards from Frosted collection) Fancy Pants Designs *Clear stamps:* (scroll from Vintage Labels set, sentiment from Tree Trimming Trio set) Papertrey Ink *Specialty ink:* (Pure Poppy hybrid) Papertrey Ink *Accents:* (pink, green buttons) Papertrey Ink; (white pearls) Zva Creative; (white glitter) Doodlebug Design *Fibers:* (white ribbon, cream twine) Papertrey Ink *Tools:* (snowflake punch) Marvy Uchida; (border punch) Fiskars

Let There Be Peace on Earth

Designer: Monika A. Davis

① Make card from cardstock; die-cut into scalloped circle.
② Die-cut circle from cardstock; stamp wisemen and adhere rhinestone. ③ Die-cut and emboss circle from cardstock; die-cut smaller circle from piece to create frame. Stamp border.
④ Die-cut circle from transparency sheet; adhere to wisemen circle with foam tape, leaving opening at top. Place beads inside and close with foam tape. ⑤ Die-cut circle from cardstock; adhere to card. Adhere wisemen circle. Adhere frame with foam tape. ⑥ Tie on cord.

Finished size: 4¼" diameter

DESIGNER TIP
Don't use too many micro beads or they'll completely cover the image.

⦂5⦂ Merry Christmas Tree

Designer: Charlene Austin

① Make card from cardstock. ② Die-cut circles from patterned paper. Trim and adhere. ③ Tie on ribbon. ④ Apply rub-on and adhere sticker with foam tape.

Finished size: 6" x 4½"

SUPPLIES: *Cardstock:* (Night of Navy) Stampin' Up!; (white) Georgia-Pacific *Transparency sheet:* Stampin' Up! *Rubber stamps:* (wisemen, border from Christmas Treasures Borders & Centers set) JustRite *Dye ink:* (Night of Navy) Stampin' Up! *Accents:* (clear rhinestone, clear micro beads) *Fibers:* (silver cord) Stampin' Up! *Dies:* (circles, scalloped circle) Spellbinders

SUPPLIES: *Cardstock:* (white) Papertrey Ink *Patterned paper:* (green stripe, red trees from Peppermint Twist pad) K&Company; (blue snowflake from Christmas pad) Die Cuts With a View *Rub-on:* (merry Christmas) Imaginisce *Sticker:* (black chipboard tree) American Crafts *Fibers:* (pink ribbon) May Arts *Die:* (circle) Spellbinders

Kwanzaa Kinara

Designer: Teri Anderson

① Make Kinara card base. ② Cut cardstock strips and pieces; adhere together to make candles. Adhere candles to card back. ③ Adhere kinara pieces together; adhere top edge to card back. Adhere cardstock strip. ④ Tie on twine.

Finished size: 5½" x 5¾"

Pure Joy

Designer: Tiffany Johnson

① Make card from cardstock. ② Cut cardstock panel to fit card front; adhere patterned paper. Stitch border. ③ Gather ribbon on pin; adhere. Attach brads. ④ Affix sticker. ⑤ Adhere panel to card. Round bottom right corner.

Finished size: 5½" x 4¼"

DESIGNER TIP
Fold in the ends of the ribbon before threading it on the pin.

SUPPLIES: *Cardstock:* (black, white, yellow, green, red) WorldWin; (brown) Provo Craft *Fibers:* (hemp twine) DCC

SUPPLIES: *Cardstock:* (Vintage Cream) Papertrey Ink; (cream) Bazzill Basics Paper *Patterned paper:* (red polka dot glitter from Sweet Dreams Holiday Avenue pad) My Mind's Eye *Accents:* (green brads) Making Memories; (silver hat pin) Jo-Ann Stores *Sticker:* (sentiment circle) Anna Griffin *Fibers:* (black striped ribbon) May Arts *Tool:* (corner rounder punch) EK Success

⟨5 STEPS⟩ Happy Hanukkah

Designer: Rebecca Oehlers

① Make card from cardstock. ② Stamp polka dots on cardstock panel; apply glitter. Mat with cardstock. ③ Stamp menorah on cardstock. Draw border and adhere rhinestones. Double-mat with cardstock and adhere to panel with foam tape. ④ Die-cut ribbon slide from cardstock; stamp sentiment. Thread slide on ribbon, tie around panel, and adhere slide with foam tape. ⑤ Adhere panel to card.

Finished size: 4¼" x 5½"

SUPPLIES: All supplies from Papertrey Ink unless otherwise noted. *Cardstock:* (Enchanted Evening, white) *Clear stamps:* (menorah, sentiment from Mazel Tov set; polka dots from Polka Dot Basics II set) *Pigment ink:* (Fresh Snow) *Specialty ink:* (Enchanted Evening hybrid) *Color medium:* (black pen) Copic *Accents:* (clear rhinestones, clear glitter) Martha Stewart Crafts *Fibers:* (blue ribbon) *Die:* (ribbon slide) Spellbinders

⟨5 STEPS⟩ Celebrate Hanukkah

Designer: Jessica Witty

① Make card from cardstock; stitch edges. ② Round top corners of patterned paper panel. ③ Stamp candle repeatedly on cardstock. Punch into circles and adhere to panel with foam tape. ④ Stamp celebrate on cardstock and adhere; stitch left side. ⑤ Tie on floss; adhere panel with foam tape.

Finished size: 5" x 3½"

SUPPLIES: *Cardstock:* (kraft, white) Papertrey Ink *Patterned paper:* (Dark Denim Dot from Double Dot collection) BoBunny Press *Clear stamps:* (celebrate, candle from Tree Trimming Trio set) Papertrey Ink *Dye ink:* (Summer Sun) Stampin' Up! *Specialty ink:* (Enchanted Evening hybrid) Papertrey Ink *Fibers:* (blue floss) DMC *Tools:* (corner rounder punch, ½" circle punch) EK Success

Happy Hanukkah

Designer: Kim Hughes

OUTSIDE

1. Make card from cardstock.
2. Spell "Happy Hanukkah" with stickers.
3. Adhere cardstock strips.
4. Punch cardstock strip and adhere.
5. Tie ribbon and adhere.

INSIDE

1. Cut pop-up, following pattern on p. 282; adhere to card.
2. Adhere cardstock strips to cardstock panel. Cut flames from cardstock; adhere. Attach brads and tie on ribbon.
3. Adhere cardstock panel. Fold down.
4. Print sentiment on cardstock; mat with cardstock and adhere.
5. Adhere cardstock strip. Punch circles from cardstock; adhere.

Finished size: 5" x 4¼"

SUPPLIES: *Cardstock:* (Daisy, Kevin; Diamond shimmer) Bazzill Basics Paper; (Seven Seas from En Route collection) SEI; (white) *Accents:* (cream brads) American Crafts *Stickers:* (Rockabye glitter alphabet) American Crafts *Fibers:* (silver ribbon) Creative Impressions *Font:* (Alison) www.abstractfonts.com *Tool:* (border punch) Stampin' Up!

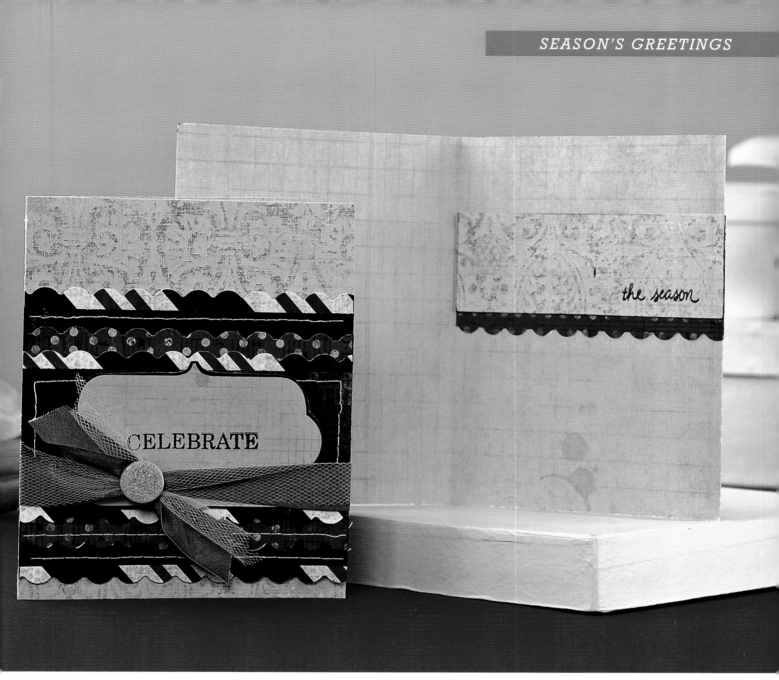

Celebrate the Season

Designer: Davinie Fiero

OUTSIDE

1. Make card from patterned paper.
2. Punch top and bottom edges of patterned paper panel. Punch and stitch patterned paper strips; layer and adhere.
3. Stamp celebrate on journaling tag; adhere.
4. Tie on tulle and ribbon; attach brad.
5. Adhere panel to card.

INSIDE

1. Punch patterned paper strip and adhere.
2. Stamp the season on patterned paper and adhere.

Finished size: 4½" x 5½"

SUPPLIES: *Patterned paper:* (North Pole, Santa's Workshop, Naughty or Nice from Mistletoe & Co. collection) Pink Paislee *Clear stamps:* (celebrate, the season from Very Merry set) October Afternoon *Solvent ink:* (Timber Brown) Tsukineko *Accents:* (blue glitter brad, journaling tag) Pink Paislee *Fibers:* (brown ribbon) SEI; (white tulle) *Tool:* (border punch) Fiskars

Celebrate Kwanzaa

Designer: Teri Anderson

OUTSIDE

1. Make card from cardstock. Cut cardstock panel to fit card front.

2. Adhere cardstock strips to panel; cut flames from cardstock and adhere.

3. Print "Celebrate" on cardstock; adhere.

4. Attach brad. Adhere panel to card.

INSIDE

1. Adhere cardstock strips to cardstock panel; cut flames from cardstock and adhere.

2. Print sentiment on cardstock; adhere.

3. Adhere panel to card.

Finished size: 5½" x 4¼"

SUPPLIES: *Cardstock: (black, white) WorldWin; (yellow) Core'dinations; (red, green) Bazzill Basics Paper Accent: (gold brad) Acco Brands Font: (CK Fresh) Creating Keepsakes*

Who's Afraid of Santa Claus?

Designer: Layle Koncar

OUTSIDE

① Make card from cardstock; adhere patterned paper panels.

② Create 3" x 4¾" project in software. Drop in photo and draw border. Type sentiment. Print on photo paper.

③ Mat photo with cardstock and adhere.

INSIDE

① Adhere patterned paper.

② Print sentiment on photo paper; adhere.

③ Affix stickers.

Finished size: 4¼" x 6"

SUPPLIES: *Cardstock:* (black, kraft) Bazzill Basics Paper *Patterned paper:* (Aggie from June Bug collection; Peppermint Twist from Eskimo Kisses collection) BasicGrey *Specialty paper:* (photo) Kodak *Stickers:* (flourish, dots) BasicGrey *Font:* (Weathered SF) www.fontcubes.com *Software:* (photo editing) *Other:* (digital photo) Microsoft

Pine Tree Joy

Designer: Teri Anderson

OUTSIDE

1. Make card from cardstock.

2. Pierce tree on cardstock using template. Stitch with floss. Adhere buttons.

3. Stamp joy on cardstock, circle-punch, and adhere. Adhere cardstock snow.

4. Double-mat piece with cardstock; adhere.

INSIDE

1. Adhere cardstock strips.

2. Stamp to the world on cardstock strip; adhere. Adhere button.

Finished size: 4¼" square

SUPPLIES: *Cardstock:* (tan) Neenah Paper; (red, brown) Provo Craft; (white) WorldWin; (green) Bazzill Basics Paper *Clear stamps:* (joy to the world from Peace, Joy, Love set) Technique Tuesday *Dye ink:* (Tuxedo Black) Tsukineko *Accents:* (red buttons) *Fibers:* (brown, green floss) *Template:* (tree) Timeless Touches *Tool:* (circle punch) Fiskars

Peace

Designer: Kalyn Kepner

OUTSIDE

1. Make card from cardstock.
2. Trim felt with decorative-edge scissors and adhere.
3. Die-cut squares from patterned paper; adhere to cardstock. Stitch squares; zigzag-stitch edges.
4. Ink edges of cardstock panel and adhere.
5. Die-cut trees from patterned paper and ink edges. Die-cut trunks from cardstock, color with marker, and assemble trees. Adhere with foam tape.
6. Die-cut "Peace" from cardstock and adhere.
7. Adhere ribbon and tie on twine. Adhere rhinestones.

INSIDE

1. Trim felt with decorative-edge scissors and adhere.
2. Print sentiment on patterned paper; ink edges. Mat with patterned paper and zigzag-stitch edges. Adhere panel.
3. Die-cut trees from patterned paper and trunks from cardstock. Color trunks, assemble, and adhere with foam tape.
4. Adhere rhinestones.

Finished size: 4¼" x 5½"

SUPPLIES: *Cardstock:* (brown, kraft, white) Bazzill Basics Paper *Patterned paper:* (Spice Tea, Tree Lot, Falling Snow, Merry Happy, Olive Branch from Wassail collection) BasicGrey; (Mitten Mitten from Oh Joy collection) Cosmo Cricket *Chalk ink:* (Chestnut Roan) Clearsnap *Color medium:* (brown marker) *Accents:* (red, clear rhinestones) *Fibers:* (green ribbon) SEI; (jute twine) Westrim Crafts *Fonts:* (Chopin Script) www.dafont.com; (Arial Black) www.fonts.com *Dies:* (Reuse alphabet, trees, square) QuicKutz *Tool:* (decorative-edge scissors) *Other:* (white felt)

Wishing You Peace

Designer: Heidi Van Laar

OUTSIDE

1. Make card from cardstock; cover with cardstock.

2. Stamp sentiment on cardstock panel. Trim felt and stitch with floss; tie on. Adhere panel.

3. Adhere cardstock square. Cut out window panes.

INSIDE

1. Stamp sentiment on cardstock; adhere.

2. Trim felt and stitch with floss; adhere.

3. Stamp snowman body pieces on cardstock; cut out, cover with glitter, and adhere with foam tape.

4. Stamp snowman arms and hat on cardstock; cut out and adhere arms. Color hat, adhere, and adhere pompom and pearls.

Finished size: 5" x 7"

SUPPLIES: *Cardstock:* (white) Georgia-Pacific; (Bazzill Red, Teal, Pebble) Bazzill Basics Paper *Clear stamps:* (snowman pieces from Create Your Own set; sentiment from Holiday Sayings set) Hero Arts *Chalk ink:* (Blackbird) Clearsnap *Color medium:* (white gel pen) Sakura *Accents:* (iridescent glitter) Martha Stewart Crafts; (white pompom) Fibre-Craft; (black pearls) Kaisercraft *Fibers:* (red floss) DMC; (white floss) Coats & Clark *Other:* (white felt)

No Peeking

Designer: Becky Olsen

OUTSIDE

1. Make card from cardstock; adhere patterned paper.

2. Punch patterned paper strip and adhere.

3. Adhere patterned paper strip.

4. Stamp image and no peeking! on cardstock; color. Stitch edges with floss and attach brads.

5. Mat stamped panel with cardstock and adhere with foam tape.

6. Tie ribbon bow and adhere.

INSIDE

1. Adhere patterned paper.

2. Stamp sentiment on cardstock; mat with cardstock and adhere.

3. Punch patterned paper strip; adhere patterned paper strips.

Finished size: 5½" x 4¼"

SUPPLIES: *Cardstock:* (white) Cornish Heritage Farms; (aqua) Core'dinations *Patterned paper:* (Fruity Dots from Surfer Girl collection, Fruity Stripes from Lovin' Life collection, Sandy Shores from Summertime Girl collection) My Mind's Eye *Rubber stamps:* (image, no peeking! from Night Before Christmas set; sentiment from Joyeux Noel set) Cornish Heritage Farms *Dye ink:* (Espresso) Ranger Industries *Color medium:* (blue, brown colored pencils) Prismacolor *Accents:* (aqua glitter brads) KI Memories *Fibers:* (white ribbon) Creative Impressions; (pink floss) DMC *Tool:* (border punch) Stampin' Up!

Patchwork Merry Christmas

Designer: Jessica Witty

OUTSIDE

1. Make card from cardstock.
2. Cut three strips from patterned paper in varying widths; adhere strips side-by-side on cardstock, forming patchwork sheet.
3. Cut four strips from patchwork sheet.
4. Adhere three strips to cardstock panel.
5. Stamp "Merry Christmas" on panel and adhere.
6. Thread buttons with twine and tie on.

INSIDE

1. Stamp "Happy new year" on cardstock; adhere.
2. Adhere patchwork patterned paper strip.

Finished size: 5" x 3½"

SUPPLIES: *Cardstock:* (kraft, white) Papertrey Ink *Patterned paper:* (Chopped Tomatoes from Minestrone collection) Jillibean Soup; (Mellow Yellow Dot from Double Dot collection) BoBunny Press; (Sunrise from Early Bird collection; Sunday from Girl Friday collection) Cosmo Cricket; (Naturally Sweet from Sweet Shoppe collection) Collage Press; (Varnished Vine from Paperie collection; Battenburg from Love Notes collection) Making Memories *Clear stamps:* (Simple alphabet) Papertrey Ink *Specialty ink:* (Ripe Avocado hybrid) Papertrey Ink *Accents:* (red, yellow, green buttons) Autumn Leaves *Fibers:* (red twine) Martha Stewart Crafts

Deck the Halls

Designer: Charlene Austin

OUTSIDE

1. Make card from cardstock; adhere patterned paper.
2. Punch cardstock strip and adhere.
3. Tie on ribbon. Tie on bells with cord.
4. Apply rub-on to cardstock; adhere.
5. Adhere frame.

INSIDE

1. Adhere patterned paper strip.
2. Print sentiment on cardstock; die-cut and emboss labels from cardstock. Layer labels and adhere.
3. Emboss cardstock. Die-cut holly and adhere.
4. Adhere rhinestones.

Finished size: 4¼" x 6"

SUPPLIES: *Cardstock:* (Pure Poppy, Rustic White) Papertrey Ink; (green) *Patterned paper:* (green snowflake from Hannah Christmas pack) Anna Griffin *Accents:* (silver bells) Westrim Crafts; (cream chipboard frame) Tattered Angels; (red rhinestones) Queen & Co. *Rub-on:* (deck the halls) American Crafts *Fibers:* (red ribbon) Offray; (silver cord) *Font:* (Blimpo) www.font-zone.com *Template:* (Swiss Dots embossing) Provo Craft *Dies:* (labels) Spellbinders; (holly) Provo Craft *Tool:* (border punch) Fiskars

Get Cozy

Designer: Kim Kesti

OUTSIDE

1 Make card, following pattern on p. 283.

2 Cut hat and brim, following pattern on p. 283. Ink edges and adhere, using foam tape for brim.

3 Spell "Get cozy" with stickers.

4 Make pompom from yarn; adhere.

INSIDE

1 Cut hat and brim from patterned paper, following pattern on p. 283. Ink edges and adhere. *Note: Leave part of brim top edge unadhered to form pocket.*

2 Spell "This holiday" with stickers.

3 Trace gift card onto patterned paper; cut out. Tie on yarn.

4 Adhere gift card to patterned paper. Place gift card in pocket.

Finished size: 5¾" x 4½"

SUPPLIES: *Cardstock:* (Parakeet) Bazzill Basics Paper *Patterned paper:* (Frosted Berry, Tee Time from Lemonade collection) BasicGrey *Chalk ink:* (Lime Pastel, pink) Clearsnap *Stickers:* (Lemonade alphabet) BasicGrey *Fibers:* (pink yarn) Coats & Clark *Other:* (gift card)

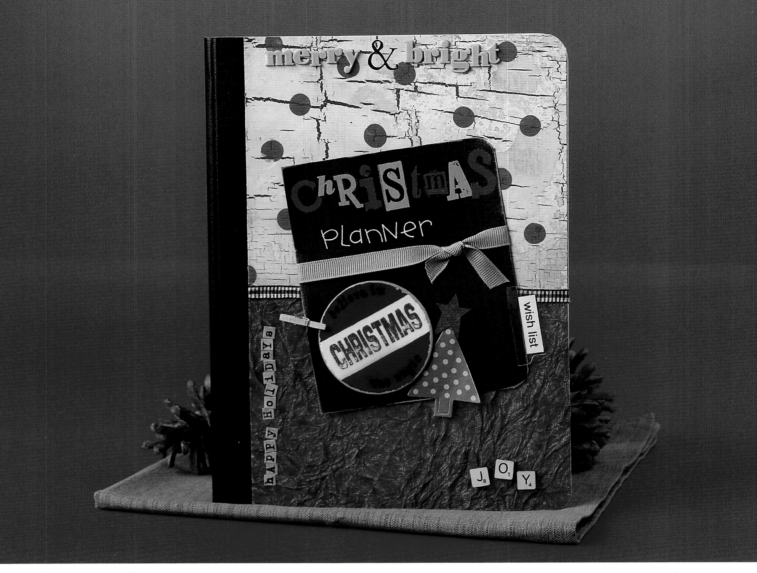

Christmas Planner

Designer: Wendy Johnson

Finished size: 7½" x 9¾"

Combine raised textures (handmade paper, wood
and acrylic accents) and flat textures (crackled
paper, funky rub-ons).

SUPPLIES: *Patterned cardstock:* (Black) Provo Craft *Patterned paper:*
(American Dots) Rusty Pickle *Specialty paper:* (Red textured) Provo Craft
Pigment ink: (Frost White) Clearsnap *Accents:* (green plastic letters, index
tab) Heidi Swapp; (Christmas chipboard coaster) Li'l Davis Designs; (Scrabble
tile accents) EK Success; (tree die cut) Moonshine Design; (mini clothespin)
Artmark Chicago Ltd.; (rusty metal star) Rusty Tin *Font:* (Arial) Microsoft *Rub-
ons:* (green, red alphabets) Making Memories; (white alphabet) Doodlebug
Design *Fibers:* (black gingham ribbon) Offray; (green grosgrain ribbon)
Stickers: (ampersand) Creative Imaginations; (brown alphabet) Karen Foster
Design *Tools:* corner rounder punch *Other:* (composition notebook) Mead

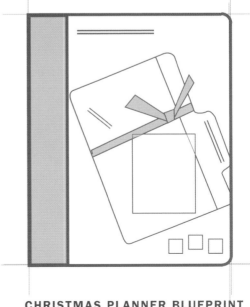

CHRISTMAS PLANNER BLUEPRINT

5 Colorful Tree Gift Box
STEPS

Designer: Danielle Flanders

① Make tree box, following pattern p. 282. ② Cut strip of patterned paper; adhere. ③ Trim sentiment die cut and adhere with foam tape. ④ Adhere beaded swirl. ⑤ Wrap ribbon around top; tie bow.

Finished size: 8½" x 9" x 8½"

SUPPLIES: *Patterned paper:* (White Christmas, 5th Avenue from Tinsel Town collection) Pink Paislee *Accents:* (sentiment die cut) Pink Paislee; (black rhinestone swirl) Prima *Fibers:* (pink ribbon) Offray *Adhesive:* (foam tape)

Pretty Paper Tags

Designer: Kristen Swain

LOVE

1 Cut patterned paper to finished size, using decorative-edge scissors. **2** Cut rectangle of patterned paper; mat with patterned paper and adhere. **3** Cut square of patterned paper; adhere. **4** Cut triangles and strips of patterned paper; adhere to create trees. *Note: Adhere one tree with foam tape.* **5** Adhere buttons; tie twine bow and adhere. **6** Cut rectangle of patterned paper; attach brad and spell "Love" with stickers. Adhere. **7** Set eyelets; knot ribbon ends through eyelets to create hanger.

NOEL

1 Cut patterned paper to finished size, using decorative-edge scissors. **2** Cut rectangle of patterned paper; mat with patterned paper and adhere. **3** Cut rectangle of patterned paper; adhere. **4** Cut rectangle of patterned paper; attach brad and spell "Noel" with stickers. Adhere. **5** Die-cut snowflakes from patterned paper; adhere. *Note: Adhere one snowflake with foam tape.* **6** Thread button with twine; tie bow and adhere. **7** Set eyelets; knot ribbon ends through eyelets to create hanger.

JOY

1 Cut patterned paper to finished size, using decorative-edge scissors. **2** Cut rectangle of patterned paper; mat with patterned paper and adhere. **3** Cut strip of patterned paper; adhere. **4** Cut rectangle of patterned paper; attach brad and spell "Joy" with stickers. Adhere. **5** Cut out bird from patterned paper; adhere. **6** Cut wing shape from patterned paper; adhere with foam tape. Thread button with twine; tie bow and adhere. **7** Set eyelets; knot ribbon ends through eyelets to create hanger.

Finished size: love 3" x 4½", noel 4¾" x 3¼", joy 3¼" x 4¾"

SUPPLIES: *Patterned paper:* (Grey Cube on Worn Background; Landings Way, Whitaker Street, River Walk, Lockwood Lane, Baywood Lane from Laurel collection) Scenic Route *Accents:* (pearlescent buttons) BoBunny Press; (assorted yellow, blue buttons) Darice; (orange, pink, blue brads) Jo-Ann Stores; (green, pink eyelets) We R Memory Keepers *Stickers:* (Tiny Alpha alphabet) Making Memories *Fibers:* (pink stitched, orange ribbon) We R Memory Keepers; (yellow twine) The Beadery *Adhesive:* (foam tape) 3M *Dies:* (snowflakes) Provo Craft *Tool:* (decorative-edge scissors) Jo-Ann Stores

Embossed Snowflake Gift Bag

Designer: Lisa Johnson

1 Stamp snowflakes on bag; adhere glitter. **2** Cut rectangle of cardstock; ink edges, stamp sentiment, and adhere with foam tape. **3** Punch scalloped circles from cardstock; stamp snowflakes and emboss. Adhere with foam tape. **4** Cut strip of cardstock; ink edges. Stamp snow; emboss. Adhere strip with foam tape. **5** Knot ribbon; adhere.

Finished size: 4¾" x 9"

SUPPLIES: *Cardstock:* (Night Sky Shimmer, Spring Moss, Pure Poppy, Dark Chocolate) Papertrey Ink *Clear stamps:* (snowflakes, snow, sentiment from Rustic Snowflakes set) Papertrey Ink *Pigment ink:* (Fresh Snow) Papertrey Ink *Specialty ink:* (Dark Chocolate hybrid) Papertrey Ink *Embossing powder:* (white) Stewart Superior Corp. *Accent:* (pearlescent glitter) Stewart Superior Corp. *Fibers:* (red ribbon) Papertrey Ink *Adhesive:* (foam tape) *Tool:* (scalloped circle punch) Marvy Uchida *Other:* (kraft paper bag) Papertrey Ink

White Poinsettia Gift Wrap

Designer: Kim Hughes

1 Stamp images on cardstock. **2** Cut 12 petals from cardstock; adhere glitter. Roll petals over finger to add dimension; adhere in layers. **3** Adhere rhinestones.

Finished size: As needed

SUPPLIES: *Cardstock:* (Tawny Light) Prism; (white) Core'dinations *Rubber stamps:* (Pin Dot Scrapblock, Aged Sheet Music Scrapblock) Cornish Heritage Farms *Dye ink:* (Sand Castle) Storage Units, Ink *Paint:* (white) *Accents:* (white glitter) Doodlebug Design; (green rhinestones) Me & My Big Ideas

Merry Christmas Tag

Designer: Sharon Laakkonen

❶ Create 2¼" x 3" project in software.
❷ Drop in borders and lines. ❸ Type "Merry Christmas!", "To:", and "From:".
❹ Print on cardstock; trim. ❺ Fold ribbon into V; staple to tag. ❻ Write names.

Finished size: 1½" x 2¼"

SUPPLIES: All supplies from Papertrey Ink unless otherwise noted. *Cardstock:* (Vintage Cream) *Clear stamps:* (swirl, star from Out of the Box set; sentiment from Out of the Box Sentiments set) *Specialty ink:* (Ripe Avocado, Spring Moss, Pure Poppy, Dark Chocolate hybrid) *Accent:* (pearlescent glitter) Stewart Superior Corp. *Fibers:* (cream stitched, green ribbon); (white string) no source *Tool:* (tag punch) Marvy Uchida

5 STEPS Shiny Star Tag

Designer: Lisa Johnson

❶ Punch tag from cardstock; ink edges.
❷ Stamp swirl, stars, and sentiment. Adhere glitter. ❸ Layer ribbon; tie bow and attach to tag with string.

Finished size: 2½" x 3⅛"

SUPPLIES: *Cardstock:* (kraft) *Color medium:* (black pen) EK Success *Accents:* (staples) *Digital elements:* (floral border, journaling lines from Vintage Garden kit) www.primahybrid.com *Fibers:* (red ribbon) *Font:* (Times New Roman) Microsoft *Software:* (photo editing) Adobe

5 STEPS Classic Christmas Tags

Designer: Ivanka Lentle

❶ Die-cut label and frame from patterned paper; adhere together to create tag. Punch hole; thread with twine. ❷ Adhere flowers; thread button with twine and adhere.
❸ Spell sentiment with stickers. ❹ Tie on ribbon.

Finished size: 2½" x 3½"

SUPPLIES: *Patterned paper:* (Merry Christmas from Cheer collection) Kaisercraft *Accents:* (newsprint flowers) Prima; (burgundy flowers) Hero Arts; (green buttons) BasicGrey *Stickers:* (Tiny Alpha alphabet) Making Memories *Fibers:* (burgundy, green ribbon; twine) May Arts *Dies:* (label, label frame) QuicKutz

Christmas Cookie Jar

Designer: Lisa Johnson

❶ Paint container lid, let dry, and adhere ribbon. ❷ Punch circle from cardstock, ink edges, and adhere. ❸ Stamp trees and sentiment on cardstock. Stamp remaining images on cardstock to create snowman. ❹ Color stamped piece with markers. Tear cardstock edge and adhere. ❺ Cut stamped piece into circle; ink edges. ❻ Adhere liquid appliqué and glitter. Adhere piece to container lid.

Finished size: 4½" diameter x 6¼" height

DESIGNER TIP

If you're feeling ambitious, make your favorite cookies and include them in the jar. If you're pressed for time, fill the container with store-bought cookies...your recipient will never know the difference!

SUPPLIES: *Cardstock:* (kraft, white) Papertrey Ink *Clear stamps:* (snowman, face, mittens, scarf, trees, arms from Made of Snow set; Christmas cookies from Holiday Treats set) Papertrey Ink *Pigment ink:* (Fresh Snow) Papertrey Ink *Specialty ink:* (True Black hybrid) Papertrey Ink *Color medium:* (assorted markers) Copic *Paint:* (Metallic Gray) Delta *Accent:* (white glitter) Stewart Superior Corp. *Fibers:* (blue ribbon) Papertrey Ink *Adhesive:* (foam tape) *Tool:* (circle punch) Marvy Uchida *Other:* (white liquid appliqué) Marvy Uchida; (plastic container)

MAKE YOUR OWN SUGAR SCRUB

INGREDIENTS
½ c. olive oil
1 c. sugar
10 drops peppermint oil

DIRECTIONS
Combine olive oil and sugar in bowl.
Mix well. Stir in peppermint oil.

Christmas Cardinal Bookmark

Designer: Aaron Brown

❶ Stamp leaves and branches on cardstock. Trim and double-mat with cardstock. ❷ Stamp cardinal on cardstock. Trim, ink edges, and accent with marker and glitter. Adhere pieces together. Adhere piece to bookmark with foam tape. ❸ String bead on ribbon, knot end, and adhere to back of bookmark. ❹ Adhere cardstock to back of bookmark.

Finished size: 2½" square

SUPPLIES: *Cardstock:* (Cranberry, Colonial White, black) Close To My Heart *Clear stamps:* (branch, leaves from Take a Bough set) Papertrey Ink; (cardinal from Bird Basics set) Close To My Heart *Dye ink:* (Cranberry, Chocolate, New England Ivy, black) Close To My Heart *Color medium:* (black marker) Close To My Heart *Accents:* (clear bead) Michaels; (yellow glitter) *Fibers:* (black striped ribbon) Close To My Heart *Adhesive:* (foam tape)

Peppermint Sugar Scrub

Designer: Leslie Webster

❶ Fill jar with sugar scrub. Tie lid with ribbon and tulle. ❷ Die-cut label from patterned paper; adhere. ❸ Print sentiment and border on cardstock; adhere. Adhere candy cane.

Finished size: 4" diameter x 3" height

SUPPLIES: *Cardstock:* (white) *Patterned paper:* (Sonoma Scrap Strip 2) Scenic Route *Accent:* (candy cane) Michaels *Fibers:* (red dotted ribbon) Michaels *Font:* (Chocolate Box) www.dafont.com *Die:* (label) Provo Craft *Other:* (white tulle, jar, sugar scrub)

A Cup of Cheer Gift Bag

Designer: Kim Hughes

❶ Cut rectangle of cardstock; stitch border and adhere. ❷ Cut strips of patterned paper; stitch borders and adhere. ❸ Cut cup and handle from patterned paper; stitch borders and adhere. ❹ Cut holly leaves from patterned paper; crease slightly and adhere. Attach brads. ❺ Cut steam swirl from vellum; adhere. ❻ Cut strip of patterned paper; stitch border. Cut strip of patterned paper; trim with decorative-edge scissors and adhere to stitched strip. Wrap ribbon around strip, tie knot, and adhere strip to gift bag. ❼ Spell "Warm wishes" with stickers. *Note: Color letters in "wishes" with pencil and marker.*

Finished size: 5¼" x 8½"

SUPPLIES: *Cardstock:* (Picket Fence) Core'dinations *Patterned paper:* (Arabella from Porcelain collection; Stone Wall, Finch from Wisteria collection) BasicGrey *Vellum:* WorldWin *Color media:* (brown colored pencil) Prismacolor; (sepia marker) Copic *Accents:* (gold glitter brads) Imaginisce *Stickers:* (Tiny Alpha, Noteworthy alphabets) Making Memories *Fibers:* (brown ribbon) Beaux Regards *Tool:* (decorative-edge scissors) Fiskars *Other:* (kraft gift bag)

Krafty Gift Wrap

Designer: Becky Olsen

❶ Cut paper to desired size. ❷ Stamp Pin Dot Scrapblock. ❸ Stamp sentiment and other images as desired. ❹ Tie wrapped gift with ribbon.

Finished size: As needed

BONUS IDEA

If you're using cling-mounted stamps, you can save a little time by creating the random pattern on a large block and stamping the paper in sections rather than stamp by stamp.

SUPPLIES: *Rubber stamps:* (snowflakes, snowman from Winter Wishes set; sentiment from Christmas Critters set; Pin Dot Scrapblock) Cornish Heritage Farms *Solvent ink:* (Opaque Cotton White) Tsukineko *Fibers:* (cream ribbon) Creative Impressions *Other:* (kraft painter's drop paper) Home Depot

5 STEPS Happy Chanukah Gift Bag
Designer: Dawn McVey

❶ Cut cardstock to fit bag front; stamp star randomly. ❷ Cut strip of cardstock; stamp menorahs and emboss. Adhere to star piece. ❸ Cut strip of cardstock; punch edge and adhere to piece. ❹ Wrap twill around piece; tie bow and adhere entire piece to bag front. ❺ Stamp dreidel on cardstock; emboss and punch into scalloped oval. Stamp sentiment on cardstock; round two corners. Punch holes in stamped pieces; tie to bag with ribbon.

Finished size: 3¼" x 7¼"

5 STEPS Tiny Hanukkah Gift Box
Designer: Alicia Thelin

❶ Make box from cardstock. ❷ Cut strip of cardstock; fold around box and adhere. ❸ Wrap ribbon around box; tie knot and adhere. ❹ Stamp sentiment and gift on cardstock; punch circle. ❺ Punch tag from cardstock; adhere stamped circle with foam tape. Attach to box with string.

Finished size: 1½" x 3¾" x 2"

SUPPLIES: All supplies from Papertrey Ink unless otherwise noted. *Cardstock:* (Night Sky Shimmer, Silver Shimmer, white) *Clear stamps:* (sentiment, menorah, dreidel from Mazel Tov set; star from Mazel Tov Additions set) *Dye ink:* (Night of Navy) Stampin' Up! *Watermark ink:* Tsukineko *Embossing powder:* (silver) *Fibers:* (white twill, silver ribbon) *Tools:* (corner rounder, scallop punches) Stampin' Up!; (scalloped oval punch) Marvy Uchida; (1/8" circle punch) *Other:* (white coffee bag)

SUPPLIES: *Cardstock:* (light blue, turquoise, yellow, white) *Rubber stamps:* (sentiment from Fancy Flexible Phrases set) Stampin' Up!; (gift) *Dye ink:* (blue, yellow) *Fibers:* (blue striped ribbon, white string) *Adhesive:* (foam tape) *Tools:* (tag, circle punches)

Christmas List Ensemble

Designer: Debbie Olson

CLIPBOARD

❶ Remove clip from board; adhere patterned paper and lightly sand edges. ❷ Mat strip of patterned paper with patterned paper. Stitch edges and adhere. ❸ Re-attach clip to board; adhere ribbon. ❹ Thread button with string; adhere. Tie ribbon with string.

NOTEBOOK

❶ Adhere patterned paper to notebook cover. Stitch patterned paper strip. ❷ Mask and stamp trees on cardstock. Apply glitter glue to star. ❸ Die-cut and emboss piece, ink edges, and adhere with foam tape. ❹ Stamp Christmas and "List" on cardstock. Die-cut and emboss, ink edges, and tie on string. Adhere with foam tape. ❺ Adhere ribbon behind tag. ❻ Thread string through button; adhere. ❼ Adhere loop of ribbon to back cover. Place rolled patterned paper in barrel of pen. Place pen in ribbon loop.

Finished sizes: clipboard 4½" x 9", notebook 3" x 5"

SUPPLIES: Cardstock: (Vintage Cream) Papertrey Ink Patterned paper: (Cup O' Cheer, Tinsel to the Top from Snowy Jo collection) Imaginisce Clear stamps: (Christmas from Merry & Bright set; circled tree, flourished tree, swirled tree from Merry & Bright Additions set; Simple Alphabet) Papertrey Ink Dye ink: (Antique Linen) Ranger Industries Pigment ink: (Oasis Green, Tea Leaves, Red Magic, Gingerbread) Tsukineko Accents: (ivory buttons) Papertrey Ink; (blue glitter glue) Ranger Industries Fibers: (green, blue stitched ribbon) Papertrey Ink; (white string) Adhesive: (foam tape) Dies: (deckled edge rectangle, tag) Spellbinders Other: (clipboard) Stampin' Up!; (pen, notepad)

Metallic Monogram Ornament

Designer: Layle Koncar

❶ Adhere patterned paper behind light switch cover. Affix sticker. ❷ Tie on ribbons. ❸ Attach jump rings to star, pendant, and key. Attach to ribbon.

Finished size: 3" x 8"

Merry & Bright Ornament

Designer: Juliana Michaels

❶ Cut ball in half. ❷ Cut circles from patterned paper; distress and ink edges. Layer and adhere to cut face of ball, using pins to secure. Adhere chipboard sentiment. ❸ Punch circles from patterned paper. Thread bead on pin, stick through patterned paper circle. Thread another bead and larger circle; attach to ball. Repeat until ball is covered. ❹ Tie ribbon; attach with pin.

Finished size: 3" diameter

SUPPLIES: *Patterned paper:* (Black Bookprint from Vintage collection) Jenni Bowlin *Accents:* (silver jump rings) Beadalon; (gold star) Nunn Design; (clear glass pendant) Elizabeth Ward & Co.; (black vintage key) *Sticker:* (foam letter) Adornit-Carolee's Creations *Fibers:* (black, brown ribbon) May Arts *Other:* (chrome light switch cover) Home Depot

SUPPLIES: *Patterned paper:* (Scrap Strip 2, Rosalie Drive, Verano Avenue, Madera Street from Sonoma collection) Scenic Route *Chalk ink:* (brown) Clearsnap *Accents:* (chipboard sentiment) Scenic Route; (silver stick pins, silver beads) *Tools:* (½", 1" circle punches) Stampin' Up! *Other:* (styrofoam ball) Hobby Lobby

Red-Nosed Rudolph Treat Jar

Designer: Tenia Nelson

❶ Cut strip of patterned paper; wrap around jar and adhere.
❷ Punch circle from cardstock; adhere to lid. ❸ Punch scalloped circle from cardstock; adhere rhinestones and adhere to jar with foam tape. ❹ Stamp image on cardstock; punch circle, mat with cardstock, and adhere with foam tape. Adhere rhinestone.
❺ Wrap ribbon around jar and tie bow.

Finished size: 2" x 3" x 2"

Let It Snow Gift Jar

Designer: Melissa Phillips

❶ Cut tag from cardstock. ❷ Stamp snowflakes; emboss and adhere glitter. Punch hole and adhere crocheted trim. ❸ Stamp sentiment on cardstock; cut out and punch hole. ❹ Cut square of fabric with decorative-edge scissors; Cover lid with fabric; wrap ribbon around and tie bow. ❺ Attach tag and sentiment with twine.

Finished size: 2¾" diameter x 2½" height

SUPPLIES: All supplies from Stampin' Up! unless otherwise noted. *Cardstock:* (Real Red, Old Olive, Very Vanilla) *Patterned paper:* (large dots from Dashing collection) *Rubber stamp:* (reindeer from Merry & Bright set) *Dye ink:* (Chocolate Chip) *Accents:* (red rhinestones) Mark Richards *Fibers:* (red ribbon) *Adhesive:* (foam tape) *Tools:* (scalloped circle, 1¼" circle, 1⅜" circle punches) *Other:* (plastic jar with lid) Making Memories

SUPPLIES: *Cardstock:* (white) Papertrey Ink *Clear stamps:* (snowflakes, sentiment from Merry & Bright set) Papertrey Ink *Pigment ink:* (Vintage Cream) Papertrey Ink *Specialty ink:* (Pure Poppy hybrid) Papertrey Ink *Embossing powder:* (clear) Ranger Industries *Accent:* (white glitter) Doodlebug Design *Fibers:* (red ribbon) Papertrey Ink; (white crocheted trim, twine) *Tools:* (⅛" circle punch, decorative-edge scissors) *Other:* (green plaid fabric; glass jar with lid)

Homespun Christmas

Celebrate the holidays with these paper creations that show off touches of homemade charm.

HAPPY HOLIDAYS

DESIGNER TIP
Save time and supplies by stitching the buttons directly onto the wreath.

DESIGNER TIP
When picking a font to use for your sentiment, use a thin stroke so that it's easily covered by your floss.

Winter Wishes Wreath Card

Designer: Sarah Martina Parker

1. Make card from cardstock. Ink edges.
2. Die-cut scalloped circle from felt; die-cut circle from piece to form wreath. Stitch buttons on using twine and adhere twine bow.
3. Adhere felt leaves and adhere wreath.
4. Stamp winter wishes and stitch x's with twine.

Finished size: 4¼" x 5½"

Hand-Stitched Merry Card

Designer: Courtney Baker

1. Make card from cardstock. Stamp lace background.
2. Print "Merry" on patterned paper, trim, and stitch sentiment with floss.
3. Border-punch strips of cardstock, adhere to patterned paper, and adhere.
4. Stamp Christmas on cardstock, trim, and adhere using foam tape.
5. Tie on ribbon.

Finished size: 4" x 5½"

SUPPLIES: *Cardstock:* (kraft) Clear & Simple Stamps *Clear stamp:* (winter wishes from Holly Jolly set) Clear & Simple Stamps *Pigment ink:* (Cloud White) Tsukineko *Specialty ink:* (red hybrid) Clear & Simple Stamps *Accents:* (red buttons) Clear & Simple Stamps; (green felt leaves) Making Memories *Fibers:* (natural twine) Papertrey Ink *Dies:* (circle, scalloped circle) Spellbinders *Other:* (white felt)

SUPPLIES: *Cardstock:* (ivory) Gina K Designs; (Old Olive) Stampin' Up! *Patterned paper:* (Ledger from Kismet collection) Glitz Design *Rubber stamp:* (Lace Background) Hero Arts *Clear stamp:* (Christmas from Holiday Sayings set) Hero Arts *Pigment ink:* (Cranberry) Clearsnap *Watermark ink:* Tsukineko *Fibers:* (cream twill) Papertrey Ink; (white floss) DMC *Font:* (Bradley Hand) www.fonts.com *Tool:* (border punch) Fiskars

DESIGNER TIP

Julie used a glass mat to stick her colored masking tape on so she could play with the lengths first to get the tree shape before sticking it on the cardstock. If you want to be really precise, measure the strips

BONUS IDEA

Cut the masking tape in half, width wise, and make mini tree gift tags. Use a star brad instead of the die cut.

:5: Doily Peace Card

Designer: Anabelle O'Malley

1 Make card from cardstock, round right corners, and adhere doily.
2 Adhere bingo card to patterned paper and tie on twine. Adhere.
3 Paint dove, affix mistletoe sticker, and adhere.
4 Thread button with floss and adhere.

Finished size: 4¼" x 4½"

:5: Masking Tape Tree Card

Designer: Julie Day

1 Make card from cardstock.
2 Adhere strip of cardstock.
3 Rip five lengths of masking tape, color, and affix in tree shape.
4 Adhere buttons and apply rub-on. Tie on twine.
5 Die-cut star from cardstock and adhere using foam tape.

Finished size: 5½" square

SUPPLIES: *Cardstock:* (Vintage Cream) Papertrey Ink *Patterned paper:* (Peppermint Twist from Eskimo Kisses collection) BasicGrey *Paint:* (cream) Delta *Accents:* (bingo card) Jenni Bowlin Studio; (chipboard dove) Tattered Angels; (doily) Wilton Enterprises *Sticker:* (chipboard mistletoe) Making Memories *Fibers:* (natural twine, black floss) *Tool:* (corner rounder punch) EK Success

SUPPLIES: All supplies from Stampin' Up! unless otherwise noted. *Cardstock:* (Chocolate Chip, yellow, kraft) *Color medium:* (Old Olive marker) *Accents:* (red buttons) *Rub-on:* (be merry) *Fibers:* (natural twine) *Die:* (star) Provo Craft *Other:* (masking tape)

Believe Card

Designer: Tina Quinata

1. Make card from cardstock. Adhere patterned paper.
2. Tie on ribbon.
3. Apply rub-on to journaling card, trim, and adhere with foam tape.
4. Attach brad to snowflakes and adhere.

Finished size: 6¼" x 4¼"

Merry Ribbon Ornament Card

Designer: Ellie Augustin

1. Make card from cardstock. Ink edges.
2. Trim circle from cardstock and ink edges.
3. Bunch ribbon and adhere to circle. Adhere circle to card.
4. Punch cardstock piece to create ornament top. Adhere cord and adhere piece with foam tape.
5. Tie bow with twine and adhere.
6. Stamp Merry Christmas.

Finished size: 4¼" x 5½"

SUPPLIES: *Cardstock:* (red) Michaels *Patterned paper:* (No. 2 Flower Stripes from Out & About collection) My Mind's Eye *Accents:* (white glitter snowflakes) Hobby Lobby; (blue jeweled fabric brad) K&Company; (journaling card) Luxe Designs *Rub-on:* (believe) Melissa Frances *Fibers:* (red gingham ribbon) Hobby Lobby *Tool:* (decorative-edge scissors) EK Success

SUPPLIES: *Cardstock:* (black, white, kraft) Papertrey Ink *Rubber stamp:* (merry Christmas from Teeny Tiny Wishes set) Stampin' Up! *Dye ink:* (Chamomile) Papertrey Ink; (Whisper White) Stampin' Up! *Specialty ink:* (True Black hybrid) Papertrey Ink *Fibers:* (silver cord) Michaels; (cream twine) Papertrey Ink; (red, green ribbon) Stampin' Up! *Tools:* (border punch; circle cutter) Stampin' Up!

BONUS IDEAS

Change the size of the crochet hook and thread to create different sized flowers.

Change the saying and the center of the flowers to make a lovely wedding invitation.

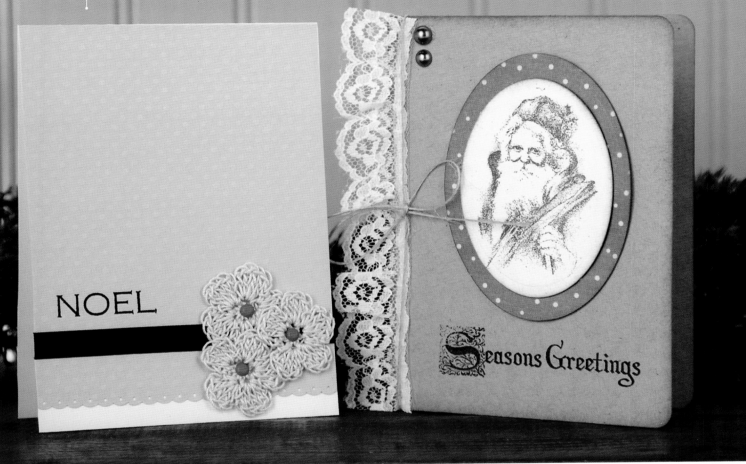

Crocheted Noel Card

Designer: Asela Hopkins

1. Make card from cardstock.
2. Trim cardstock, border punch, and stamp noel.
3. Adhere ribbon.
4. Crochet flowers using following pattern: Round 1: Chain 2, 5 single crochets from hook. Join with slip stitch to first single crochet. (Chain 2, 3 double crochets, chain 2, slip stitch in the same single crochet.) Do 5 times making 5 petals. Trim. Repeat 2 times.
5. Attach flowers using brads.
6. Adhere panel.

Finished size: 4¼" x 5½"

:5: Vintage Santa Greetings Card

Designer: Kelley Eubanks

1. Make card from cardstock, round right corners, and ink edges.
2. Stamp santa on cardstock, die-cut into oval, and ink edges. Mat with die-cut patterned paper oval. Adhere.
3. Stamp season's greetings.
4. Adhere lace, tie on twine, and adhere pearls.

Finished size: 4¼" x 5½"

SUPPLIES: *Cardstock:* (ivory) Neenah Paper; (Sandbox embossed) Bazzill Basics Paper *Rubber stamp:* (noel from First Christmas set) Gina K Designs *Specialty ink:* (black hybrid) Stewart Superior Corp. *Accents:* (orange brads) Stampin' Up! *Fibers:* (cream crochet thread) DMC; (black ribbon) *Tools:* (border punch) EK Success; (size 3/D crochet hook)

SUPPLIES: *Cardstock:* (Vintage Cream, kraft) Papertrey Ink *Patterned paper:* (The Night Before Christmas from Christmas Past collection) Graphic 45 *Clear stamps:* (season's greetings, santa from Vintage Christmas set) Crafty Secrets *Dye ink:* (Vintage Photo) Ranger Industries; (Real Red) Stampin' Up! *Specialty ink:* (True Black hybrid) Papertrey Ink *Accents:* (silver pearls) Prima *Fibers:* (natural twine) Papertrey Ink; (cream lace) Hobby Lobby *Dies:* (ovals) Spellbinders *Tool:* (corner rounder punch) Stampin' Up!

DESIGNER TIP

Adhering the center of the banner to the card first helps ensure the placement of the outer elements are even.

BONUS IDEA

This card design and color scheme works well for any Jewish holiday such as Rosh Hashana or Passover.

DESIGNER TIPS

Use a sewing machine without thread to poke even stitching holes before hand-stitching.

Trace around stickers to get the perfect shape for stitching, as Kim did for the heart.

Chanukah Blessings Card

Designer: Allison Landy

1. Make card from cardstock. Adhere patterned paper and zigzag-stitch border.
2. Spray patterned paper with ink, adhere to chipboard banners, and trim.
3. Adhere banners together to create stars.
4. Punch stars, tie together with twine, and adhere. Staple.
5. Affix stickers to spell "Chanukah blessings".
6. Thread twine through button and adhere.

Finished size: 6¾" x 5"

Green Peace on Earth Card

Designer: Kim Hughes

1. Make card from cardstock.
2. Trim patterned paper, stitch with floss, and adhere.
3. Stitch heart with floss.
4. Affix globe and earth stickers. Write "Peace on" with pen.

Finished size: 3½" x 6"

SUPPLIES: *Cardstock:* (Espresso) Bazzill Basics Paper *Patterned paper:* (Slate from Little Sprout collection) Crate Paper; (Typo from Anthology collection) Studio Calico *Specialty ink:* (Latte spray) Maya Road *Accents:* (white button) Jesse James & Co.; (mini chipboard banner) Maya Road; (white staples) *Stickers:* (Tiny Alpha alphabet) Making Memories *Fibers:* (brown twine) May Arts *Tool:* (⅛" circle punch)

SUPPLIES: *Cardstock:* (Snowflake) Core'dinations *Patterned paper:* (Butter Creams from Christmas Mint collection) SEI *Color medium:* (black pen) Sakura *Stickers:* (globe, earth) Doodlebug Design *Fibers:* (green floss) DMC

BONUS IDEA
You could easily use a lovely holiday sentiment stamp for this card instead of the sticker sentiment used here.

Holiday Recipes Album Cover

Designer: Betsy Veldman

COVER

❶ Make album cover from cardstock. Ink edges of patterned paper and adhere.

❷ Trim oval from patterned paper; ink edges. Mat with cardstock and trim with decorative-edge scissors. Stitch and adhere.

❸ Stamp holiday recipes on cardstock, trim, and ink edges. Adhere.

❹ Trim strip of patterned paper; fan-fold to create apron skirt. Trim apron top from patterned paper and adhere to skirt. Adhere.

❺ Adhere twill and twine bow. Thread buttons with twine and adhere.

❻ Punch heart from patterned paper and adhere using foam tape.

ALBUM

❶ Die-cut patterned paper to create divider pages.

❷ Stamp cookies, treats, and chocolates on cardstock; trim, and adhere.

❸ Trim cardstock pieces to create pages and back cover.

❹ Bind pages, dividers, and covers using binding machine.

Finished size: 5½" x 5"

Just for You Card

Designer: Amy Heller

❶ Make card from cardstock, round top corners, and border punch right side.

❷ Trim patterned paper, round top corners, and adhere.

❸ Adhere rickrack, affix sticker, and adhere rhinestones.

❹ Adhere felt poinsettia.

Finished size: 4¼" x 6½"

SUPPLIES: *Cardstock:* (Ripe Avocado, Pure Poppy, Rustic Cream) Papertrey Ink *Patterned paper:* (Fill the Stockings, Sing the Carols, Wrap the Presents, Write the Cards from Very Merry collection; Ice Cream from Fly a Kite collection) October Afternoon *Clear stamps:* (holiday recipes from Holiday Button Bits set; cookies, treats, chocolates from Just for You set) Papertrey Ink *Pigment ink:* (Fresh Snow) Papertrey Ink *Chalk ink:* (Creamy Brown) Clearsnap *Specialty ink:* (Pure Poppy hybrid) Papertrey Ink *Accents:* (red buttons) Papertrey Ink *Fibers:* (red twill, cream twine) Papertrey Ink *Die:* (recipe divider page) Provo Craft *Tools:* (decorative-edge scissors) Provo Craft; (heart punch) EK Success; (binding machine) Zutter *Other:* (white binding wires) Zutter

SUPPLIES: *Cardstock:* (cream) Bazzill Basics Paper *Patterned paper:* (Powdered Sugar from Eskimo Kisses collection) BasicGrey *Accents:* (felt poinsettia) BasicGrey; (pink rhinestones) Michaels *Sticker:* (sentiment) October Afternoon *Fibers:* (pink rickrack) Close To My Heart *Tools:* (corner rounder punch; border punch) Fiskars

DESIGNER TIP

Lightly draw the swirl using a pencil before hand-stitching.

BONUS IDEA

This card would look lovely with either an angel or snowman in the "snow" as well.

DESIGNER TIP

Let the ink dry completely before cutting and stitching.

BONUS IDEA

Try stamping a variety of images on felt to create a homemade embellishment for any occasion. Darker inks stand out and work the best on felt.

Snowy Christmas Tree Card

Designer: Laura Onosato

1. Make card from cardstock.
2. Stamp sheet music on cardstock, trim, and adhere.
3. Zigzag-stitch border and stitch swirl.
4. Die-cut Christmas tree from patterned paper, wrap with twine, and adhere.
5. Die-cut trunk from cardstock and adhere. Attach brad.

Finished size: 5" x 4¼"

Holiday Greetings Card

Designer: Maile Belles

1. Make card from cardstock.
2. Trim circle from cardstock and adhere using foam tape.
3. Stamp tree and trunk on felt, trim, and adhere together. Stitch and sew on buttons with floss. Adhere.
4. Stamp holiday greetings and tie on ribbon.

Finished size: 4" x 5½"

SUPPLIES: *Cardstock:* (Melon Berry, kraft) Papertrey Ink; (dark brown) Bazzill Basics Paper *Patterned paper:* (green dot from 2008 Bitty Dot Basics collection) Papertrey Ink *Rubber stamp:* (Aged Sheet Music) Cornish Heritage Farms *Watermark ink:* Tsukineko *Accent:* (white glitter brad) We R Memory Keepers *Fibers:* (natural twine) Papertrey Ink *Die:* (Christmas tree) Provo Craft

SUPPLIES: All supplies from Papertrey Ink unless otherwise noted. *Cardstock:* (white, kraft) *Clear stamps:* (tree, trunk from Tree Trimming Trio set; holiday greetings from Signature Christmas set) *Specialty ink:* (Ripe Avocado, Dark Chocolate hybrid) *Accents:* (pink buttons) *Fibers:* (aqua ribbon); (aqua, white floss) DMC *Tool:* (circle cutter) Provo Craft *Other:* (cream felt)

Candy Cane & Cocoa Card

Designer: Kim Kesti

1. Make card from cardstock.
2. Trim cardstock, stamp sentiment, and round corners.
3. Tie on ribbon and adhere.
4. Stamp candy cane and hot cocoa, stitch with floss, and round corners.
5. Mat with batting, stitch, and adhere.

Finished size: 4¼" x 6¾"

Season's Greetings Bird Card

Designer: Betsy Veldman

1. Make card from cardstock. Apply bird transfer using iron.
2. Stamp season's greetings and adhere rhinestones.
3. Die-cut border from felt and adhere; zigzag-stitch.
4. Adhere strip of patterned paper and zigzag-stitch.
5. Thread ribbon with twine and tie on.

Finished size: 4¼" x 5½"

SUPPLIES: Cardstock: (Candy Apple, Vanilla, kraft) Bazzill Basics Paper Clear stamps: (candy cane, hot cocoa, sentiment from Cozy Moments set) Hero Arts Pigment ink: (Cardinal, black) Tsukineko Fibers: (red ribbon) Offray; (red floss) Tool: (corner rounder punch) Other: (cotton batting)

SUPPLIES: Cardstock: (Vintage Cream) Papertrey Ink Patterned paper: (Wrap the Presents from Very Merry collection) October Afternoon Clear stamp: (season's greetings from Communique Curves set) Papertrey Ink Chalk ink: (Creamy Brown) Clearsnap Specialty ink: (Pure Poppy hybrid) Papertrey Ink Accents: (red button) Papertrey Ink; (red rhinestones) Kaisercraft Fibers: (natural twine) Papertrey Ink Die: (eyelet lace border) Papertrey Ink Other: (white felt) Papertrey Ink; (vintage bird transfer)

For the Love of Music

Sheet music prints are all the trendy rage right now, and it's easy to master the musical motif with inspiration from these projects that are sure to make your recipients sing with delight!

DID YOU KNOW?
Look closely at Lisa's poinsettia stamp.
It subtly continues the music motif!

5 STEPS Holiday Cheer Card

Designer: Lisa Henke

1. Make card from cardstock.
2. Stamp poinsettias and holiday cheer.
3. Affix candy cane.
4. Tie on ribbon. Thread twine through button and tie to bow.

Finished size: 4¼" x 5½"

Love Songbird Card

Designer: Kazan Clark

1. Make card from cardstock.
2. Trim patterned paper and adhere. Die-cut border strips from patterned paper; adhere and bend edges up slightly. Trim card bottom to match border strip.
3. Adhere ribbon. Stitch with floss.
4. Stamp bird; emboss.
5. Trim patterned paper in spiral and fold to form rose; adhere. Thread button with floss and adhere.
6. Stamp sentiment on cardstock. Trim into tag and ink edges. Attach eyelet; tie on twine and adhere.

Finished size: 4½" x 5½"

SUPPLIES: *Cardstock:* (kraft) Stampin' Up! *Rubber stamp:* (poinsettia from Hodge Podge of Happiness set) Unity Stamp Co. *Clear stamp:* (holiday cheer from Holiday Treats set) Papertrey Ink *Dye ink:* (Real Red) Stampin' Up! *Pigment ink:* (Whisper White) Stampin' Up! *Accent:* (red button) Papertrey Ink *Sticker:* (chipboard candy cane) Cosmo Cricket *Fibers:* (ivory twine) Papertrey Ink; (black ribbon) Stampin' Up!

SUPPLIES: *Cardstock:* (Creamy Cocoa) WorldWin *Patterned paper:* (Festive Floral/Red Herringbone from Christmas Magic collection) Little Yellow Bicycle; (Good Junk from Thrift Shop collection) October Afternoon *Clear stamps:* (sentiment from Very Square Sentiments set, bird from Birds Galore set) Inkadinkado *Embossing powder:* (glitter black) American Crafts *Accents:* (gold eyelet) Eyelet Outlet; (red button) *Fibers:* (black ribbon) Hobby Lobby; (tan, black floss) Prism; (natural twine) *Die:* (border) Spellbinders

BONUS IDEAS

You can make a flower without shimmer spray, but be sure to dampen the punched circles first to make the paper easier to crumple.

Add an aged effect by inking the edges of the punched circles before assembling the flower.

Joyeux Noel Card

Designer: Erica Hettwer

1. Make card from cardstock. Draw stitches around edges with pen.
2. Stamp joyeux noel. Punch border strip from cardstock and adhere.
3. Punch seven scalloped circles from sheet music; spray with shimmer spray and crumple.
4. Thread twine through button and center of stacked circles to create flower; adhere.

Finished size: 5½" x 4¼"

Vintage Happy Birthday Card

Designer: Ingrid Danvers

Ink all edges.

1. Make card from cardstock. Adhere patterned paper strip.
2. Trim patterned paper panel. Die-cut border strip from book page; adhere to panel.
3. Tie ribbon around panel; thread twine through button and tie to ribbon. Adhere panel to card.
4. Thread twine through buttons; knot ends and adhere.
5. Stamp text backround on tag; stamp damask border and sentiment. Adhere tag to card with foam tape.

Finished size: 4" x 5½"

SUPPLIES: *Cardstock:* (kraft) Stampin' Up; (black) Bazzill Basics Paper *Clear stamp:* (joyeux noel from Mistletoe & Co. set) Pink Paislee *Dye ink:* (Tuxedo Black) Tsukineko *Specialty ink:* (Old Lace shimmer spray) Tattered Angels *Color medium:* (black pen) EK Success *Accent:* (tan button) American Crafts *Fibers:* (natural twine) *Tools:* (border punch) Fiskars; (scalloped circle punch) Marvy Uchida *Other:* (vintage sheet music)

SUPPLIES: *Cardstock:* (Smokey Shadow, Rustic Cream) Papertrey Ink *Patterned paper:* (Good Junk from The Thrift Shop collection) October Afternoon *Clear stamps:* (damask border, sentiment from Damask Designs set; text background from Background Basics; Text Style II set) Papertrey Ink *Dye ink:* (Tuxedo Black) Tsukineko; (Chamomile, Chai) Papertrey Ink *Pigment ink:* (Pinecone) Tsukineko *Accents:* (black buttons) Autumn Leaves; (ivory button) Papertrey Ink *Fibers:* (black striped ribbon) May Arts *Die:* (border) Papertrey Ink *Other:* (tag, book page)

:5: Musical Joy Card

Designer: Kelley Eubanks

❶ Make card from cardstock; round bottom corners.

❷ Trim and adhere sheet music.

❸ Apply joy rub-on.

❹ Tie on twill.

Finished size: 5½" x 4¼"

:5: Follow Your Dreams Card

Designer: Clouds Shadler

❶ Make card from cardstock.

❷ Stamp Music Score on cardstock; stamp butterflies. Trim and mat with cardstock.

❸ Tie on ribbon and adhere with foam tape.

❹ Punch five scalloped circles from book pages; thread twine through button and center of stacked circles to create flower; crumple edges and adhere.

❺ Stamp sentiment on cardstock; trim and adhere with foam tape. Adhere pearls.

Finished size: 3¾" x 5¼"

SUPPLIES: *Cardstock:* (black) Papertrey Ink *Rub-on:* (joy) Hambly Screen Prints *Fibers:* (red twill) May Arts *Tool:* (corner rounder punch) Stampin' Up! *Other:* (sheet music)

SUPPLIES: *Cardstock:* (Sahara Sand, white) Stampin' Up!; (black) Bazzill Basics Paper *Rubber stamps:* (Music Score) Stampendous!; (butterfly from Charming set) Stampin' Up! *Clear stamp:* (sentiment from Fillable Frames #3 set) Papertrey Ink *Dye ink:* (Basic Black, Going Gray) Stampin' Up! *Accents:* (white button) Papertrey Ink; (white pearls) Michaels *Fibers:* (ivory ribbon) Offray *Tool:* (scalloped circle punch) Stampin' Up! *Other:* (book pages)

DESIGNER TIP

Positioning a clear stamp well on an acrylic block can be tricky. Try laying the stamp face down on a piece of scrap paper and bringing the block to it. You'll find it a lot easier to stamp a straight image when the stamp and block are lined up.

DESIGNER TIP

Adhere your cardstock tree trunk with a bit of the strip hanging off the tag. Flip it over and trim off the excess, using the circle edge as your guide.

BONUS IDEA

This simple card lends itself well to mass production, but pre-made embellishments could get pricey. Try substituting a punched butterfly, and add your own rhinestones.

Musical Tree Tag

Designer: Courtney Baker

1. Die-cut circles from cardstock and patterned paper; adhere patterned paper to cardstock.
2. Stamp background on cardstock; trim into tree shape.
3. Trim trunk from cardstock. Adhere tree and trunk.
4. Stamp sentiment on cardstock and adhere with foam tape.
5. Attach eyelet; tie on twine.

Finished size: 2¾" diameter

Christmas Butterfly Card

Designer: Kelly Marie Alvarez

1. Make card from cardstock.
2. Stamp merry Christmas.
3. Adhere butterfly.

Finished size: 3" square

SUPPLIES: *Cardstock:* (Spring Moss) Papertrey Ink.; (ivory) Gina K Designs *Patterned paper:* (Ledger from Kismet collection) Glitz Design *Clear stamps:* (music background from Distressing 2 set) Glitz Design; (sentiment from Holiday Sayings set) Hero Arts *Pigment ink:* (Onyx Black) Tsukineko *Specialty ink:* (Moulin Rouge hybrid) Stewart Superior Corp. *Accent:* (green eyelet) Making Memories *Fibers:* (brown/white twine) Daisy Bucket Designs *Dies:* (circles) Spellbinders

SUPPLIES: *Cardstock:* (Desert Storm) Neenah Paper *Clear stamp:* (merry Christmas from Holiday Sayings set) Hero Arts *Pigment ink:* (Red Magic) Tsukineko *Accent:* (embellished butterfly) Jenni Bowlin Studio

DESIGNER TIPS

To cut letters from patterned paper without the outline showing, create sentiment in Microsoft Word using Word Art and reverse the text using the "Flip Horizontal" rotation option. Print on the back of patterned paper and cut out.

When using patterned letters, mount on cardstock in a strong contrasting color and keep the rest of your design simple.

5 Colorful Noel Card

Designer: Charity Hassel

1. Make card from cardstock.
2. Trim patterned paper into strips; loop, staple ends, and adhere.
3. Trim patterned paper and adhere with foam tape; adhere rhinestones.
4. Affix stickers to spell "Noel".

Finished size: 6½" x 4"

5 Heaven & Nature Sing Card

Designer: Beth Opel

1. Make card from cardstock; print "Heaven & nature" on card.
2. Trim and adhere cardstock.
3. Print "Sing" on patterned paper (see "Designer Tip"); fussy-cut and adhere with foam tape.
4. Adhere trim.
5. Thread button with floss and adhere with foam tape.

Finished size: 4" x 5½"

SUPPLIES: *Cardstock:* (ivory) Prism *Patterned paper:* (Sing the Carols, Fill the Stockings from Very Merry collection) October Afternoon *Accents:* (clear rhinestones) Doodlebug Design *Stickers:* (Very Merry alphabet) October Afternoon

SUPPLIES: *Cardstock:* (white) American Crafts; (blue) Die Cuts With a View *Patterned paper:* (Sprightly from Nerdy Bird collection) Sassafras *Accent:* (red button) *Fibers:* (red pom-pom trim) We R Memory Keepers; (blue floss) Bazzill Basics Paper *Fonts:* (Century Gothic) www.fonts.com; (Elephant) Microsoft *Software:* (word processing) Microsoft

DESIGNER TIP
Use a bit of repositionable adhesive to hold the die in place while you die-cut a stamped image.

Jingle Bells Card

Designer: Kimberly Crawford

1. Make card from cardstock.
2. Trim and adhere cardstock.
3. Trim patterned paper; distress edges and adhere. Adhere lace.
4. Stamp star on cardstock twice. Stamp sentiment in the center of one star.
5. Die-cut first stamped star; die-cut circle from center of second star. Adhere center to star with foam tape.
6. Tie ribbon and twine into bow; attach brad through center and attach to star. Adhere star to card with foam tape.

Finished size: 4¼" x 5½"

Musical Bird Card

Designer: Vanessa Menhorn
Ink all edges.

1. Make card from cardstock.
2. Trim patterned paper panel to fit card front. Trim patterned paper; zigzag-stitch edge and stamp thank you. Adhere to panel.
3. Die-cut label from sheet music; stamp bird and adhere to panel.
4. Stamp bird on cardstock; color with markers and fussy-cut body; adhere with foam tape.
5. Adhere pleated ribbon; tie twine around panel. Tie ribbon into bow; thread twine through button and around bow. Adhere to panel.
6. Adhere panel to card. Adhere buttons and pearls.

Finished size: 5½" x 4¼"

SUPPLIES: *Cardstock:* (Slate) WorldWin; (Vintage Cream) Papertrey Ink *Patterned paper:* (Golden Gleam from Dear Lizzy collection) American Crafts *Clear stamps:* (star, sentiment from Seasons of Love set) Waltzingmouse Stamps *Specialty ink:* (Charcoal hybrid) Stewart Superior Corp. *Accent:* (gray velvet brad) Crate Paper *Fibers:* (gray ribbon) American Crafts; (ivory twine) May Arts; (ivory lace) Wrights *Dies:* (circle, star) Spellbinders

SUPPLIES: *Cardstock:* (Vintage Cream) Papertrey Ink *Patterned paper:* (Think Big from 365 Degrees collection) Pink Paislee; (Nijo from Tea & Silk collection) Prima *Clear stamps:* (bird from Two Birds set) Hero Arts; (thank you from Loving Words set) Technique Tuesday *Dye ink:* (Tuxedo Black) Tsukineko; (Walnut Stain) Ranger Industries *Color medium:* (light, dark brown markers) Copic *Accents:* (blue pearls) Prima; (blue buttons) Papertrey Ink *Fibers:* (green pleated ribbon) Pink Paislee; (ivory ribbon) Papertrey Ink; (natural twine) *Die:* (label) Spellbinders *Other:* (sheet music)

DESIGNER TIP

Markers allow you to ink stamps for a multi-colored image. Since they dry quickly, make sure to "huff" on the stamp to remoisten the ink before you stamp the image.

Oh What Fun Tag

Designer: Windy Robinson

1. Make tag from cardstock.
2. Stamp Recital on tag.
3. Trim and adhere patterned paper; adhere rhinestones.
4. Punch and adhere cardstock circle; punch hole and thread with twine.
5. Tie on ribbon; string buttons on ribbon and tie to bow.

Finished size: 3" x 5¾"

Sing It Loud Card

Designer: Michele Gross

1. Make card from cardstock.
2. Stamp background on cardstock; emboss, mat with cardstock, and adhere.
3. Color sentiment stamp with markers and stamp on card.
4. Adhere ribbon strip; make ribbon bow and adhere.

Finished size: 4¼" x 5½"

SUPPLIES: *Cardstock:* (kraft) DMD, Inc.; (ivory) The Paper Company *Patterned paper:* (Elements from Jolly By Golly collection) Cosmo Cricket *Clear stamp:* (Recital) Prima *Dye ink:* (Tea Dye) Ranger Industries *Accents:* (clear rhinestone buttons) Blumenthal Lansing; (clear rhinestones) Zva Creative *Fibers:* (green ribbon) Michaels; (natural twine) May Arts *Tool:* (circle punch)

SUPPLIES: *Cardstock:* (white) Stampin' Up!; (black) Bazzill Basics Paper *Rubber stamps:* (music background, sentiment from Music of My Heart set) Ippity by Unity Stamp Co. *Pigment ink:* (black) Tsukineko *Embossing powder:* (clear) Stampin' Up! *Color medium:* (black, orange markers) Stampin' Up! *Fibers:* (orange stitched ribbon) American Crafts

All Creatures Great & Small

Celebrate the holidays with these trendy critters!

Discover how to incorporate bees, beasts, and birds of all feathers into cute Christmas cards drawn from a menagerie of festive friends.

Bee Merry Card

Designer: Kim Hughes

1. Make card from cardstock.
2. Cut rectangle of patterned paper; punch border and adhere. Stitch border.
3. Cut strip of patterned paper; zigzag-stitch and adhere.
4. Thread buttons with twine; adhere. Adhere patterned paper strip.
5. Trim tree; stitch edges and adhere. Tie bow with twine; adhere.
6. Trim bee from patterned paper; adhere.
7. Spell sentiment on cardstock with rub-ons; trim and adhere.

Finished size: 3¾" x 4"

5 STEPS All Creatures Great & Small Card

Designer: Kim Kesti

1. Make card from cardstock.
2. Print sentiment on cardstock and adhere.
3. Stamp image; color, apply glitter glue, punch, and mat with cardstock.
4. Adhere with foam tape.

Finished size: 4¾" square

SUPPLIES: *Cardstock:* (orange) *Patterned paper:* (Daintily from Vintage Yummy collection) Sassafras Lass; (Fuzzy Navel from Lime Rickey collection, Greenhouse from Wisteria collection) BasicGrey; (brown stripes from Celebrate pad) Me & My Big Ideas *Accents:* (green buttons) BasicGrey *Rub-ons:* (Hildi alphabet) American Crafts *Fibers:* (twine) *Tool:* (border punch) Fiskars

SUPPLIES: *Cardstock:* (Red Devil, Limeade, white) Bazzill Basics Paper *Rubber stamp:* (Kelly's Gnome with Mouse) Just Johanna Rubber Stamps *Solvent ink:* (black) Tsukineko *Color medium:* (assorted markers) Copic *Accent:* (red glitter glue) Ranger Industries *Font:* (Cambria) Microsoft *Tools:* (1¾", 2" circle punches) EK Success

Good Cheer Card

Designer: Barbara Housner

1. Make card from patterned paper.
2. Adhere strip of patterned paper.
3. Affix sticker.
4. Apply rub-ons.

Finished size: 5½" x 3¼"

DESIGNER TIP

Instead of using cardstock as your card base, use a heavier-weight patterned paper. This is a great way to add instant contrast without layering.

Be Merry Owl Card

Designer: Rae Barthel

1. Make card from cardstock. Adhere rectangle of patterned paper.
2. Cut strip of patterned paper; punch border, tie on ribbon, and adhere.
3. Adhere scalloped circle; apply rub-on.
4. Adhere owl with foam tape.

Finished size: 4" x 6"

DESIGNER TIP

Add variety to your card by mixing and matching seasons. Use elements from spring, summer, or fall in holiday cards when the colors match.

SUPPLIES: All supplies from October Afternoon unless otherwise noted. *Patterned paper:* (Falling Snow, Sleigh Bells from Good Cheer collection) *Rub-ons:* (sentiment, music notes) *Sticker:* (bird branch) Colorbok

SUPPLIES: *Cardstock:* (red) Bazzill Basics Paper *Patterned paper:* (Peppermint Sticks from Good Cheer collection) October Afternoon *Accents:* (chipboard owl) Colorbok; (scalloped circle die cut) Jenni Bowlin Studio *Rub-on:* (sentiment) Creative Imaginations *Fibers:* (light blue ribbon) Fiskars *Tool:* (border punch) Wrights

Merry Kiss-mas Card

Designer: Bethany Kartchner

1. Make card from cardstock. Draw and color border.
2. Punch heart; adhere. Draw and color border around heart.
3. Trim birds, mistletoe, and hats from patterned paper. Adhere.
4. Color birds. Outline with black pen.
5. Draw mistletoe string and bird legs, tails, and feet.
6. Cover brads with glitter glue; attach.

Finished size: 6" square

5 STEPS Happy Howlidays Card

Designer: Julie Campbell

1. Make card from cardstock.
2. Print "Happy Howlidays" on cardstock. Sand edges.
3. Adhere patterned paper strip and ribbon. Adhere piece to card.
4. Stamp dogs on patterned paper, mat with cardstock, and adhere.

Finished size: 5½" square

DESIGNER TIPS

If you don't have the right color of brad, cover it with glitter glue to make it match. When covering brads with glitter glue, stick them into a piece of foam to hold them in place.

If your card elements don't seem to stand out enough, outline them using a fine-tip pen to really make them pop!

DESIGNER TIP

Always print computer-generated sentiments on scrap paper first to check for size and placement. This will save you from wasting expensive cardstock.

SUPPLIES: *Cardstock:* (red, kraft) Bazzill Basics Paper *Patterned paper:* (Garland, Pine from Candy Cane collection; Loved from Color Me collection) Luxe Designs *Color media:* (red, green colored pencils) Prismacolor; (black pen) American Crafts; (white pen) Sanford *Accents:* (silver brads) Making Memories; (red glitter glue) Ranger Industries *Tool:* (heart punch) Creative Memories

SUPPLIES: *Cardstock:* (True Black) Papertrey Ink; (Parsley) Memory Box Inc. *Patterned paper:* (Milk from Urban Prairie collection) BasicGrey; (polka dots from Black & White Basics collection) Papertrey Ink *Rubber stamp:* (dachshund from Little Gal set) Cornish Heritage Farms *Dye ink:* (Lettuce) Ranger Industries; (Tuxedo Black) Tsukineko *Specialty ink:* (Pure Poppy hybrid) Papertrey Ink *Fibers:* (red ribbon) Papertrey Ink *Font:* (CK Holland Font) Creating Keepsakes

Merry Little Christmas Card

Designer: Kimberly Crawford

❶ Make card from cardstock.

❷ Stamp cardstock rectangle with Fine Houndstooth Scrapblock; adhere.

❸ Die-cut label, stamp sentiment and branches, and adhere.

❹ Stamp branches on separate piece of cardstock; trim and adhere.

❺ Stamp and flock bird; trim and adhere with foam tape.

❻ Tie on ribbon. Thread button and top of bird with twine and tie bow.

Finished size: 4¼" x 5½"

DESIGNER TIP

When using flocking powder, let the glue dry for a moment before adding it. Pour a good amount of powder over the glue, push down onto the surface, and set it aside to dry. Shake off the excess after the glue has dried.

Cozy Christmas Wishes Card

Designer: Betsy Veldman

❶ Make card from cardstock. Create top oval standup by cutting half oval from back flap of card.

❷ Adhere patterned paper. Stitch border.

❸ Stamp sentiment on patterned paper; adhere. Adhere rhinestones.

❹ Spell "Cozy" with stickers.

❺ Tie on ribbon. Thread twine through button and tie on bow.

❻ Stamp hedgehog on cardstock, punch oval, and ink edges. Hand-stitch with floss across neck several times and tie. Adhere to patterned paper.

❼ Punch scalloped oval. Adhere with foam tape.

Finished size: 4¼" x 6½"

SUPPLIES: *Cardstock:* (kraft, Pure Poppy, Vintage Cream) Papertrey Ink *Rubber stamps:* (Fine Houndstooth Scrapblock) Cornish Heritage Farms; (Bird Ornament, Merry Little Christmas) Inkadinkado; (branches) *Chalk ink:* (dark brown) Clearsnap *Specialty ink:* (Ripe Avocado hybrid) Papertrey Ink; (L'Amour hybrid) Stewart Superior Corp. *Accents:* (green button) BasicGrey; (brown flocking powder) Stampendous! *Fibers:* (red ribbon) Papertrey Ink; (twine) May Arts *Die:* (large label) Spellbinders

SUPPLIES: *Cardstock:* (Ripe Avocado, Vintage Cream) Papertrey Ink *Patterned paper:* (Snowflake from Fa La La collection) Making Memories; (Wrapping Paper from Oh Joy collection) Cosmo Cricket *Clear stamps:* (hedgehog from Forest Friends set, Christmas Wishes from Merry and Bright set) Papertrey Ink *Chalk ink:* (Creamy Brown) Clearsnap; (white) *Accents:* (brown rhinestones) Kaisercraft; (green button) Papertrey Ink *Stickers:* (Passport Canvas alphabet) Making Memories *Fibers:* (red floss) Bazzill Basics Paper; (brown ribbon) Papertrey Ink; (twine) The Beadery *Tools:* (oval punch, scalloped oval punch) Marvy Uchida; (oval cutter) Creative Memories

Simple Peace Card

Designer: Rae Barthel

1. Make card from cardstock.
2. Round corners, tie on ribbon, and adhere with foam tape.
3. Adhere snowflake.
4. Apply sentiment.
5. Affix sticker.
6. Adhere rhinestones.

Finished size: 6" x 4"

DESIGNER TIP

Sometimes less is more. Let white space draw attention to the accents on your projects.

5 STEPS 'Tis the Season Card

Designer: Maren Benedict

1. Make card from cardstock.
2. Adhere patterned paper rectangles.
3. Affix stickers.
4. Adhere rhinestones.
5. Tie on ribbon. Stitch edges.

Finished size: 4½" x 5½"

DESIGNER TIP

When you are stitching around the card border, stitch the ribbon ends to secure the bow in place.

SUPPLIES: *Cardstock:* (white embossed) Bazzill Basics Paper; (red) Hobby Lobby *Accents:* (snowflake) K&Company; (clear rhinestones) Kaisercraft *Rub-on:* (sentiment) Creative Imaginations *Sticker:* (deer) Colorbok *Fibers:* (red ribbon) Michaels *Tool:* (corner rounder punch) EK Success

SUPPLIES: *Cardstock:* (Pure Poppy) Papertrey Ink *Patterned paper:* (stripes, snowflake, 'tis the season from Wonderland pad) Cosmo Cricket *Accents:* (red, clear rhinestones) Me & My Big Ideas *Stickers:* (squirrel, hedgehog) Colorbok *Fibers:* (red ribbon) Michaels

Stinkin' Merry Christmas Card

Designer: Wendy Sue Anderson

1. Make card from cardstock.
2. Adhere patterned paper layers. Stitch edges.
3. Adhere strips of white and green ribbon. Tie bow and adhere.
4. Trim skunk from patterned paper; adhere with foam tape. Adhere Santa hat.
5. Print sentiment on cardstock; trim and adhere.
6. Affix stickers to complete sentiment.

Finished size: 5½" x 6"

Elephant Peace on Earth Card

Designer: Jessica Witty

1. Make card from cardstock.
2. Stamp leaves along bottom.
3. Stamp elephant and "Peace" on cardstock; adhere.
4. Stamp "On earth" on cardstock strip and adhere.
5. Stamp bird and small branch on cardstock. Trim and adhere.
6. Cut slit in card seam, thread ribbon, and tie bow. Tie twine around bow.

Finished size: 3½" x 5"

DESIGNER TIP

Virtually any image can be integrated into a holiday card when paired with the perfect sentiment. Having a few simple alphabet stamp sets in a variety of sizes makes it a snap to create holiday cards with even the most unlikely images!

SUPPLIES: *Cardstock:* (white) American Crafts *Patterned paper:* (Skunk from The Green Stack collection) Die Cuts With a View; (Jack Stripe from Animal Crackers collection) Making Memories *Accent:* (Santa hat) Stickopotamus *Stickers:* (Rockabye alphabet) American Crafts *Fibers:* (green polka dot ribbon) American Crafts; (white ribbon) *Font:* (Classizism Antiqua) www.abstractfonts.com

SUPPLIES: *Cardstock:* (white, Spring Moss) Papertrey Ink *Rubber stamp:* (dove from Love Ya Bunches set) Stampin' Up! *Clear stamps:* (elephant from Bitty Baby Blessings set; branch, peace from Rustic Branches set; Simple Alphabet) Papertrey Ink *Dye ink:* (Chocolate Chip, Old Olive) Stampin' Up! *Color medium:* (Chocolate Chip, Olive Old markers) Stampin' Up! *Fibers:* (green ribbon) Papertrey Ink; (twine)

Holiday Birds Card

Designer: Kalyn Kepner

Ink all edges.

① Make card from cardstock.

② Cut patterned paper to fit card front; adhere.

③ Cut strips of patterned paper; adhere.

④ Cut strip of cardstock using decorative-edge scissors; adhere.

⑤ Die-cut birds from patterned paper and cardstock.
Adhere pieces and adhere to card with foam tape.

⑥ Stamp sentiment.

Finished size: 6¼" x 4¾"

Not a Creature was Stirring Card

Designer: Kim Hughes

① Cut mouse body from patterned paper.

② Print "Not a creature was stirring…" on cardstock;
trim and adhere.

③ Cut ear flap from card.

④ Trim hat pieces from patterned paper and cardstock. Adhere
pieces. Slide hat under ear flap and adhere.

⑤ Punch eye from cardstock. Adhere eye and rhinestone nose.

⑥ Adhere pompom. Adhere twine tail.

⑦ Adhere piece to cardstock card base.

Finished size: 5" x 3½"

DESIGNER TIPS

To form mouse, trace a mug or small bowl to
get the perfect half circle.

Liquid glue works nicely when adhering twine
to keep it in place.

SUPPLIES: *Cardstock:* (tan) The Paper Company; (brown) Bazzill Basics Paper *Patterned paper:* (Snow Dust from Wassail collection) BasicGrey; (5th Avenue, Jack Frost from Tinsel Town collection) Pink Paislee *Rubber stamp:* (Happy Holidays) A Muse Artstamps *Chalk ink:* (Chestnut Roan, light brown) Clearsnap *Die:* (bird) QuicKutz *Tool:* (decorative-edge scissors) EK Success

SUPPLIES: *Cardstock:* (Snow, black) Bazzill Basics Paper *Patterned paper:* (Number Cruncher from Teacher's Pet collection) Imaginisce; (Special Swirls from Uniquely You collection) My Mind's Eye *Accents:* (pink rhinestone) Zva Creative; (white pompom) Bazzill Basics Paper *Fibers:* (jute) *Font:* (Adorable) www.dafont.com *Tool:* (1/8" hole punch) We R Memory Keepers

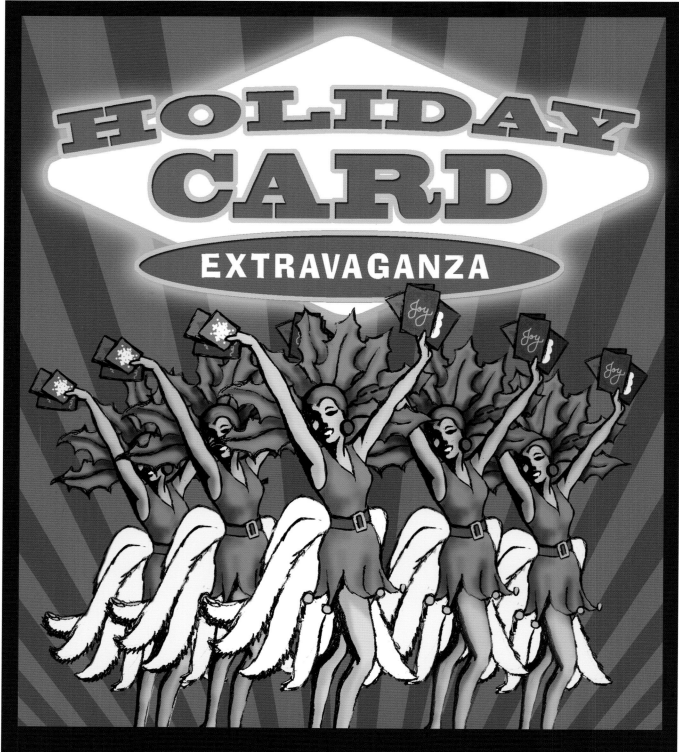

HOLIDAY CARD EXTRAVAGANZA

Family gatherings, favorite foods, and traditional songs are just a few of the signs that the holiday season has begun. What better way to kick off the holidays than by making some festive cards! With styles ranging from traditional to trendy, these cards will give you the perfect way to spread some holiday cheer.

Warm Wishes Snowman Card

Designer: Melissa Phillips

❶ Make card from cardstock.

❷ Adhere patterned paper strip and round bottom corners.

❸ Apply rub-ons.

❹ Adhere patterned paper behind heart square. Sand and stitch edges; adhere.

❺ Thread button with floss and adhere.

❻ Adhere snowman tag.

Finished size: 5" x 3¾"

SUPPLIES: *Cardstock:* (white) Bazzill Basics Paper *Patterned paper:* (Christmas Classic) Doodlebug Design; (Paisley Dot from Vintage Hip collection) Making Memories *Accents:* (chipboard heart square) Heidi Swapp; (snowman tag) Me & My Big Ideas; (green button) *Rub-ons:* (Simply Sweet alphabet) Doodlebug Design; (flourish) BasicGrey *Fibers:* (red floss) *Tool:* (corner rounder punch)

⑤ STEPS Merry & Bright Trees Card

Designer: Kim Hughes

❶ Make card from patterned paper.

❷ Adhere patterned paper strip.

❸ Adhere ribbon over seam. Affix sticker.

❹ Draw tree shapes on paper leaves, trim, and adhere.

❺ Attach brad.

Finished size: 5¼" x 4"

SUPPLIES: *Patterned paper:* (Whiting Street from Roxbury collection) Scenic Route; (Ice Capades from Candy Cane Lane collection) Imaginisce *Accents:* (green paper leaves) Prima; (red heart brad) Making Memories *Sticker:* (merry & bright) Imaginisce *Fibers:* (green velvet ribbon) Making Memories

Festive Trees Card

Designer: Stefanie Hamilton

❶ Make card from cardstock.

❷ Create finished size project in software. Open digital elements.

❸ Drop in template. Brush trees.

❹ Change color of trees and flourish.

❺ Type sentiment. Draw border.

❻ Print on photo paper; trim and adhere to card.

Finished size: 6" square

SUPPLIES: *Cardstock:* (green) *Specialty paper:* (photo) *Digital elements:* (polka dot, floral Christmas tree brushes from Holiday Trees No. 07 kit) www.designer digitals.com; (March Freebie layout template) www.crystalsdigitemplateshoppe. com *Font:* (French Script MT) www.fonts.com *Software:* (photo editing) Adobe

Naughty or Nice? Card

Designer: Melanie Douthit

❶ Make card from cardstock.

❷ Cut rectangle of cardstock, round corners, and adhere.

❸ Cut patterned paper strips, round corners, and adhere.

❹ Tie ribbon around card front.

❺ Stamp Santa and sentiment on cardstock. Color hat with pen and trim.

❻ Double-mat stamped image with cardstock and adhere.

Finished size: 5½" x 4¼"

SUPPLIES: *Cardstock:* (Flamingo) Bazzill Basics Paper; (Intense Kiwi, white) Prism; (red) *Patterned paper:* (Little Boy, Black Sheep from Ba Ba Black Sheep collection) Piggy Tales *Rubber stamps:* (Santa, naughty or nice from Christmas Cheer set) Cornish Heritage Farms *Dye ink:* (Lipstick) Paper Salon *Color medium:* (red gel pen) Sakura *Fibers:* (lime ribbon) Piggy Tales *Tool:* (corner rounder punch)

 Peace & Love Card

Designer: Melissa Phillips

❶ Make card from cardstock.

❷ Cut patterned paper slightly smaller than card front, ink edges, and adhere.

❸ Cut strip of patterned paper, trim one edge with decorative-edge scissors, and punch holes; adhere.

❹ Tie ribbon around front flap. Attach brad to holly leaves; adhere. Adhere rhinestone.

❺ Ink edges of sticker; affix.

Finished size: 4½" x 5¼"

Christmas Joy Card

Designer: Danni Reid

❶ Make card from cardstock.

❷ Cut cardstock slightly smaller than card front, emboss using template, and adhere.

❸ Cut patterned paper strip and round bottom corners. Adhere ribbon, stitch top side edges, and adhere.

❹ Cut star from cardstock, emboss, and punch edges using oval and rectangle punches.

❺ Adhere chipboard pieces. Thread button with floss and adhere.

❻ Adhere star to card using foam tape.

Finished size: 4" x 6½"

SUPPLIES: *Cardstock:* (red) Bazzill Basics Paper *Patterned paper:* (Snowflake, Flocked Holly from St. Nick Vintage collection) Making Memories *Dye ink:* (Old Paper) Ranger Industries *Accents:* (green holly leaves, purple brad) Heidi Grace Designs; (white glitter chipboard holly leaves) Melissa Frances; (red rhinestone) Doodlebug Design *Sticker:* (peace & love scalloped circle) Making Memories *Fibers:* (red gingham ribbon) *Tool:* (decorative-edge scissors) Provo Craft

SUPPLIES: *Cardstock:* (white) Bazzill Basics Paper *Patterned paper:* (Flocked Holly from St. Nick Vintage collection) Making Memories *Accents:* (chipboard Christmas) Scenic Route; (green chipboard alphabet, brackets, circle) Making Memories; (white button) Creative Café *Fibers:* (red gingham ribbon) Offray; (red floss) *Adhesive:* (foam tape) *Templates:* (embossing swirl) Provo Craft; (star) *Tools:* (oval punch, ¼" rectangle punch) Fiskars; (embossing machine) Provo Craft; (corner rounder punch)

⑤ Santa Sketch Card

Designer: Wendy Sue Anderson

❶ Make card from cardstock.

❷ Adhere scalloped cardstock and patterned paper strips.

❸ Adhere velvet ribbon. Tie bow and adhere iridescent ribbon.

❹ Apply rub-on.

❺ Trim Santa image from patterned paper, mat with cardstock, and adhere with foam tape.

Finished size: 9" x 4"

⑤ Joys Be Many Card

Designer: Anabelle O'Malley

❶ Make card from cardstock.

❷ Adhere patterned paper strips.

❸ Attach brad to chipboard star and adhere.

❹ Tie ribbon around card front.

❺ Mat Santa card with cardstock. Adhere glitter to chipboard holly and adhere to piece. Adhere piece to card using foam tape.

Finished size: 5" square

SUPPLIES: *Cardstock:* (green scalloped) Bazzill Basics Paper; (tan, red) *Patterned paper:* (Collage from St. Nick Vintage collection) Making Memories *Rub-ons:* (celebrate the season) Crate Paper *Fibers:* (red velvet ribbon) SEI; (green/red iridescent ribbon) *Adhesive:* (foam tape)

SUPPLIES: *Cardstock:* (Natural) Bazzill Basics Paper *Patterned paper:* (Holly, Wenceslaus) Melissa Frances *Accents:* (white glitter chipboard star, holly leaves) Melissa Frances; (epoxy poinsettia brad) Making Memories; (red glitter glue) Ranger Industries; (vintage Santa card) Crafty Secrets *Fibers:* (pale green ribbon) Michaels *Adhesive:* (foam tape)

Deck the Halls Card

Designer: Anabelle O'Malley

❶ Make card from cardstock; round top corners.

❷ Stamp flourish; emboss.

❸ Cut strip of cardstock and stamp flourish; emboss.

❹ Align embossed images; adhere strip.

❺ Affix deck the halls, stars, and dots stickers.

❻ Affix ornament frame sticker to cardstock. Trim, color image with markers, and adhere with foam tape.

Finished size: 5¼" x 4"

SUPPLIES: *Cardstock:* (Hot Pink, Fussy) Bazzill Basics Paper; (white) The Paper Company *Rubber stamp:* (flourish from Flurries set) Inque Boutique *Pigment ink:* (white) Stampin' Up! *Embossing powder:* (white) Ranger Industries *Color medium:* (pink, green markers) Copic Marker *Stickers:* (ornament frame, deck the halls, stars, dots) Magenta Style *Adhesive:* (foam tape) *Tool:* (corner rounder punch) Marvy Uchida

Christmas Bell Card

Designer: Beatriz Jennings

❶ Make card from cardstock.

❷ Cut patterned paper, ink edges, and adhere. Adhere rickrack.

❸ Cut strip of cardstock; adhere. Stitch edges.

❹ Stamp sentiment.

❺ Cut cardstock strip with decorative-edge scissors; adhere.

❻ Tie ribbon bow; adhere. Adhere jingle bell.

Finished size: 4" x 4½"

SUPPLIES: *Cardstock:* (pink) Bazzill Basics Paper; (green) *Patterned paper:* (pink floral from Christmas Stack) Die Cuts With a View *Clear stamp:* (Merry Christmas from Whimsical Holiday set) Junkitz *Dye ink:* (Old Paper) Ranger Industries; (black) *Accents:* (jingle bell) *Fibers:* (red ribbon, red rickrack) *Tool:* (decorative-edge scissors) Provo Craft

Happy Kwanzaa Card

Designer: Teri Anderson

1 Make card from cardstock; round bottom corners.

2 Adhere cardstock strips.

3 Spell "kwanzaa" with stickers.

4 Apply rub-on.

5 Knot jute and tie around card.

Finished size: 5½" x 4¼"

Noel Greetings Card

Designer: Dawn McVey

1 Make card from cardstock. Stitch top edge and sides.

2 Cut patterned paper strip, sand edges, and adhere.

3 Cut cardstock strip, stamp noel, and adhere.

4 Tie ribbon around card front.

5 Stamp pine cones and branches on cardstock; trim. Punch circles from cardstock and adhere to pine cones.

6 Adhere branches to card. Adhere pine cones using foam tape.

Finished size: 5½" x 4¼"

SUPPLIES: *Cardstock:* (white, red, black, green) Bazzill Basics Paper *Rub-on:* (happy) American Crafts *Stickers:* (Whistle Stop alphabet) American Crafts *Fibers:* (jute) DCC *Tool:* (corner rounder punch)

SUPPLIES: All supplies from Stampin' Up! *Cardstock:* (Real Red, Certainly Celery, Close to Cocoa, kraft) *Patterned paper:* (Real Red dots/diamonds from Designer Series Prints pack) *Rubber stamps:* (pine cone, branch from Peaceful Wishes set; noel from Many Merry Messages set) *Dye ink:* (Chocolate Chip, Always Artichoke) *Fibers:* (tan ribbon) *Adhesive:* (foam tape)

Wise Men Joyeux Noel Card

Designer: Becky Olsen, courtesy of Cornish Heritage Farms

❶ Make card from cardstock. Stamp Scratched Grid Backgrounder.

❷ Cut square of cardstock slightly smaller than card front; adhere.

❸ Cut square of cardstock and stamp Scratched Grid Backgrounder; ink edges and adhere.

❹ Stamp Joyeux Noel.

❺ Stamp Three Wise Men on cardstock; trim and adhere with foam tape.

❻ Stamp Modern Star with adhesive ink. Cover with gold foil and rub to burnish image.

Finished size: 5½" x 4¼"

⑤ Bright & Happy Hanukkah Card

Designer: Tresa Black

❶ Make card from cardstock. Sand edges.

❷ Cut patterned paper slightly smaller than card front, sand edges, and adhere.

❸ Print sentiment on patterned paper. Trim, ink edges, and adhere.

❹ Cut circle from cardstock using template; ink edges. Stamp image, watercolor, and adhere.

❺ Punch holes, attach conchos, and tie twine.

Finished size: 7" x 5"

DESIGNER TIP

To add sparkle to this design, apply glitter to candle flames and stars.

SUPPLIES: *Cardstock:* (cream) Prism; (Dark Denim Dot from Double Dot collection) Bo-Bunny Press *Rubber stamps:* (Joyeux Noel, Three Wise Men, Modern Star, Scratched Grid Backgrounder) Cornish Heritage Farms *Dye ink:* (Old Paper, Antique Linen) Ranger Industries *Pigment ink:* (Night Sky) Tsukineko *Specialty ink:* (adhesive) Tsukineko *Adhesive:* (foam tape) Therm O Web *Other:* (gold foil) 7gypsies

SUPPLIES: *Cardstock:* (Desert Sand, White Daisy) Close To My Heart *Patterned paper:* (Blue Trees, Tan Snowflakes from Aspen Level 2 Paper Pack) Close To My Heart *Clear stamp:* (menorah from Jewish Remembrance set) Close To My Heart *Dye ink:* (Goldrush, Dutch Blue, Sunny Yellow, Desert Sand) Close To My Heart *Solvent ink:* (black) Tsukineko *Accents:* (pewter conchos) Close To My Heart *Fibers:* (hemp twine) *Font:* (Marydale) www.fonts.com *Template:* (circle) Provo Craft *Tool:* (water brush)

GIFTY Gift Card HOLDERS

Do you have people on your gift list who are difficult to shop for? Gift cards are often a great solution, but they don't always have packaging that matches their quality. Here, we show you how to create paper-crafted packaging that will allow you to add a personal touch to your gift cards.

Do Not Open Pillow Box

Designer: Andrea Bowden, courtesy of Stampin' Up!

❶ Cut pillow box from cardstock, using template. Assemble box; adhere.

❷ Punch three circles from cardstock; adhere to box.

❸ Cut rectangle of cardstock, stamp snowflakes, and adhere to box with foam tape.

❹ Stamp sentiment on cardstock; trim and adhere with foam tape.

❺ Tie ribbon around box.

Finished size: 4¼" x 3"

Happy Holidays Box

Designer: Lisa Johnson

❶ Trim patterned paper to fit inside box; adhere.

❷ Adhere ribbon and bow to lid.

❸ Stamp sentiment on cardstock and punch into circle. Ink edges and adhere rhinestones.

❹ Punch hole in circle. Attach circle to bow with thread.

Finished size: 2¼" x 4¼" x 2¼"

DESIGNER TIP
Fill the box with candy to make this gift extra sweet.

SUPPLIES: All supplies from Stampin' Up! unless otherwise noted. *Cardstock:* (kraft, Old Olive, Riding Hood Red, Very Vanilla) *Rubber stamps:* (snowflake, do not open from Winter Post set) *Dye ink:* (Old Olive, Riding Hood Red) *Fibers:* (brown/red/green striped ribbon) *Adhesive:* (foam tape) *Template:* (pillow box) no source

SUPPLIES: *Patterned paper:* (Happy Holidays, I Believe Swirls from Happy Holidays collection) Adornit-Carolee's Creations *Clear stamp:* (happy holidays from Holiday set) My Sentiments Exactly! *Dye ink:* (Vintage Green, Brown) Clearsnap *Accents:* (red rhinestones) Hero Arts *Fibers:* (olive ribbon) Papillon Ribbon & Bow; (linen thread) Stampin' Up! *Tools:* (¹⁄₁₆", 1¼" circle punches) Marvy Uchida *Other:* (acrylic box) Michaels

BACK

5 STEPS Christmas Tin

Designer: Michele Boyer

1 Cut patterned paper slightly smaller than tin top. Round corners, attach brads, and adhere.

2 Stamp sentiment and flourish on cardstock; trim and ink edges. Draw berries with marker. Mat with cardstock and adhere.

3 Adhere patterned paper strips to tin sides.

Finished size: 3¾" x 2¼" x ¾"

Night Before Christmas Envelope

Designer: Lisa Dorsey

PREPARE

Make envelope from cardstock, using template. Ink edges.

FRONT

1 Mat patterned paper with cardstock; ink and stitch edges. Adhere.

2 Punch photo corners from patterned paper, ink edges, and adhere. Adhere beads.

3 Adhere vintage tag. Trim Santa image from second tag and adhere with foam tape.

4 Adhere beads around tag. Tie ribbon bow and adhere.

BACK

1 Attach buttons to envelope with brads.

2 Tie floss around buttons for envelope closure.

Finished size: 4½" x 6¼"

DESIGNER TIP

Use a family photo instead of a tag to personalize the envelope.

SUPPLIES: *Cardstock:* (Crabapple Dark, Natural Smooth) Prism *Patterned paper:* (Holly Paisley Snowbell from Snowflakes & Holly collection) Daisy D's *Rubber stamps:* (flourish from Beautiful set, Merry Christmas from The Art of Framing set) Cornish Heritage Farms *Dye ink:* (Raisin, Oregano, Latte) Ranger Industries *Color medium:* (Cardinal marker) Copic Marker *Accents:* (gold brads) Making Memories *Tool:* (corner rounder punch) EK Success *Other:* (tin) Altoids

SUPPLIES: *Cardstock:* (tan, light blue) Bazzill Basics Paper *Patterned paper:* (Berry from Color Connect Elegant collection) The Paper Company; (White Paisley from Kraft collection) Making Memories *Pigment ink:* (black, white, brown) Clearsnap *Accents:* (vintage gift tag) Melissa Frances; (clear glass beads) Create-a-Craft; (red buttons) Autumn Leaves; (black brads) *Fibers:* (red ribbon) Michaels; (white floss) DMC *Adhesive:* (foam tape) *Template:* (envelope) *Tools:* (corner rounder punch, photo corner punch) EK Success

INSIDE

Davis

⑤ Matryoshka Doll Gift Card Holder

Designer: Kim Kesti

❶ Cut doll from cardstock, following pattern on p. 284. Cut bonnet and apron from cardstock, following patterns. Punch two circles for doll's head from cardstock. Trim one circle into hair shape.

❷ Adhere hair to circle. Apply chalk for cheeks and draw eyes and mouth with markers; adhere piece to bonnet.

❸ Punch pop up flower from cardstock; adhere button. Adhere piece to apron. Punch border along apron bottom edge. Adhere cardstock behind border. Adhere apron to doll.

❹ Layer doll pieces and stitch edges, leaving top open for gift card.

❺ Layer bonnet pieces and stitch edges, leaving bottom open for gift card. *Note: The inserted gift card will hold both pieces of the doll together.*

Finished size: 3½" x 5¾"

⑤ Penguin Gift Card Holder

Designer: Wendy Gallamore

❶ Make tag from cardstock; round top corners. Cut square of cardstock; punch half-circle. Adhere, leaving top open for pocket.

❷ Trim cardstock strips and adhere. *Note: Trim top edges in a wave.*

❸ Die-cut penguin, assemble pieces, and adhere. Adhere eyes.

❹ Die-cut letters for recipient's name; adhere.

❺ Adhere ribbon and button. Insert gift card in pocket.

Finished size: 3½" x 4¾"

SUPPLIES: *Cardstock:* (Parakeet, Berrylicious, Pumpkin Seed, Snowcone, Lemon Lime, brown, white) Bazzill Basics Paper *Color media:* (pink chalk) Pebbles Inc.; (black, red markers) *Accent:* (red flower button) KI Memories *Fibers:* (green, red floss) *Tools:* (1½" circle punch, pop up flower punch) EK Success; (scallop border punch) Fiskars *Other:* (gift card)

SUPPLIES: *Cardstock:* (Beetle Black, Vibrant Blue, Sunshine, Ruby Slipper, white) Bazzill Basics Paper *Accents:* (wiggle eyes) Westrim Crafts; (black button) Doodlebug Design *Fibers:* (red ribbon) Offray *Dies:* (penguin) Provo Craft; (Khaki SkinniMini alphabet) QuicKutz *Tools:* (die cut machine) Provo Craft, QuicKutz; (½" circle punch) EK Success; (corner rounder punch) *Other:* (gift card)

5 STEPS Noel Gift Card Holder

Designer: Terri Davenport

❶ Cut circles from chipboard and patterned paper. Adhere patterned paper to both sides of chipboard circle.

❷ Cut circle from patterned paper; cut in half. Adhere edges only to form pocket.

❸ Adhere ribbon. Form ribbon loop; adhere.

❹ Draw star on chipboard, trim, and cover with patterned paper. Sand edges.

❺ Thread buttons with floss and adhere to star; adhere piece.

Finished size: 5¼" diameter

Christmas Joy Mailbox

Designer: Lisa Dorsey

❶ Cover top and ends of mailbox with patterned paper.

❷ Adhere patterned paper strips to sides. Adhere ribbon over seams.

❸ Affix sticker to cardstock, trim, and adhere to flag. Tie ribbons to flag. Draw stitches on ribbon with marker.

❹ Cut strips of cardstock, trim one side using decorative-edge scissors, and adhere. Detail with marker.

❺ Affix sentiment sticker to cardstock, trim, and adhere to mailbox front.

❻ Adhere chipboard star, affix sentiment sticker, thread button with floss, and adhere.

Finished size: 3" x 3½" x 5"

SUPPLIES: *Patterned paper:* (Jailbird, Hoopla from Okee Dokee collection) TaDa Creative Studios *Accents:* (red, blue, yellow buttons) Autumn Leaves *Fibers:* (red noel ribbon) KI Memories *Tool:* (circle cutter) Creative Memories *Other:* (chipboard)

SUPPLIES: *Cardstock:* (Deep Berry Red) WorldWin; (light blue) Bazzill Basics Paper *Patterned paper:* (Hillary Lace Flower from Noteworthy collection) Making Memories; (Holiday Type/ Evergreen Scroll from Home for the Holidays collection) Deja Views *Color medium:* (white paint marker) Sanford *Accents:* (blue button) Buttons Galore & More; (chipboard star) American Crafts *Stickers:* (holiday sentiments) K&Company *Fibers:* (red/white stitched ribbon) Making Memories; (blue ribbon) Offray; (red ribbon) JKM Ribbon; (white floss) *Tools:* (decorative-edge scissors) Fiskars *Other:* (mailbox) Target

INSIDE

5 STEPS — Santa Was Here Envelope

Designer: Melissa Phillips

1. Die-cut envelope from patterned paper, ink edges, and assemble.

2. Spell sentiment with rub-ons.

3. Thread ribbon through buttons, wrap around card, and knot.

4. Thread twine through metal tree and tie on ribbon.

Finished size: 3¾" x 2¼"

DESIGNER TIP
This gift card holder can be used as an ornament by hanging it from the twine.

5 STEPS — For You Gift Card Holder

Designer: Teri Anderson

1. Make card from cardstock. Cover with patterned paper. Round corners.

2. Adhere rhinestones.

3. Spell "for you" with stickers.

4. Knot ribbon and adhere.

5. Cut strip of patterned paper and round bottom corners. Adhere edges inside card to create pocket.

Finished size: 3½" x 4½"

SUPPLIES: *Patterned paper:* (Lime Dot paper from Spirit collection) Creative Café *Dye ink:* (Old Paper) Ranger Industries *Accents:* (red buttons) Creative Café; (metal tree) Making Memories *Rub-ons:* (red alphabet) Creative Café *Fibers:* (green gingham ribbon) Making Memories; (red/white twine) Martha Stewart Crafts *Die:* (business card envelope) AccuCut *Tool:* (die cut machine) AccuCut

SUPPLIES: *Cardstock:* (white) Provo Craft *Patterned paper:* (Twinkle Twinkle, Gift Wrap from Christmas Party collection) American Traditional Designs *Accents:* (red rhinestones) Me & My Big Ideas *Stickers:* (Smooth alphabet) Colorbok *Fibers:* (red ribbon) *Tool:* (corner rounder punch) Marvy Uchida *Other:* (gift card)

Fancy Ornament Gift Card Holder

Designer: Anabelle O'Malley

❶ Make two ornaments from patterned paper and cardstock, following pattern on p. 282. Layer together and stitch edges, leaving top open for tag.

❷ Cut patterned paper strip, using ornament edge as guide. Ink edges and adhere.

❸ Punch circles from patterned paper, ink edges, and adhere with foam tape. Adhere rhinestones.

❹ Make tag from cardstock, following pattern. Round edges using corner rounder punch. Make ornament top from patterned paper, following pattern. Adhere to tag. Adhere gift card.

❺ Make topper, following pattern. Draw curved line with pencil. Adhere to tag. Insert tag in ornament.

❻ Tie ribbon around ornament top.

❼ Die-cut tags from patterned paper, stamp sentiments, ink edges, and attach to ribbon with safety pin.

Finished size: 5¼" x 6"

SUPPLIES: *Cardstock:* (white) The Paper Company; (Parakeet) Bazzill Basics Paper *Patterned paper:* (Crimson, Jubilant from Deck the Halls collection) Fontwerks; (Ledger Text from Noteworthy collection) Making Memories *Rubber stamps:* (joy, to/from from Mini-Christmas set) Inque Boutique *Pigment ink:* (Merlot) Clearsnap *Color medium:* (red pencil) *Accents:* (clear rhinestones) Heidi Swapp; (white safety pin) Making Memories *Fibers:* (teal ribbon) SEI *Adhesive:* (foam tape) *Dies:* (tags) Provo Craft *Tools:* (die cut machine) Provo Craft; (1¼" circle punch, corner rounder punch) *Other:* (gift card)

Season's Greetings Pocket

Designer: Lisa Johnson

❶ Trim patterned paper and fold in half to create pocket. Round top corners. Punch half circle in pocket front. Sand edges.

❷ Stitch edges, leaving top open for pocket.

❸ Stamp sentiment; emboss.

❹ Punch snowflake from patterned paper; stitch and adhere.

❺ Apply glitter glue and adhere rhinestones.

❻ Make tag from patterned paper, round corners, and sand edges.

❼ Punch tab from patterned paper, sand edges, and stitch to piece. *Note: Adhere gift card to center of tag and place inside pocket.*

Finished size: 4¼" x 5¼"

SUPPLIES: *Patterned paper:* (Candied Apples, Sleigh Belle, Ribbon Candy from Ting-a-Ling collection) Webster's Pages *Clear stamp:* (season's greetings from Holiday Sentiments set) My Sentiments Exactly! *Watermark ink:* Clearsnap *Embossing powder:* (silver) Clearsnap *Accents:* (iridescent glitter glue) Ranger Industries; (clear rhinestones) Hero Arts *Tools:* (corner rounder punch, 2" circle punch, snowflake punch) Marvy Uchida; (tab punch) Stampin' Up! *Other:* (gift card)

Merry Pillow Box

Designer: Alisa Bangerter

❶ Assemble pillow box die cut; adhere.

❷ Sand box band die cut edges; mat with cardstock. Wrap piece around pillow box and adhere ends together.

❸ Sand edges of merry circle die cut; adhere holly leaves die cut. Thread buttons with floss and adhere to piece.

❹ Adhere piece with foam tape.

Finished size: 7" x 4"

Christmas Tree Gift Card Holder

Designer: Teri Anderson

❶ Cut tree shape from cardstock.

❷ Cut triangle of patterned paper slightly smaller than tree base; adhere. *Note: When adhering patterned paper, leave middle section of right edge open for gift card.*

❸ Adhere cardstock strip for trunk.

❹ Trim heart from cardstock and adhere.

❺ Insert gift card.

Finished size: 4¼" x 6½"

SUPPLIES: *Cardstock:* (black) *Accents:* (pink buttons) Making Memories; (pillow box, box band, holly leaves, merry circle die cuts) One Heart One Mind *Fibers:* (white, black floss) *Adhesive:* (foam tape)

SUPPLIES: *Cardstock:* (kraft, white) Provo Craft; (pink) Bazzill Basics Paper *Patterned paper:* (Noel Tinsel from Love, Elsie collection) KI Memories *Other:* (gift card)

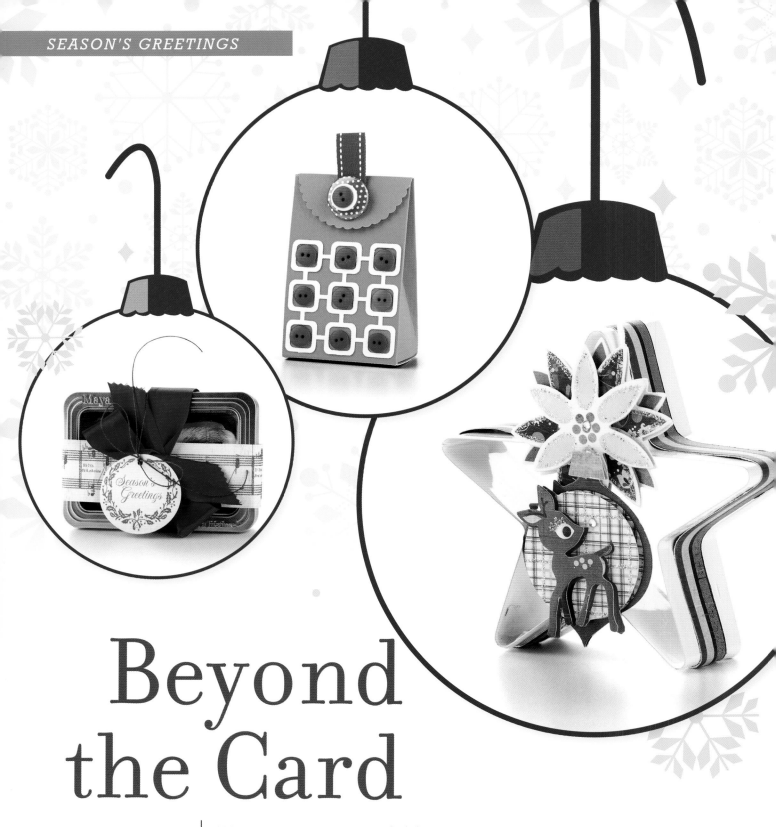

Beyond the Card

We invite you to join us on a holiday journey – one that takes you beyond the card and into a world of paper crafting inspiration that includes tags, bags, boxes, album covers, ornaments, home decor, and even a bottle wrap. Holiday gifts never looked this good!

Mini Merry Tag Trio

Designer: Kelley Eubanks

1. Die-cut and emboss tags from cardstock.
2. Die-cut trees, bird, and snowflake from cardstock; adhere with foam tape. *Note: Adhere one tree without foam tape.*
3. Adhere rhinestones.
4. Tie on twine.

Finished size: 1½" x 2¼"

Gingerbread Gift Bag

Designer: Kalyn Kepner

1. Mat cardstock with cardstock panel; draw border.
2. Attach brads and adhere rhinestone.
3. Trim cardstock strip with decorative-edge scissors; adhere. Adhere ribbon.
4. Adhere sticker with foam tape.
5. Adhere panel to bag with foam tape.
6. Tie on ribbons.

Finished size: 3¾" x 9"

SUPPLIES: *Cardstock:* (Pure Poppy, Enchanted Evening, New Leaf, Ripe Avocado, white) Papertrey Ink *Accents:* (red, green, blue rhinestones) Little Yellow Bicycle *Fibers:* (blue/white twine, red/white twine, green/white twine) Daisy Bucket Designs *Dies:* (trees, bird, snowflake, embossed tag) Ellison

SUPPLIES: *Cardstock:* (kraft, pink, white) Bazzill Basics Paper *Color medium:* (white gel pen) Sakura *Accents:* (green mint brad, pink glitter heart brad) Doodlebug Design; (red rhinestone) *Sticker:* (gingerbread house) Doodlebug Design *Fibers:* (green, red, red polka dot ribbon) *Tool:* (decorative-edge scissors) Provo Craft *Other:* (white gift bag)

DESIGNER TIP
Stamping on both sides of the glass creates a cool 3-D effect.

Blessed Family Ornament

Designer: Nina Brackett

1. Die-cut label from cardstock and patterned paper; adhere together and ink edges. Stamp background.
2. Adhere lace and tie on ribbon.
3. Die-cut scalloped circle from cardstock; adhere. Die-cut photo into circle; adhere.
4. Stamp family on cardstock. Round corners, ink edges, and adhere with foam tape.
5. Adhere sentiment strips, buttons, and flower.
6. Thread button with twine and adhere.

Finished size: 4" x 5½"

Joy Ornament

Designer: Deb Rymer

1. Stamp snowflakes on back of glass. Stamp joy on front; emboss.
2. Attach frame.
3. Tie on ribbon.

Finished size: 2" square

SUPPLIES: *Cardstock:* (Lipstick Red, Ivory) Gina K Designs *Patterned paper:* (Tea Pots from Nook & Pantry collection) BasicGrey *Rubber stamps:* (family from Sweetest Memories set; music background from Vintage Borders set) Gina K Designs *Dye ink:* (Rich Cocoa) Tsukineko *Accents:* (green, red buttons) Gina K Designs; (paper flower, sentiment strips) Making Memories *Fibers:* (white ribbon) Gina K Designs; (natural twine) May Arts; (cream lace) *Dies:* (label, circle, scalloped circle) Spellbinders *Tool:* (corner rounder punch) Fiskars *Other:* (photo)

SUPPLIES: *Clear stamps:* (joy, snowflakes from Snowflake Serenade set) Papertrey Ink *Solvent ink:* (Cotton White) Tsukineko *Embossing powder:* (Sterling Silver) Stampin' Up! *Fibers:* (red ribbon) Michaels *Other:* (silver frame, frosted glass) Ranger Industries

12 Days of Cookies Album

Designer: Valerie Mangan

1. Punch circles from patterned paper and adhere.
2. Trim patterned paper into tag; punch edge. Trim cardstock into tag; punch edge. Adhere to patterned paper tag.
3. Affix stickers. Stitch around tag and stickers. Adhere.
4. Print "Days of cookies" on cardstock. Trim and adhere.
5. Punch circle and scalloped circle from patterned paper; layer and adhere.
6. Tie on twine and ribbon.

Finished size: 9¾" x 6¾"

5 Season's Greetings Wall Décor

Designer: Sherry Wright

1. Distress edges of patterned paper and adhere inside shadowbox.
2. Adhere appliqué.
3. Trim branches from patterned paper and adhere.
4. Affix stickers and apply glitter glue.

Finished size: 6" square

SUPPLIES: *Cardstock:* (kraft) Bazzill Basics Paper; (teal) Core'dinations *Patterned paper:* (Alpine, Rooftop from Eskimo Kisses collection) BasicGrey; (Red Medium Polka Dots from Lush collection) My Mind's Eye *Stickers:* (numbers) Making Memories *Fibers:* (red/white twine) Martha Stewart Crafts; (teal ribbon) *Font:* (French Script) www.fonts.com *Tools:* (border punch) Stampin' Up!; (1½" circle punch, 2" scalloped circle punch) EK Success *Other:* (album) American Crafts

SUPPLIES: *Patterned paper:* (Cranberry Sauce, French Hens from Wassail collection) BasicGrey *Accents:* (gold glitter glue) Ranger Industries; (white rose resin appliqué) Melissa Frances *Stickers:* (chipboard flowers) BasicGrey; (season's greetings oval) Making Memories *Other:* (cream shadowbox)

DESIGNER TIP

Include a picture of you with your recipient for a fun friend gift or use as place settings by including photos of your guests.

Merry Christmas Treat Box

Designer: Jennifer Biederman

1. Cut patterned paper to fit around box. Ink edges, mat with cardstock, and adhere ends together to form band.
2. Tie on ribbon.
3. Stamp Merry Christmas Logo on cardstock with watermark ink; emboss. Ink tree image, wipe off excess, and punch into circle. Mat with patterned paper, and adhere. Adhere rhinestones.
4. Stamp Merry Christmas Logo on cardstock, punch into circle, and punch out center. Adhere with foam tape.
5. Slide band over box.

Finished size: 4¼" x 4¼" x 1"

Homespun Frame

Designer: Juliana Michaels

1. Cover chipboard bird and inside frame with patterned paper.
2. Attach brad and adhere rhinestones and trim to frame.
3. Attach brad to flowers; adhere.
4. Sand edges of bird; apply glitter glue and adhere.

Finished size: 3½" x 4¼"

SUPPLIES: *Cardstock:* (white) Papertrey Ink *Patterned paper:* (Dot from Persuasion collection, Blush Dot from Double Dot collection) BoBunny Press *Rubber stamp:* (Merry Christmas Logo) Purple Onion Designs *Dye ink:* (Peeled Paint, Vintage Photo) Ranger Industries *Watermark ink; Embossing powder:* (clear) American Crafts *Accents:* (pink rhinestones) BasicGrey *Fibers:* (green ribbon) Creative Impressions *Tools:* (1", 1¾" circle punches) EK Success *Other:* (clear box) Clearbags

SUPPLIES: *Patterned paper:* (Pink Sparkle, Pink Stitchery from Homespun Chic collection) GCD Studios *Accents:* (chipboard bird, layered frame; pink, white decorative brads) GCD Studios; (pink felt flowers) Stampin' Up!; (pink rhinestones) BoBunny Press; (iridescent glitter glue) Ranger Industries *Fibers:* (white pompom trim)

Celebrate Gift Bag

Designer: Carolyn King

1 Adhere patterned paper to bag; affix tape.
2 Make card from cardstock. Ink edges of patterned paper strip and adhere.
3 Stamp sentiment on cardstock. Distress and ink edges; adhere.
4 Punch patterned paper. Distress and ink edges; adhere.
5 Affix tape and adhere flower with foam tape.
6 Thread button with floss and adhere.
7 Adhere card to bag. Tie on twine.

Finished size: 5¼" x 8½"

5 STEPS Vintage Christmas Album Cover

Designer: Anabelle O'Malley

1 Punch holes in book covers; attach rings.
2 Adhere die cuts and scene.
3 Adhere snowflake with foam tape.
4 Punch hole in oval. Thread ribbon and seam binding through oval and ring; tie on.

Finished size: 7" x 4½"

SUPPLIES: *Cardstock:* (Ivory) Gina K Designs *Patterned paper:* (Gingerbread from Good Cheer collection; Fireflies from Fly a Kite collection) October Afternoon *Rubber stamp:* (sentiment from Christmas Treasures Borders & Centers set) JustRite *Dye ink:* (Frayed Burlap) Ranger Industries *Color medium:* (red, black markers) Stampin' Up! *Accents:* (green flower, red button) Jillibean Soup *Stickers:* (black polka dot tape) Making Memories *Fibers:* (natural jute twine) Westrim Crafts; (red floss) *Tool:* (border punch) Stampin' Up! *Other:* (kraft gift bag)

SUPPLIES: *Accents:* (silver rings) Staples; (chipboard snowflake, sentiment oval, children scene) K&Company; (holly, label die cuts) Mamelok Press *Fibers:* (green ribbon) Michaels; (cream seam binding) MemrieMare *Tool:* (³⁄₁₆" circle punch) *Other:* (book covers) 7gypsies

5 STEPS 'Tis the Season Gift Tin

Designer: Kalyn Kepner

1. Cover tin with patterned paper.
2. Trim patterned paper strip with decorative-edge scissors; adhere.
3. Tie on ribbon.
4. Adhere circle die cut to lid. Adhere star, snowflake, and sentiment die cuts with foam tape.

Finished size: 2¼" diameter x 2¼" height

5 STEPS Be Jolly Treat Box

Designer: Teri Anderson

1. Punch circle from patterned paper. Mat with circle punched from cardstock; adhere to box.
2. Spell "Be jolly" with stickers.
3. Adhere poinsettia.
4. Tie on ribbon.

Finished size: 2½" x 2½" x 1"

SUPPLIES: *Patterned paper:* (Snowflake Stripes from Colorful Christmas collection) My Mind's Eye *Accents:* (star, snowflake, circle, sentiment die cuts) My Mind's Eye *Fibers:* (orange ribbon) *Tool:* (decorative-edge scissors) Provo Craft *Other:* (white tin) Westrim Crafts

SUPPLIES: *Cardstock:* (white) Georgia-Pacific *Patterned paper:* (Sage Green from Juliette collection) A Muse Artstamps *Accent:* (red/pink poinsettia) BasicGrey *Stickers:* (Mini alphabet) My Little Shoebox *Fibers:* (red ribbon) Stampin' Up! *Tools:* (1¾", 2" circle punches) EK Success, Fiskars *Other:* (clear box) Denami Design

5 STEPS · Homespun Noel Tag

Designer: Kelley Eubanks

1. Ink edges of tag; adhere patterned paper.
2. Trim image from vintage tag; adhere, using foam tape for image.
3. Stamp noel.
4. Adhere ribbon. Tie on twine.

Finished size: 2½" x 5¼"

5 STEPS · Poinsettia Noel Tag

Designer: Kelley Eubanks

1. Die-cut labels from cardstock. Stamp labels and noel on cardstock labels; layer with foam tape.
2. Attach brad to poinsettia and adhere with foam tape.
3. Punch hole and tie on twine.

Finished size: 2¼" x 3¾"

5 STEPS · Shabby Joy Tag

Designer: Sherry Wright

1. Trim cardstock into tag; ink edges.
2. Distress edges of patterned paper and adhere.
3. Stamp sentiment on cardstock and adhere.
4. Ink edges of chipboard frame. Adhere frame, trim, flourish, and flower.
5. Tie ribbon bow and adhere. Tie button with twine and adhere.

Finished size: 2¾" x 5¼"

SUPPLIES: *Patterned paper:* (Letters to Santa from Christmas Past collection) Graphic 45 *Clear stamp:* (noel from Tree Trimming Trio set) Papertrey Ink *Dye ink:* (Vintage Photo) Ranger Industries *Specialty ink:* (True Black hybrid) Papertrey Ink *Accent:* (red vintage tag) Graphic 45 *Fibers:* (red pleated ribbon) Pink Paislee; (natural twine) Papertrey Ink *Other:* (cream tag) DMD, Inc.

SUPPLIES: *Cardstock:* (Scarlet Jewel, Rustic Cream) Papertrey Ink *Clear stamps:* (noel from Signature Christmas set) Papertrey Ink; (labels from Very Vintage Labels No. 4 set) Waltzingmouse Stamps *Specialty ink:* (True Black hybrid) Papertrey Ink *Accents:* (red poinsettia) Hero Arts; (silver glitter brad) Little Yellow Bicycle *Fibers:* (natural jute twine) Papertrey Ink *Dies:* (labels) Spellbinders *Tool:* (1/16" circle punch)

SUPPLIES: *Cardstock:* (white) *Patterned paper:* (Cranberry Sauce from Wassail collection) BasicGrey *Clear stamp:* (sentiment from Signature Christmas set) Papertrey Ink *Chalk ink:* (Chestnut Roan) Clearsnap *Accents:* (white chipboard frame) Tattered Angels; (white flower, burgundy pearl flourish) Zva Creative; (cream button) *Fibers:* (cream ribbon) Offray; (white trim) Webster's Pages; (brown twine)

christmas Gifts for the Neighbors

Any neighbor would love to find one of these clever handmade packages on their doorstep this holiday season. From gift bags to festive tins this assortment of quick gifts is guaranteed to bring a smile to your friends' faces and a little more holiday cheer to your neighborhood!

You're So Cool Gift Bag

Designer: Kim Kesti

① Fold top of bag to finished size.

② Trim cardstock; adhere to bag.

③ Trim patterned paper; mat with cardstock.

④ Stamp sentiment on cardstock; trim and adhere.

⑤ Attach brad.

⑥ Adhere glitter.

⑦ Punch hole in tag, tie to bag with ribbon, and adhere.

Finished size: 4¼" x 8¼"

DESIGNER TIP

Fill the gift bag with cool-flavored treats like peppermint fudge, mint hot chocolate mix, or mint-flavored candies.

5 STEPS Season of Joy Tin

Designer: Susan Neal

① Cover tin with patterned paper.

② Adhere rhinestones.

③ Create bow from patterned paper strips (see "How to Create Bow").

④ Adhere bow.

Finished size: 3" diameter x 9½" height

HOW TO CREATE BOW

a Lay strip horizontally and hold down midpoint. Fold left end down across midpoint; repeat with right end.
Note: The folded strip resembles "awareness" ribbons.

b Repeat; staple set of two folded strips at tail ends.

c Adhere two sets at tail ends to create four corners.

d Repeat steps a–c and layer groups as desired.

e Fold two strips into loops; flatten slightly, layer, and adhere to create center.

SUPPLIES: *Cardstock:* (Lily White, Ocean scalloped) Bazzill Basics Paper *Patterned paper:* (Cary Grant from Noir Blanc collection) Tinkering Ink *Clear stamp:* (you're so cool from Zoology set) Technique Tuesday *Solvent ink:* (Jet Black) Tsukineko *Accents:* (blue penguin brad) Creative Imaginations; (clear glitter) FloraCraft *Fibers:* (black dotted ribbon) Adornit-Carolee's Creations *Other:* (white gift bag)

SUPPLIES: *Patterned paper:* (Naughty & Nice, Fruit Cake from Season of Joy collection) Scrapworks *Accents:* (clear rhinestones) *Other:* (white tin) Provo Craft

INSIDE

Enjoy a night
at the movies on us!

Merry Christmas,
The O'Malleys

Happy Holidays

Tree Gift Box

Designer: Melissa Phillips

❶ Die-cut box from cardstock; trim acrylic frame to fit window and adhere.

❷ Insert candy; secure box closed.

❸ Adhere chipboard wreath. Tie floss through button and adhere to chipboard circle; adhere.

❹ Tie ribbon around box.

❺ Adhere chipboard tag.

Finished size: 5¼" x 6" x ¾"

Movie Ticket Tin

Designer: Anabelle O'Malley

❶ Paint tin.

❷ Trim patterned paper to cover tin; sand and adhere.

❸ Ink journaling card; adhere.

❹ Affix sticker.

❺ Adhere chipboard snowflake. Tie floss through button and knot; adhere.

❻ Trim patterned paper to fit inside tin; print sentiment, ink edges, and fold.

Finished size: 5" x ¾" x 3¼"

DESIGNER TIPS
- Sand the paper edges to give the tin a shabby feel.
- Tuck tickets to a local children's production or play in the tin instead of movie tickets.

SUPPLIES: *Cardstock:* (Ladybug glitter) Doodlebug Design *Accents:* (acrylic swirl frame) My Mind's Eye; (chipboard wreath, circle, tag) Making Memories; (white button) Melissa Frances *Fibers:* (white ribbon) Wrights; (red floss) *Die:* (tree box) Provo Craft *Tool:* (die cut machine) Provo Craft *Other:* (candy)

SUPPLIES: *Patterned paper:* (Dots/Blue from Merry Christmas collection) My Mind's Eye *Pigment ink:* (Dune) Clearsnap *Chalk ink:* (Creamy Brown) Clearsnap *Paint:* (white) Delta *Accents:* (blue journaling card) My Mind's Eye; (chipboard glitter snowflake) Melissa Frances; (blue button) Autumn Leaves *Stickers:* (green flourish) Creative Imaginations *Fibers:* (red floss) DMC *Font:* (Amazone BT) www.fontstock.net *Other:* (silver tin) Michaels

5 steps Happy Holidays Bag

Designer: Alisa Bangerter

❶ Cut cardstock slightly smaller than bag front; mat with cardstock and stitch edges. Adhere.

❷ Adhere patterned paper.

❸ Adhere buttons.

❹ Mat sticker with cardstock; adhere with foam tape.

❺ Tie ribbon to handle.

Finished size: 5½" x 8½"

Noel Cookie Mix Jar

Designer: Melissa Phillips

❶ Affix label sticker. Fill jar with cookie mix.

❷ Cut circles from fabric using decorative-edge scissors, layer, and secure to jar lid with rubber band.

❸ Wrap ribbon around lid and tie bow. Adhere flat pearl.

❹ Affix sticker to tag. Tie thread through buttons; adhere.

❺ Thread twine through tag, wrap around lid, and tie bow.

❻ Cover chipboard star with sheet music; adhere.

Finished size: 3½" diameter x 6¾" height

BONUS IDEA
Fill the jar with your favorite homemade soup for an alternative to sweet treats.

SUPPLIES: All supplies from Making Memories unless otherwise noted. *Cardstock:* (Lily Pad, brown) Bazzill Basics Paper *Patterned paper:* (Scallop Circle from Fa La La collection) *Accents:* (green, brown, white, ivory buttons) *Stickers:* (sentiment epoxy) *Fibers:* (green stitched ribbon) *Adhesive:* (foam tape) *Other:* (kraft gift bag) DMD, Inc.

SUPPLIES: *Accents:* (green Santa tag, chipboard star; white, clear buttons) Melissa Frances; (flat pearl) *Stickers:* (pinecone label, Noel) Melissa Frances *Fibers:* (red ribbon, twine) *Tool:* (decorative-edge scissors) *Other:* (gingham, striped fabric; canning jar, sheet music, cookie mix)

Celebrate Gable Box
Designer: Susan Neal

❶ Cover gable box with patterned paper.

❷ Tie fibers to handle.

❸ Trim sticker from sheet; punch hole. Tie sticker to ribbon with cording.

Finished size: 4" x 5½" x 2½"

Sweet Sentiments Box
Designer: Kim Kesti

❶ Apply rub-ons.

❷ Cut window in patterned paper; adhere to lid.

❸ Adhere photo corners.

❹ Trim patterned paper strips; adhere to lid.

Finished size: 6¼" x 6¼" x 3¼"

SUPPLIES: *Patterned paper:* (Peppermint Twist from Peppermint Twist Paper Pad) K&Company *Sticker:* (bell) K&Company *Fibers:* (pink sheer ribbon) Karen Foster Design; (gold cording) *Other:* (white gable box) XPedX

SUPPLIES: All supplies from One Heart One Mind unless otherwise noted. *Patterned paper:* (Jingle Jingle Coverall from Merry Merry collection) *Accents:* (pink, white photo corners) *Rub-ons:* (holiday sentiments) *Other:* (white window box) no source

5 STEP Musical Gift Bag

Designer: Heidi Sonboul

① Cover bag front with patterned paper; trim strip of patterned paper with decorative-edge scissors and adhere.

② Cut cardstock rectangle; ink edges. Cut cardstock strips with decorative-edge scissors; adhere. Stitch edges and adhere.

③ Cut cardstock rectangle; mat with patterned paper. Cut patterned paper rectangle with decorative-edge scissors; adhere. Stitch edges and adhere with foam tape.

④ Affix stickers.

⑤ Set eyelets; thread ribbon through eyelets and knot.

Finished size: 7¼" x 8½"

Santa Tussie

Designer: Melissa Phillips

① Trim 9" square of patterned paper and make cone.

② Cut patterned paper strip with decorative-edge scissors; adhere.

③ Adhere trim.

④ Attach ribbon and buttons to create hanger. Attach ribbon inside cone bottom.

⑤ Affix family sticker.

⑥ Adhere glitter to chipboard deer; tie ribbon. Adhere. Affix believe tag sticker.

⑦ Adhere glitter to bells; adhere.

Finished size: 3¼" diameter x 9½" long

SUPPLIES: *Cardstock:* (Parakeet, white) Bazzill Basics Paper *Patterned paper:* (Red Damask from Dorothy collection, Music from Blythe collection) Anna Griffin *Dye ink:* (Garden Green) Stampin' Up! *Accents:* (white square eyelets) Making Memories *Stickers:* (tree, gifts) Anna Griffin *Fibers:* (green stitched ribbon) Anna Griffin *Adhesive:* (foam tape) *Tool:* (decorative-edge scissors) Fiskars *Other:* (white gift bag)

SUPPLIES: *Patterned paper:* (Collage, Flocked Poinsettia from St. Nick Vintage collection) Making Memories *Accents:* (chipboard reindeer; white, gold glitter) Melissa Frances; (gold jingle bells) Darice; (gold buttons) *Stickers:* (family, believe tag) Melissa Frances *Fibers:* (cream lace trim) Prima; (red ribbon) Making Memories; (green velvet ribbon) Maya Road *Tool:* (decorative-edge scissors) Provo Craft

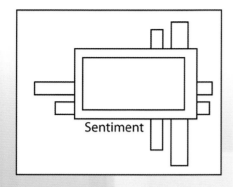

Sentiment

DESIGNER TIP

Punch up the flair of decorative tapes by adding fun stitching over them.

Holly Jolly Card

Designer: Sarah Martina Parker

❶ Make card from cardstock. Ink edges.

❷ Affix tape strips and zigzag-stitch.

❸ Trim cardstock, ink edges, and mat with cardstock. Adhere.

❹ Adhere tag using foam tape.

❺ Stamp sentiment.

Finished size: 5½" x 4¼"

SUPPLIES: *Cardstock:* (white, kraft) Papertrey Ink *Clear stamp:* (sentiment from Holly Jolly set) Clear & Simple Stamps *Pigment ink:* (Sahara Sand) Tsukineko *Accent:* (Christmas tag) Creative Imaginations *Sticker:* (red polka dot tape) Love My Tapes

Cute Happy Holidays Card

Designer: Melissa Elsner

SUPPLIES: *Cardstock:* (Salt embossed) Bazzill Basics Paper *Patterned paper:* (Accessory Sheet from Colorful Christmas collection) My Mind's Eye *Rubber stamp:* (Happy Holidays) Studio G *Pigment ink:* (Onyx Black) Tsukineko *Accents:* (green rhinestones) Kaisercraft

Finished size: 5½" x 4¼"

Snowman Warm Winter Wishes Card

Designer: Betsy Veldman

SUPPLIES: *Cardstock:* (white, kraft) Papertrey Ink *Patterned paper:* (Wrap the Presents from Very Merry collection; Ice Cream from Fly a Kite collection) October Afternoon; (Travel Ticking from On Holiday collection) The Girls' Paperie; (blue grid from 2008 Bitty Box Basics collection) Papertrey Ink *Clear stamps:* (sentiment from Merry & Bright set; snowman from Holiday Tree set) Papertrey Ink *Pigment ink:* (Fresh Snow, Spring Rain) Papertrey Ink *Chalk ink:* (Creamy Brown) Clearsnap *Specialty ink:* (Dark Chocolate hybrid) Papertrey Ink *Accents:* (red rhinestones) Kaisercraft *Die:* (tree) Provo Craft

Finished size: 5½" x 4¼"

Joyous Kwanzaa Gift Bag

Designer: Kim Hughes

SUPPLIES: *Cardstock:* (Wool Scarf, Pumpkin Vine, Maple Leaf, Candied Apple) Couture Cardstock; (Tawny Light) Bazzill Basics Paper; (Nightfall, Snowflake) Core'dinations *Patterned paper:* (Draft from Basics collection) BasicGrey *Accents:* (light orange rhinestones) Zva Creative *Stickers:* (Tiny Alpha alphabet) Making Memories *Fibers:* (green twill) Papertrey Ink *Tool:* (decorative-edge scissors) Fiskars *Other:* (kraft bag)

Finished size: 5¼" x 6"

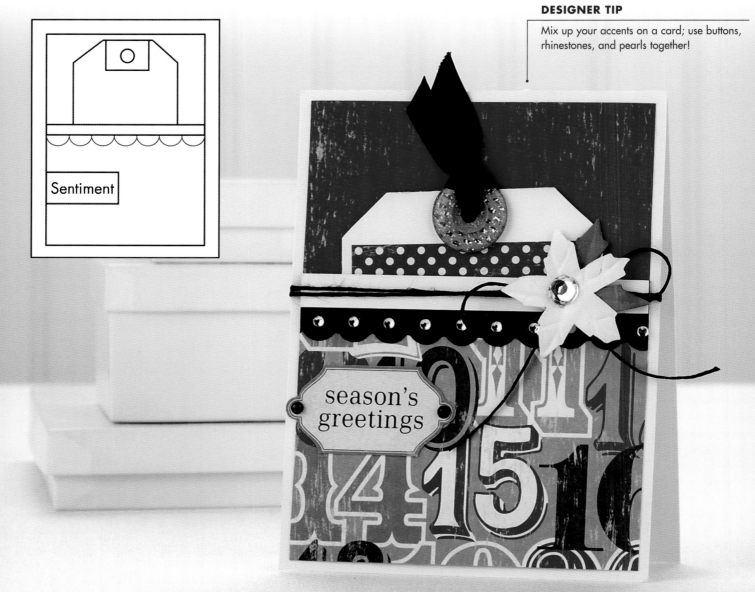

DESIGNER TIP

Mix up your accents on a card; use buttons, rhinestones, and pearls together!

Season's Greetings Card

Designer: Rae Barthel

❶ Make card from cardstock. Adhere patterned paper square to top.

❷ Adhere patterned paper to bottom. *Note: Adhere only on sides and bottom; leave top open to create pocket.*

❸ Border-punch strip of cardstock, adhere, and adhere strip of cardstock.

❹ Adhere rhinestones, tie on string, and adhere flower. Adhere rhinestone.

❺ Adhere sentiment die cut and pearls.

❻ Trim cardstock to make tag, adhere patterned paper, and punch hole.

❼ Adhere button, tie on ribbon, and tuck tag into pocket.

Finished size: 4¼" x 5½"

SUPPLIES: *Cardstock:* (Vintage Cream) Papertrey Ink; (black) Bazzill Basics Paper *Patterned paper:* (Advent, Argyle, Die-Cut Glitter Mini Red Dot from Mistletoe collection) Making Memories *Accents:* (green button, white flower, sentiment die cut) Making Memories; (clear rhinestones) Michaels; (black pearls) Queen & Co. *Fibers:* (black ribbon) Hobby Lobby; (black string) *Tool:* (border punch) Fiskars

DESIGNER TIP

To make your cardstock stickers even more versatile, you can adhere them to cardstock, trim, and then use foam tape to attach them to your project.

DESIGNER TIPS

Consider using both sides of an embossing folder as they can have very different effects.

Because there are so many layers in the flower, it's best to sew them together rather than use adhesive

Enjoy Gift Card Holder

Designer: Kathi F. Rerek

SUPPLIES: *Cardstock:* (white) Bazzill Basics Paper *Patterned paper:* (Vintage Plaid, Admiral from June Bug collection) BasicGrey *Vellum:* Strathmore Artist Papers *Dye ink:* (Black Soot) Ranger Industries *Accents:* (red rhinestones) Michaels *Stickers:* (Metro Shimmer alphabet) Making Memories *Die:* (ticket strip) Ellison *Tools:* (border punch) Fiskars; (corner rounder punch) Tonic Studios; (slot punch) Stampin' Up! *Other:* (gift card)

Finished size: 4¼" x 5½"

The Best Birthday Card

Designer: Chan Vuong

SUPPLIES: *Cardstock:* (Lemon Tart, Aqua Mist, Melon Berry) Papertrey Ink *Patterned paper:* (Confection from Sweet Marmalade collection) Sassafras Lass; (Tossed Salad from Garden Variety collection) Cosmo Cricket; (bird from The Songbird Stack pad) Die Cuts With a View *Clear stamp:* (sentiment from Delta Series set) BasicGrey *Pigment ink:* (Onyx Black) Tsukineko *Sticker:* (flag banner) Sassafras Lass *Fibers:* (aqua polka dot ribbon) American Crafts *Template:* (Small Polka Dots embossing) QuicKutz *Die:* (tag) Provo Craft *Tools:* (corner rounder punch) Marvy Uchida; (decorative-edge scissors)

Finished size: 4¼" x 5½"

Pretty Thank You Card

Designer: Lisette Gibbons

SUPPLIES: *Cardstock:* (Cream Puff) Bazzill Basics Paper *Patterned paper:* (One-of-a-Kind, Needs Paint, Collector's Item from The Thrift Shop collection) October Afternoon *Clear stamp:* (thank you from Communique Curves Sentiments set) Papertrey Ink *Dye ink:* (Antique Linen) Ranger Industries *Solvent ink:* (Timber Brown) Tsukineko *Accents:* (white pearls) Kaisercraft *Sticker:* (red frame) October Afternoon *Fibers:* (red twill) *Template:* (Diamonds & Dots embossing) Provo Craft *Dies:* (large scalloped border, flowers) Papertrey Ink *Other:* (red crepe paper)

Finished size: 5¼" x 6"

Glitter is Glam

Try these nine stunning ways to incorporate glitter into your next paper-crafted project.

Shaker card. Place chunky glitter inside a transparent pocket.

Glitter borders. Adhere glitter to double-sided adhesive strips.

Enhance stamped images. Stamp an image with a glue pad and adhere glitter.

Add eye-catching detail. Apply glitter glue to motifs on patterned paper.

Make custom accents. Cover chipboard with adhesive and glitter.

Create dimension. Adhere coarse glitter to cardstock edges.

Customize buttons. Adhere glitter to the backs of clear buttons.

Create Faux mats. Trace borders with a glue pen and apply glitter.

Create patterned paper. Expose double-sided adhesive one square at a time and apply glitter.

DESIGNER TIP

Make your adhesive do double duty! Seal the tin and adhere your ribbon by affixing liner tape to the outside edges of your project.

5 STEPS Joy to the World Ornament

Designer: Jessica Witty

❶ Adhere patterned paper to inside of tin.

❷ Accent house and tree stickers with glitter. Adhere inside tin with foam tape.

❸ Pour glitter inside tin and close lid. Adhere ribbon around tin; knot on top.

❹ Stamp sentiment on cardstock; trim.

❺ Brush back of button with liquid adhesive; apply glitter. Tie button, sentiment, and snowflake sticker to ribbon with string.

Finished size: 3½" x 5½" x 1"

SUPPLIES: *Cardstock:* (white) Papertrey Ink *Patterned paper:* (Ocean Dot from Double Dot collection) BoBunny Press *Clear stamp:* (sentiment from Daily Designs Sentiments set) Papertrey Ink *Specialty ink:* (New Leaf hybrid) Papertrey Ink *Accents:* (clear button) 7gypsies; (clear glitter) Chenille Kraft; (blue glitter) *Stickers:* (chipboard houses, tree, snowflake) Cosmo Cricket *Fibers:* (pink striped ribbon) Hobby Lobby; (blue striped string) Martha Stewart Crafts *Other:* (white rectangle tin)

Snowballs Bucket
Designer: Davinie Fiero

❶ Punch circles from patterned paper. Layer and attach to foam balls with stick pins.
❷ Trim patterned paper strip with decorative-edge scissors; adhere to bucket. ❸ Ink large tag. Stamp "Snowballs" and staple to veneer strip. Cover chipboard snowflake with glitter; adhere. ❹ Spell "5¢" with stickers on price tag; attach to sign. Tie on ribbon. ❺ Place sign in bucket; fill most of bucket with felt. Arrange snowballs.

Finished size: 6½" diameter x 11½" height

SUPPLIES: *Patterned paper:* (Jack Frost, 34th Street, 5th Avenue from Tinsel Town collection) Pink Paislee *Clear stamps:* (Vintage Pop Alphabet) Pink Paislee *Dye ink:* (brown) *Solvent ink:* (green) Tsukineko *Accents:* (silver glitter) Pink Paislee; (chipboard snowflake) Maya Road; (large tag) 7gypsies; (silver stick pins) Jo-Ann Stores; (price tag, staples) *Stickers:* (Holly Doodle alphabet) Pink Paislee *Fibers:* (pink stitched ribbon) Offray *Tools:* (circle punches) EK Success; (decorative-edge scissors) *Other:* (white felt, foam balls, silver bucket) Michaels; (wood veneer strip)

Cold Winter Fun Album

Designer: Beatriz Jennings

❶ Paint edges of album; let dry. ❷ Trim cardstock to fit covers and spine. Trim slightly smaller piece of patterned paper. Ink and distress edges. Stitch to cardstock and adhere pieces to album. ❸ Adhere lace and ribbon. *Note: Leave excess ribbon on side to tie closed.* ❹ Apply rub-on. ❺ Adhere pompoms and letters. Attach brad to snowflake and adhere. ❻ Tie string through buttons and adhere to spine.

Finished size: 5¾" x 3"

SUPPLIES: Cardstock: (Lily White glitter) Doodlebug Design Patterned paper: (Cassy) Melissa Frances Dye ink: (Old Paper) Ranger Industries Paint: (white) Accents: (white chipboard snowflake) Melissa Frances; (silver chipboard letters, blue/cream brad) K&Company; (white pompoms, pink buttons) Rub-on: (winter fun) Melissa Frances Fibers: (blue ribbon) Martha Stewart Crafts; (cream lace, red/pink string) Other: (chipboard album) Maya Road

No Winter
Lasts Card

Designer: Susan Neal

1 Make card from cardstock.

2 Cut patterned paper slightly smaller than card front; ink edges. *Note: Cut with cloud pattern at top of piece.*

3 Print sentiment on piece; adhere.

4 Cut cardstock piece; tear edge and adhere.

5 Adhere die cuts, some with foam tape.

Finished size: 3¾" x 8½"

SUPPLIES: *Cardstock:* (Camouflage, Chocolate) Bazzill Basics Paper *Patterned paper:* (Lenient from Mellow collection) BasicGrey *Chalk ink:* (Olive) Clearsnap *Accents:* (tree, leaf die cuts) BasicGrey *Font:* (AshleyCapitaliSofia) www.abstract-fonts.com *Adhesive:* (foam tape) Therm O Web

Winter Wishes Gift Set

Designer: Susan Neal

TRAY

1 Paint sides and edges; sand. 2 Adhere patterned paper to sides. Sand and ink edges. 3 Ink edges of striped paper; adhere. 4 Print sentiment on cardstock; stamp snowflakes and ink edges. Mat with cardstock; adhere.

BUCKET

1 Paint edges and handle. Sand. 2 Adhere patterned paper. Sand and ink edges. 3 Mat cardstock strip with cardstock; adhere. 4 Print recipe on journaling block. Ink edges. Stamp snowflakes. Adhere to bucket.

CINNAMON STICK TAG

1 Tie cinnamon sticks together with ribbon. 2 Print sentiment on tag die cut; ink edges. 3 Tie to ribbon with jingle bell.

Finished sizes: tray 13½" x 10¼" x 1¼", bucket 4½" x 4" x 3", cinnamon sticks tag 2" x 1½"

SUPPLIES: *Cardstock:* (Natural, Skyline, Bitter Chocolate) Bazzill Basics Paper *Patterned paper:* (Scarf Stripes from Frost collection, Reindeer from Festive collection) My Mind's Eye *Rubber stamp:* (snowflake) *Chalk ink:* (Prussian Blue, Chestnut Roan) Clearsnap *Paint:* (Brown Iron Oxide) Delta *Accents:* (journaling block, tag die cuts) My Mind's Eye; (gold jingle bells) *Fibers:* (brown jute twine, striped jute ribbon) *Font:* (TXT Antique Poster) www.scrapnfonts.com *Tools:* (die cut machine) Provo Craft; (⅛" circle punch) Marvy Uchida *Other:* (wood bucket) Provo Craft; (wood tray, apple cider spice mix, cinnamon sticks, plastic bag)

Download sentiments at www.PaperCraftsMag.com

"When witches go riding,
and black cats are seen,
the moon laughs and whispers,
'tis near Halloween."

YOU'RE INVITED

"Backward, turn backward,
O Time, in your flight
make me a child again
just for to-night!"
—*Elizabeth Akers Allen*

HAPPY HALLOWEEN

"Once in a young lifetime one should
be allowed to have as much sweetness
as one can possibly want and hold."
—Judith Olney

BEWARE
OF THINGS THAT GO
BUMP IN THE NIGHT

Finish What You Started

Use these spooky quotes to help you create a sentiment perfectly customized for any occasion or recipient.

Front of Card	Inside Card
"Backward, turn backward, O Time, in your flight make me a child again just for to-night!" —*Elizabeth Akers Allen*	Channel your inner child at our annual costume party. For details call 123-4567.
"Once in a young lifetime one should be allowed to have as much sweetness as one can possibly want and hold." —*Judith Olney*	Wishing you and yours a very sweet and happy Halloween.
Beware of things that go bump in the night	It just might be another birthday creeping up on you. Happy 50th!

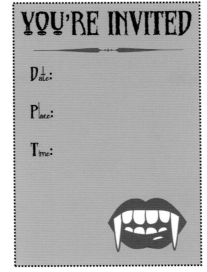

YOU'RE INVITED

Date:

Place:

Time:

HAPPY HALLOWEEN

EAT, DRINK, & BE
SCARY.

happy haunting!

Come with me
All Hallows night
We'll **FRIGHTEN** everyone in sight
Such pranks for once, are justified
And **FUN** and **FROLIC** amplified.
—19th Century Halloween postcard

When witches go riding
and black cats are seen,
the moon laughs and whispers
Happy Halloween!

Clothes make a statement.
Costumes tell a *story.*
—Mason Cooley

DOUBLE, DOUBLE
toil AND TROUBLE,
fire burn and
cauldron bubble
—William Shakespeare

Finish What You Started

Use these seasonal quotes to help you create a sentiment perfectly customized for any recipient.

Front of Card	Inside Card
"Clothes make a statement. Costumes tell a story." —Mason Cooley	Make a statement AND tell a story at our annual costume party.
"Double, double toil and trouble; fire burn and cauldron bubble." —William Shakespeare	Wishing you a Halloween "bubbling over" with fun!

JOY TO the WORLD

all is calm, all is bright.

Wise Men
Still Seek Him

Christmas
waves a magic wand over
this world, and behold, everything
is softer and more beautiful.

--Norman Vincent Peale

Peace on earth will come to stay,
when we live Christmas every day.

--Helen Steiner Rice

There's
no place like
home for the holidays.

And He
shall reign
forever & ever.

WE WISH YOU A
MERRY CHRISTMAS...

...AND A HAPPY NEW YEAR.

Joyeux Noel

Finish What You Started

Use these quotes to help you create a sentiment perfectly
customized for any Yule-time recipient.

Front of Card	Inside Card
Wise Men Still Seek Him.	May His love fill your home this Christmas.
Joyeux Noel	In any language, we send you love and peace at Christmas.

Teacher says,
"Every time a bell rings,
an angel gets
his wings."

--It's a Wonderful Life

Finish What You Started

Use these quotes to help you create your holiday cards from the outside in!

Front of Card	Inside Card
Have yourself a merry little Christmas…	…and a happy New Year
Season's Greetings	From our home to yours!
Mele Kalikimaka	Wishing you a warm holiday season!

PATTERNS

MARTINI GLASS PATTERN p.8
ENLARGE 200%

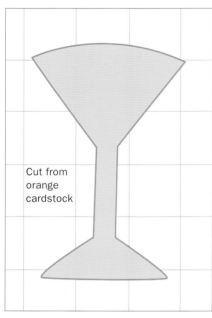

Cut from orange cardstock

Each square = 1". Cut on solid lines.

FANCY ORNAMENT GIFT CARD HOLDER p.252   ENLARGE 350%

TOPPER
Cut 1 Parakeet cardstock

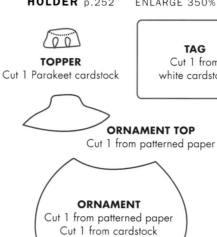

TAG
Cut 1 from white cardstock

ORNAMENT TOP
Cut 1 from patterned paper

ORNAMENT
Cut 1 from patterned paper
Cut 1 from cardstock

SCALLOPED OWL CARD PATTERN
p.117   ENLARGE 300%

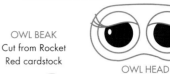

OWL BEAK
Cut from Rocket Red cardstock

OWL HEAD
Cut from Kraft cardstock
OWL EYES
Cut from white cardstock
OWL EYELIDS
Cut from Rocket Red cardstock

OWL BELLY
Cut from white cardstock

OWL BODY
Mirror body pattern and cut 1 from kraft cardstock

Cut 1 front only from Red Rocket cardstock

OWL WINGS
Cut from kraft cardstock

SPARKLING HANUKKAH
p.190   ENLARGE 265%

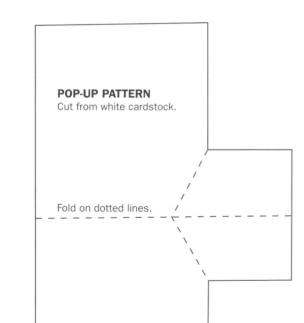

POP-UP PATTERN
Cut from white cardstock.

Fold on dotted lines.

WITCH HAT PATTERN p.97
ENLARGE 375%

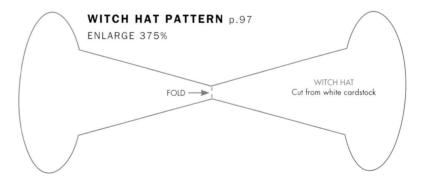

FOLD →

WITCH HAT
Cut from white cardstock

COLORFUL TREE GIFT BOX p.202
ENLARGE 400%

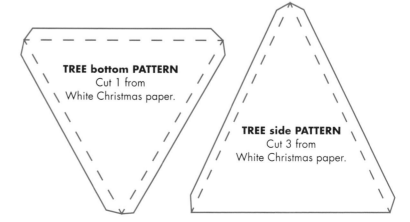

TREE bottom PATTERN
Cut 1 from White Christmas paper.

TREE side PATTERN
Cut 3 from White Christmas paper.

YOU MAKE MY HEART MELT p.19
ENLARGE 350%

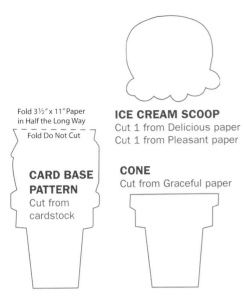

Fold 3½" x 11" Paper in Half the Long Way

Fold Do Not Cut

CARD BASE PATTERN
Cut from cardstock

ICE CREAM SCOOP
Cut 1 from Delicious paper
Cut 1 from Pleasant paper

CONE
Cut from Graceful paper

YOU HOLD THE KEY p.23
ENLARGE 310%

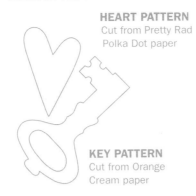

HEART PATTERN
Cut from Pretty Rad Polka Dot paper

KEY PATTERN
Cut from Orange Cream paper

GET COZY p.200
ENLARGE 260%

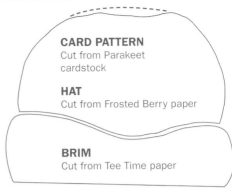

CARD PATTERN
Cut from Parakeet cardstock

HAT
Cut from Frosted Berry paper

BRIM
Cut from Tee Time paper

PUMPKIN WALL HANGING PATTERNS
P.164   ENLARGE 400%

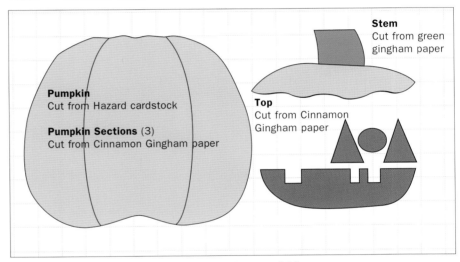

Pumpkin
Cut from Hazard cardstock

Pumpkin Sections (3)
Cut from Cinnamon Gingham paper

Stem
Cut from green gingham paper

Top
Cut from Cinnamon Gingham paper

Each square = 1". Cut on solid lines.

WITCH'S BREW CARD PATTERN
P.161   ENLARGE 275%

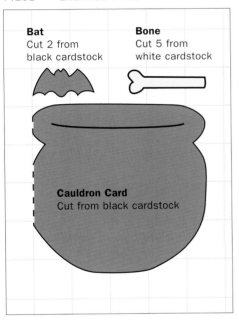

Bat
Cut 2 from black cardstock

Bone
Cut 5 from white cardstock

Cauldron Card
Cut from black cardstock

TREAT BOX PATTERN P.160
ENLARGE 275%

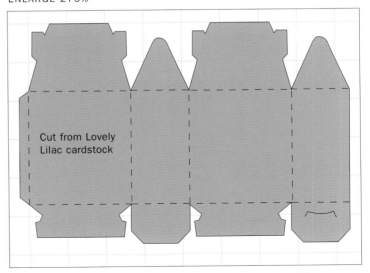

Cut from Lovely Lilac cardstock

Each square = 1". Cut on solid lines. Fold on dashed lines.

TEQUILA MAKES ME SMILE GLASS PATTERN p.77
ENLARGE 350%

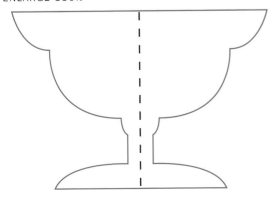

BEWITCHED HAT
CARD PATTERN p.129
ENLARGE 140%

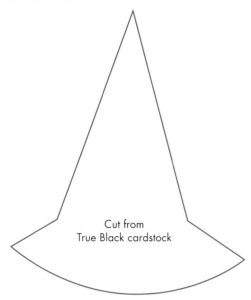

Cut from
True Black cardstock

BOO GIFT BAG PATTERN p.116
ENLARGE 300%

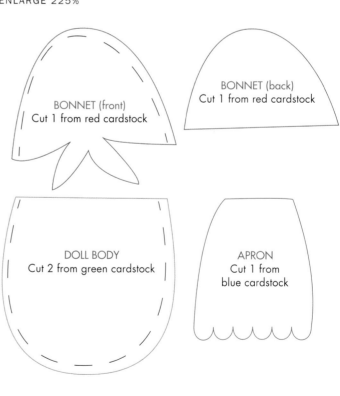

EYES & MOUTH
Cut from Suede
Brown Dark cardstock

GHOST BODY
Cut from Butter
Cream cardstock

BAT PATTERN p.145

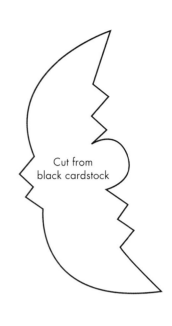

Cut from
black cardstock

WITCH BOOT PATTERN p.125
ENLARGE 250%

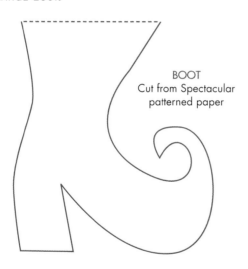

BOOT
Cut from Spectacular
patterned paper

MATRYOSHKA DOLL GIFT CARD PATTERN p.249
ENLARGE 225%

BONNET (front)
Cut 1 from red cardstock

BONNET (back)
Cut 1 from red cardstock

DOLL BODY
Cut 2 from green cardstock

APRON
Cut 1 from
blue cardstock

LOVE YOU BERRY MUCH,
STRAWBERRY PATTERN p.13
ENLARGE 225%

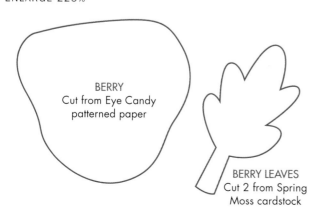

BERRY
Cut from Eye Candy
patterned paper

BERRY LEAVES
Cut 2 from Spring
Moss cardstock